Donated by

Wallace Dace

PLAYS AND PREFACES

Wallace Dace

VANTAGE PRESS
New York

To Hal, Teddy, and the memory of Beth and Judy

Contents

HITLER IN LANDSBERG, A Play in Two Acts   1

     Preface: On Hitler   3
     Text   19

FATE, FORTUNE, AND FINAL SOLUTIONS, A Stoic Comedy   75

     Preface: On Suicide   77
     Text   95

THE FEAST OF THYESTES, A Tragedy in Two Acts   145

     Preface: On Famine   147
     Text   153

EPILOGUE: On Violence   207

Hitler in Landsberg

A Play in Two Acts

Preface: On Hitler

Adolf Hitler (1889–1945) is one of the perennially fascinating figures of the twentieth century. A hero to millions of his countrymen in the 1930s and a villain to everybody else, he embodied a certain Teutonic way of looking at things, a *Weltanschauung,* present in many Germans, that expresses an inherited belief that they are members of a race of people superior to all other peoples on earth.

Hitler led his people into a world war more devastating to Germany than the Thirty Years War of 1618–48. His armies were crushed, his cities reduced to rubble, and his people's cherished belief in their racial superiority badly shaken. Today, the Germans hover unobtrusively in the background of European affairs, quietly making money while attracting as little attention as possible. Their Constitution forbids them to wage aggressive warfare against any other country or people. They will not let themselves build nuclear weapons. The defense of the realm is left to NATO and a modest home army. The present German *Weltanschauung* reminds one of some lines from a Franz Lehár operetta:

> Immer nur lächeln, immer vergnügt,
> Immer zufrieden, wie's immer sich fügt.
> Lächeln trotz Weh und tausend Schmerzen.

> [Always smiling, always joyful,
> Always ready to make oneself useful.
> Smiling in spite of woe and pain.]

Recently, German parliamentarians engaged in strenuous debate in their *Bundestag* about whether German radar technicians should make up part of the crews of AWACS planes flying over Bosnia or a small unit of German infantry should be made available to the United Nations for peacekeeping duties in Somalia (they voted a reluctant "Ja" to both proposals). Their *Bundeswehr,* inheritor of the stirring traditions of German armies of yore, prides itself on the formation of three new infantry divisions made up of German-French, German-Dutch, and German-American soldiers.

Peace has come to Europe. Acceptance by all the European states of liberal democracy—the greatest achievement of the human imagination—is complete. Fascism and Communism are utterly discredited; democracy is seen everywhere as the key to universal peace. At no point in history has a genuine liberal democracy ever attacked another country. The democracies have shown that they will defend themselves, but they will not attack first. This is because the people do not like war and, if the people have *real* control of a country, they will not allow their leaders to declare war on another country simply to acquire some territory. They will live within the territory they have rather than try to get more by military action.

Hitler, then, represents the final (hopefully) embodiment in history of a long line of conqueror-adventurers, from Alexander the Great to Hannibal, from Julius Caesar to Genghis Khan, from Frederick the Great to Napoléon—outsize mortals, to be sure, convinced of their own greatness and the greatness of their people.

What was Hitler like?

A few snapshots:

August Kubizek, who was born in the Austrian provincial capital of Linz in 1888, was Hitler's closest boyhood friend. In his book, *The Young Hitler I Knew,* Kubizek provides many images of Hitler growing up in Linz. At sixteen, for example, Hitler fell in love with Stefanie, "a distinguished-looking girl, tall and slim with beautiful eyes." Hitler and Kubizek would wait every day at five o'clock at the Schmiedtoreck to observe Stefanie and her mother as they took their afternoon stroll along the Landstraße, chatting and looking in the shop windows. Hitler never dared speak to Stephanie, but she became aware of him, and once, during the Flower Festival of June 1906, when she passed him in a flower-decked carriage, she threw him a smile and a red poppy. Kubizek reports:

> Never again did I see Adolf as happy as he was at that moment. When the carriage had passed he dragged me aside and with emotion he gazed at the flower, this visible pledge of her love. I can still hear his voice trembling with excitement, "She loves me! You have seen! She loves me!" (65)

Adolf's love for Stefanie lasted over four years, and he was true to her alone.

He imagined her as Elsa in *Lohengrin* and wrote her love poems. "Hymn to the Beloved" was the title of one of them that he read to Kubizek: "Stefanie, a high born damsel in a dark blue, flowing velvet gown, rode on a white steed over the flowering meadows, her loose hair fell in golden waves on her shoulders. Everything was pure, radiant joy." (59)

Kubizek, who regarded all this as an evasion of reality, reminded his friend that he didn't even know this girl. Hitler replied that once he met Stefanie, everything would be clear. For two such extraordinary beings, routine communication was unnecessary. They would understand each other by intuition.

Kubizek was charged, finally, with obtaining information about Stefanie. Through a friend who knew her, Kubizek discovered that she was not engaged and that she loved to dance. Here was Adolf's opportunity: invite her to a dance somewhere. But Hitler was horrified. Waltz his Elsa around some pedestrian dance floor? Never! A vision of purgatory! Besides, he had never learned to dance. Dancing was a pastime for the insane. To this, Kubizek inquires rhetorically:

> What was the origin of this strange, almost ascetic trait in him that made him reject all the pleasures of youth? . . . After all, he was a most presentable young man, well built, slender, and his somewhat severe and exaggeratedly serious features were enlivened by his extraordinary eyes, whose peculiar brilliance made one forget the sickly pallor of his face. And yet—dancing was as contrary to his nature as smoking or drinking beer at a pub. These things simply did not exist for him, although nobody, not even his mother, encouraged him in this attitude. (62)

Years later, after Hitler became Chancellor, a young woman mentioned to him at a party that Napoléon had been an accomplished ballroom dancer, to which Hitler replied, "All the more reason why I should abstain!"

Hitler never did say "Guten Tag" to Stefanie. He instinctively kept his idealized dream of union with his beloved separate from what it probably would have been like in reality—a routine, middle-class life of marriage, work, children, ennui, and demise—a life hard to imagine with Hitler at the center of it.

Another of Kubizek's vivid impressions of Hitler emerged from a visit to the Staatsoper Linz, a good provincial company with a substantial tax subsidy. They possessed sufficient vocal resources to perform Wagner's third opera, *Rienzi,* a tale that the composer adapted from a novel by the

English writer and political figure Edward Bulwer-Lytton. The opera depicts the rise of a man of the people in fourteenth-century Rome to the rank of tribune. He struggles with the Roman nobility to preserve the people's rights, but his enemies get the better of him and at the end he dies with his sister and her lover as the burning capitol building collapses on them.

It was past midnight when *Rienzi* ended (even Wagner thought it was too long) and Kubizek and Hitler gained the street. Kubizek remembers a cold, foggy, unpleasant November evening, his friend unusually silent, absorbed in his thoughts, leading the way toward a mountain that overlooks the city and the Danube flowing through it, called the Freinberg. They climbed the heights in silence. At the top, Kubizek recalls a change from the foggy darkness below to a scene bathed in brilliant starlight. Suddenly Hitler exploded:

> Adolf stood in front of me; and now he gripped both my hands and held them tight. He had never made such a gesture before. I felt from the grasp of his hands how deeply moved he was. His eyes were feverish with excitement. The words did not come smoothly from his mouth as they usually did, but rather erupted, hoarse and raucous. From his voice I could tell even more how much this experience had shaken him. . . .
>
> I cannot repeat every word that my friend uttered. I was struck by something strange, that I had never noticed before, even when he had talked to me in moments of the greatest excitement. It was as if another being spoke out of his body, and moved him as much as it did me. It wasn't at all a case of a speaker being carried away by his own words. On the contrary; I rather felt as though he himself listened with astonishment and emotion to what burst forth from him with elemental force. (99–100)

Over thirty years later, when Hitler had invited Kubizek to the Bayreuth Festival of 1939 and both were guests of Frau Winifred Wagner at Villa Wahnfried, Hitler recounted to her and her family this most significant experience of his youth in Linz. As he put it in conclusion, "In that hour, it began."

Kubizek joined Hitler in Vienna for a time but, unable to find suitable employment, he returned to Linz. He continued to correspond with his friend for a time but, finally, lost track of him. The First World War came and went, and Kubizek settled down to the life of a municipal clerk in the Upper Austrian town of Eferding, where he also conducted the local chorus and symphony orchestra. In the late twenties and early thirties, he began to hear of an Adolf Hitler who was making something of a political reputation in Germany but thought it must be someone else. After all, "Adolf Hitler" was a common name. But when President Hindenburg appointed Hitler Chancellor of Germany in January 1933, Kubizek finally saw a picture of him in a newspaper and, in profound astonishment, realized it was his boyhood friend of yore.

What to do? Would Hitler remember him? He tried a letter to the Reich Chancellery in Berlin and, after some months, received a warm letter from the Chancellor saying he did indeed remember Kubizek and expressing the hope that they could get together sometime so that he could "revive once more with you those memories of the best years of my life." Was there an erotic element in their relationship?

The grand reunion had to be postponed for a time due to the pressure of world events. But on the occasion of the *Anschluss* with Austria, in 1938, Hitler spent a few days in Linz and, to Kubizek's intense surprise, their reunion did indeed take place, in the Hotel Weinzinger, on April 9, 1938:

> As Hitler suddenly came out of one of the hotel rooms, he recognized me immediately and with the joyful cry, "Gustl!", he left his entourage standing there and came and took me by the arm. I still remember how he took my outstretched right hand in both of his and held it firmly, and how his eyes, which were still as bright and as piercing as ever, gazed into mine. He was obviously moved, just as I was. I could hear it in his voice. (276–7)

Hitler took his old friend to his private suite, and they had a good talk. Kubizek hadn't changed; he just looked older. Linz still looked terrible, but Hitler had plans. A new bridge was needed over the Danube—to be called the Nibelungen Bridge. A new opera house would be erected on the site of that ugly central railroad station. A new concert hall was essential if Linz was to be worthy of its reputation as the "City of Bruckner".

And what had Kubizek been doing all this time? Town Clerk at Eferding! And conductor of the Eferding Symphony Orchestra! What did they play? Schubert's *Unfinished!* Beethoven's *Third!* Mozart's *Jupiter!* Hitler would see about a tax subsidy for this admirable musical ensemble. And Hitler told Kubizek he would provide for the education of his three sons at the Bruckner Conservatory in Linz.

Kubizek saw his old friend for the last time at the Bayreuth Festival of 1939, to which the Chancellor had invited him. After a warm conversation in a private room at Villa Wahnfried, Hitler rose and solemnly motioned his friend to follow him:

> He opened the French windows and preceded me into the garden down the stone steps. Well tended paths brought us to a high, wrought-iron gate. He opened it. There were flowers and shrubs in full bloom and the mighty trees, forming a roof above us, threw the place into semi-darkness. A few more paces and we stood in front of Richard Wagner's grave. Hitler took my hand and I could feel how moved he was. It was quite still; nothing disturbed the solemn peace. Hitler broke the silence. "I am happy that we have met once more on this spot which always was the most venerable place for us both." (289)

The day Kubizek stood with Hitler before the grave or Germany's greatest dramatic poet was August 3, 1939. A month later, the world was engulfed in war.

In August 1914, when the First World War began, Hitler was in Munich, and he quickly volunteered for service in the German Army. He was posted to the List Regiment of the Sixteenth Bavarian Infantry and soon found a place in the military world as a *Meldegänger* (dispatch runner)—dangerous duty in the warfare of the time. Dispatch runners were usually sent out in pairs in the hope that if one got killed, the other might get through with the message. Hitler carried three kinds of messages: "urgent", which had to be delivered at once; "quick", which had to be delivered within twenty-four hours; and "in your own time", which could be delivered when the enemy artillery bombardment had slackened off a bit.

In the first battle of Ypres in October 1914, Hitler's regiment of 3,000 men suffered 2,500 casualties—dead, wounded, and vanished. Hitler survived with only a torn sleeve from a shell fragment. His bravery in this action was rewarded by an Iron Cross, second class, and a promotion to the rank of *Gefreiter*. *

Hitler kept notes of his wartime experiences and sometimes wrote

*One stripe. In the British Army, lance corporal; in the U.S. Army, private first class. The reason Hitler is constantly described as "corporal" is because the earliest commentators on his career who wrote in English were British. To an American, however, he was a Pfc. The rank in the German Army designates a private who is exempt from standing guard duty.

lengthy letters to friends in Germany. In a letter of February 1915 to a lawyer, Ernst Hepp, as quoted by Robert Payne in his book *The Life and Death of Adolf Hitler,* he describes his first fight with the British, mentions his Iron Cross, then relates his experiences as a *Meldegänger*:

> My job now is to carry dispatches for the staff . . . In Wytschaete during the first day of the attack three of us eight dispatch runners were killed, and one was badly wounded. The four of us survivors and the man who was wounded were cited for distinguished conduct. While they were deciding which of us should be awarded the Iron Cross, four company commanders came to the dugout. That meant that the four of us had to step out. We were standing some distance away about five minutes later when a shell slammed into the dugout, wounding Lt.-Col. Engelhardt and killing or wounding the rest of his staff. This was the most terrible moment of my life. We worshipped Lt.-Col. Engelhardt. (112–13)

Unlike his comrades, who tended to rely on luck, Hitler prepared for his dispatch runs by carefully studying the available maps to discover the safest way to reach his objective. This attention to detail helps explain how he managed to survive four brutal years of trench warfare in France and Belgium.

During his moments of rest behind the lines, Hitler kept up his painting and sketching. About forty of his wartime watercolors have survived, probably the best of which is *The Sunken Road at Wytschaete,* which "he painted with thick, heavy strokes in the autumn of 1914. He knew this road well, for he had travelled along it often when it was under heavy enemy fire . . . Hitler, no longer under the necessity of creating architectural forms, has suggested the stark horror and menace of the landscape with a minimum of means." (119) Some of his other pictures were of buildings shattered by the war, the roofs caving in and walls crumbling, and roads strewn with rubble.

During his four years in the trenches, Hitler also read a book, Schopenhauer's *The World as Will and Representation*—only one book, to be sure, but he read it over and over. It is likely that he was pleased to discover a philosophical confirmation of his lifelong belief that anything is possible if one wills it strongly enough. And Schopenhauer's opinion of women may have corresponded to his own.

In September 1917 Hitler received the Cross of Military Merit and in August 1918 the Iron Cross first class, for running a dispatch over ground under enemy shelling so intense as to render the mission almost an act of suicide. The citation, signed by his regimental commander, Baron von Godin, read as follows:

> As a dispatch runner, he has shown cold-blooded courage and exemplary boldness both in position warfare and in the war of movement, and he has always volunteered to carry messages in the most difficult situations and at the risk of his life. Under conditions of great peril, when all the communication lines were cut, the untiring and fearless activity of Pfc. Hitler made it possible for important messages to go through. (113)

Hitler's battlefield career came to an end in October 1918, during the third battle of Ypres, as the result of a British gas shell bombardment on his trench position. Chlorine gas penetrated the primitive gas mask he wore, and he soon became totally blind. He was taken to a hospital in Pasewalk a town near Stettin, where he learned in November that the Kaiser had abdicated and the German Army had surrendered. Hitler lay in the hospital for many days in a state of total despair but finally came out of it, as he regained his eyesight, returned to Munich, and took up the career for which he is remembered today.

Joseph Goebbels was a good judge of character and political talent. One night in Munich in June of 1922, he attended a big political rally at the Kirkus Krone, the largest auditorium in the city. Along with eight thousand other spectators, he watched as a man identified in the program as "Adolf Hitler" began to speak. In his diary, as quoted by Curt Riess in his biography, *Joseph Goebbels,* the future Reich Propaganda Minister wrote:

> I hardly realized that suddenly someone was standing up there and had begun to talk, hesitantly and shyly at first, as though groping for words adequate to express the thoughts whose greatness would not fit the narrow confines of ordinary language. Then, suddenly, the speech gathered momentum. I was caught. I was listening . . .
> The crowd began to stir. The haggard, gray faces were reflecting hope. Over there, someone got up, shaking his fist. Two seats farther to my left an old officer was crying like a child. I felt alternately hot and cold. I didn't know what was happening . . . I was beside myself. I was shouting hurrah! Nobody seemed surprised. The man up there looked at me for one moment. His blue eyes met my glance like a flame. This was a command! At that moment I was reborn . . . Now I knew which road to take . . . (12)

10

Another astute judge of character was Albert Speer, who became Hitler's architect and, later, his Minister of Armaments. Speer recorded, in his book *Inside the Third Reich*, many vivid portraits of a man whose confidence he enjoyed for more than ten years. He joined the Nazi party in January 1931 and in a short time began to attract the attention of party officials in Berlin, including Joseph Goebbels. After planning the decorations for a big May 1, 1933, party rally at Tempelhof Airport—that included a large platform and, behind it, three huge banners, each over one hundred feet high, illuminated by giant searchlights—Speer was called to Nuremberg to design the background for the first annual summer rally at the Zeppelin field outside the city. Speer replaced his three huge banners at Tempelhof with a gigantic eagle, over a hundred feet in wingspread, to crown his festive designs. Only Hitler could approve the décor for a Nuremberg rally, so Speer was sent with his drawings to Hitler's apartment in Munich, where he met the Chancellor face to face for the first time:

We stopped at an apartment house in the vicinity of the Prinzregenten Theater. Two flights up I was admitted to an anteroom . . . an adjutant came in, opened a door, said casually, "Go in", and I stood before Hitler, the mighty Chancellor of the Reich. On a table in front of him lay a pistol that had been taken apart; he seemed to have been cleaning it. "Put the drawings here," he said curtly. Without looking at me he pushed the parts of the pistol aside and examined my sketches with interest but without a word. "Agreed". No more. Since he turned to his pistol again, I left the room in some confusion. (28)

In time, Speer received commissions from Hitler to design various public buildings in Berlin, including the new Reich Chancellery, and eventually became a member of Hitler's inner circle. Hitler liked him. Perhaps, Speer thought, because he saw in the younger man an image of his own youthful ambition to become an architect. The possibility that the older man may have been attracted physically to the handsome younger man is not mentioned by Speer in his book, although the thought must have crossed his mind.

Speer noticed that Hitler possessed a certain inherited talent for architecture:

When buildings were in question, Hitler repeatedly displayed his ability to grasp a sketch quickly and to combine the floor plan and elevations into a three-dimensional conception. Despite all his government business and although he was often dealing with anywhere from ten to fifteen large buildings in different cities, whenever the drawings were presented to him again—often after an interval of months—he immediately found his bearings and could remember what changes he had asked for. Those that thought a request or a suggestion had long since been forgotten quickly learned otherwise. (79)

Speer devoted most of his time before the war broke out to designing several new buildings as part of Hitler's plan for a grand reconstruction of the center of Berlin, from the Victory Column south to a point just west of Tempelhof Airport. Speer constructed models of this project in his big studio in the old Berlin Academy of Arts on Pariser Platz, and Hitler delighted in bringing his dinner guests through the Chancellery gardens to see them.

During the war, Speer became Hitler's Armaments Minister and did a great deal to enable his country to keep up the vast struggle. Before long, however, it became clear that the Russian Army, after its great victory at Kursk in July 1943, could not long be kept from the gates of Berlin. By the spring of 1945, Hitler had confined himself to his bombproof bunker deep in the garden behind Speer's new Reich Chancellery building. Hitler was much changed from the old days when Speer said good-bye to him for the last time:

Now, he was shrivelling up like an old man. His limbs trembled; he walked stooped, with dragging footsteps. Even his voice became quavering and lost its old masterfulness. Its force had given way to a faltering, toneless manner of speaking. When he became excited, as he frequently did in a senile way, his voice would start breaking . . . His complexion was sallow, his face swollen; his uniform, which in the past he had kept scrupulously neat, was often neglected . . . and stained by food he had eaten with a shaking hand . . . By now it was about three o'clock in the morning . . . I sent word that I wanted to bid him good-bye. The day had worn me out, and I was afraid that I would not be able to control myself at our parting. Trembling, the prematurely aged man stood before me for the last time; the man to whom I had dedicated my life twelve years before . . . I was both moved and confused. For his part, he showed no emotion . . . His words were as cold as his hand: "So, you're leaving? Good. *Auf Wiedersehen*." No regards to my family, no wishes, no thanks, no farewell. For a moment I lost my composure, said something about coming back. But he could easily see that it was a white lie, and turned his attention to something else. I was dismissed. (472; 485)

The inner workings of Hitler's mind are not as easy to describe as his outward appearance. More than most people, he depended on intuition to guide his political and military decisions as well as those of everyday life. And this reliance on intuition made him all the more susceptible to the influence of his inherited talents and fears.

Like many others, Hitler seems to have been born with an inherited fear of debt, and—also like many others—he associated debt with the Jews. Fear of debt led him to hatred of the Jews, since we all hate the things we fear. Doubtless, his dire poverty during his Vienna years contributed to his anti-Semitism, a fixation he shared with many thousands of his German and Austrian countrymen.

Signs of this innate anti-Semitism among Germans of the nineteenth century appear in the popular literature of the time. Many writers made use of the stereotype of the Jew as rapacious, greedy, and lacking in principle. Gustav Freytag, in his *Soll und Haben* (1855), contrasts the honorable, idealistic Anton Wohlfarth with the ambitious, materialistic, and unscrupulous Jew, Veitel Itzig, who drowns, finally, after committing a murder. The same general comparison of "good" Germans with "bad" Jews also appears in Wilhelm Raabe's *Der Hungerpastor* (1864) and in Felix Dahn's immensely popular *Ein Kampf um Rom* (1867), in which the Jew, Jochem, whose face bears "all the calculated cunning of his race", betrays the city-state of Naples to Byzantium. While growing up in Passau and Linz, Hitler very likely read these and other books with similar depictions of Jewish venality. That was what was selling in those days.

Popular fear of the Jewish money lender gradually broadened to embrace the image of the all-powerful Jewish banker. In Germany, such Jewish names as Rothschild, Bleichröder, Lasker, Bamberger, and Oppenheimer were associated in the public mind not only with manipulations of the Berlin stock exchange, but also influence of political parties by means of bribery and, through this influence, power over the decisions of the Reichstag itself. During the tense days of the Weimar Republic, the idea that money could be used to buy political power became an obsession in both literature and its first cousin, the film. For instance, the film *Jud Süss,* made under the personal supervision of Joseph Goebbels in 1940 and much admired by both Himmler and Hitler, relates the story of an eighteenth-century Jewish banker from Frankfurt, Süss Oppenheimer, who comes to Stuttgart, where he contrives to be appointed Financial Adviser to the Duke of Württemberg. He soon gets the Duke into his power by loaning him money in return for control over the tax revenues of the Duchy. In the most repugnant sequence of the film, he rapes the daughter of an important government official while her husband, who has been planning an insurrection against Süss, is being tortured in a dungeon, scenes that are cross-cut more and more rapidly to good cinematic effect. Later, the daughter drowns herself in the Neckar, the Duke dies, Süss is tried for his crimes and sentenced to be suspended in an iron cage high over the city, so that the good burghers of Stuttgart can watch the evil Jew Süss as he slowly dies of thirst.

Hitler not only read anti-Semitic books as he was growing up, he also came to believe in the authenticity of an infamous document called *The Protocols of the Elders of Zion,* a purported plot by the Jews to take over the world that captured the imagination of millions at the turn of the century. The *Protocols* were forged in France during the time of the Dreyfus affair, with help from the Russian secret police, and published under the title *Protocols des Sages d'Israël.* The French government needed a document to counter the efforts of Émile Zola and others to obtain the freedom of the innocent Dreyfus from Devil's Island, and the Czar needed something to use against the Bolsheviks, who were linked in the popular mind with the Jews.

As described by George L. Nosse in his book, *Toward the Final Solution,* this notorious forgery relates a plan made by the Elders of Zion during a secret meeting in the Jewish cemetery of Prague, where they could not be spied on by the gentiles. They would employ the famous slogan of the French Revolution, "Liberty, Equality, Fraternity" to characterize their aims. They would strive to help people rid themselves of their childish belief in God. They would provoke a worldwide financial crisis and use their hoards of gold to drive up prices. Soon the only people left would be the richest Jews—the Elders—their police, their soldiers, and the starving masses. Worldwide tribute would be paid to the King of the Jews. Should the plan be discovered by the gentiles, railway trains running beneath the world's great cities would be loaded with explosives and the cities blown up, killing millions. And, as a last resort, the Elders would destroy the remaining gentiles by inoculating them with a fatal disease. (118)

The widespread belief in these absurd fantasies testifies to the power of inherited fear of debt which, as an aspect of the fear of death, is transmitted genetically from our forefathers to ourselves. No one can escape inherited fear. We can take measures against it, but it is always there, ready to break out in some unexpected way, at some inappropriate moment in our lives.

Hitler inherited his prejudice against the Jews from his Austrian forebears, just as he also inherited, from somebody in the family, his talent for oratory, a gift he discovered entirely by chance. After leaving the hospital at Pasewalk and returning to Munich, he was allowed by his Commanding officer, Capt. Ernest Roehm, to remain in the army for a time, a privilege enjoyed by very few soldiers during this period, when the German Army was being drastically reduced in size. Roehm, who probably had a homosexual relationship with Hitler, suggested to his friend that he attend an indoctrination course given at the University of Munich for soldiers who needed to be made aware of the political philosophy approved by the army. At the end of one of Professor von Mueller's lectures, a soldier rose and protested his verdict on the Jews. Hitler rose to the professor's defense and made a strong extemporaneous speech that he could see was holding his audience spellbound. Hitler had found his voice.

In his book, *The Life and Death of Adolf Hitler,* Robert Payne describes Hitler's awakening to the existence and depth of his talent as follows:

> At the Männerheim in Vienna, he had often spoken to small groups about political matters, but always with the knowledge that his words carried little weight, for he was addressing an audience without any political power. But the soldiers who attended the indoctrination courses were not powerless: they carried weapons, they had conquered Munich, and they were only too obviously impressionable. Now, day after day, Hitler got up at the end of classes at Munich University and delivered speeches attacking the Jews, vehemently insisting upon the need to preserve the purity of the German race. He had discovered that he could talk on his feet without embarrassment, defiantly, awkwardly, but nevertheless with an air of complete conviction. He was a natural orator and could swing into a speech without the slightest preparation. (128–29)

After years of aimless inactivity, entirely by chance, Hitler discovered that he had inherited a substantial talent for oratory and had possessed it all his life but had never encountered a situation that could bring it out of his unconscious. The military indoctrination course at the University of Munich in 1919 finally presented the situation, and Hitler's career as one of the most powerful political figures of modern times was launched.

A letter of Hitler's of 1919 to a certain Adolf Gemlich, describing in detail his beliefs regarding the Jews, has survived and is quoted in full in Payne's biography. In it, Hitler makes several points:

1. Jewery describes a race, not a religious community . . . There is scarcely a single race whose members belong so exclusively to a single religion . . .
2. In general, the Jew has preserved his race and character through hundreds of years of inbreeding . . .
3. The emotions of the Jews remain purely materialistic, and this is even truer of their ideas and aspirations. The dance before the Golden Calf has been transformed into a merciless struggle for precisely those possessions which we, following our innermost feelings, scarcely regard as having the highest importance, nor as the only ones worth striving for . . .
4. Their power is the power of money which, in the form of interest, endlessly and effortlessly increases, compelling the people to submit to this most dangerous yoke . . . The effect is to produce a race tuberculosis of the Folk . . .
5. Anti-Semitism arising out of purely emotional causes finds its ultimate expression in pogroms. Rational anti-Semitism must be directed toward a methodical legal struggle against them and the elimination of the privileges they possess . . .
6. The final aim must be the deliberate removal of the Jews. (130–31)*

It is clear that Hitler originally did not intend a pogrom against the Jews. He envisaged, instead, a "methodical legal struggle", the "elimination of their privileges" and their "deliberate removal" from Germany and German-controlled territory.

Of course, in calling for the expulsion of the Jews, Hitler was not proposing something new. The Jews have endured this bitter experience throughout the course of their troubled history: from the time of their expulsion from Egypt to their Babylonian captivity and from their expulsion from Jerusalem by the Romans in the first century A.D. to their expulsion

*In 1940, after the victory over the French, Hitler briefly entertained the idea of deporting the Jews to Madagascar, where they could be held under French jurisdiction.

from England in the late thirteenth century, from France in the early fourteenth, and from Spain in the fifteenth. Most of the deportees went to Germany and Austria, making these the host countries to the largest European Jewish population for a long time. The Jews were expelled from Russia after the failed Revolution of 1905. In fact, there is scarcely a major country worldwide—except the United States, to our credit—that has not, at some time in its history, expelled its Jews. We in America can't expel them on grounds that they don't belong here, because *nobody* belongs here. We are all descended from immigrants. Even Native Americans are descended from Asians who crossed, fifteen thousand years ago, to Alaska on the land bridge over the Bering Sea and settled the entire hemisphere, from the Arctic Circle to the Strait of Magellan.

During their previous expulsions, the Jews had places to which they could migrate. But when Adolf Hitler obtained the power to expel the European Jews, he ran into an unexpected obstacle. There were no foreign countries to which he could expel them. Franklin Roosevelt saw to it that very few Jews were admitted to the United States. Great Britain kept them out of Palestine, and other countries followed suit. As the war with Russia began, the resettlement of the Jews to the east or west became impossible, and Hitler decided on his bitter "Final Solution". His order was passed verbally to Himmler and Göring sometime in the midsummer of 1941, Göring sent a written order to Reinhard Heydrich on July 31, 1941, and Heydrich's conference in his villa at Grosser Wansee, January 20, 1942, set the infamous pogrom into irreversible motion.

Hitler was mainly self-educated. He was attuned to the ideas of his time, however, which is why he describes himself in *Mein Kampf* as both thinker and politician. He thought that power had to grow out of a firm intellectual base or it would waver, grope, and eventually become insecure. Power can rest only on a fanatical political and cultural *Weltanschauung* such as he himself had developed during his years in Vienna, Munich, and trenches of the Western Front, 1914–18.

The essential elements of his policy for Germany were as follows:

Internally, he intended to establish a combination of capitalism and socialism under the direction of a strong central authority, achieve rearmament and a buildup of the armed forces. "Foreign elements," such as Jews, were to be deported.

Externally, he called for a return to the 1914 geographical boundaries, meaning the reoccupation of Alsace and Lorraine from the French, the return to German hegemony of western Czechoslovakia, and the return to Germany of the Danzig area of Poland in order to reunite East Prussia with Pomerania. Finally, Germany must be reunited with its natural brother to the south, Austria. Once all this had been achieved, Hitler envisioned further territorial acquisitions in Eastern Europe—in the rest of Czechoslovakia, Poland, the Ukraine, and the Baltic states—to satisfy the historic need to obtain *Lebensraum* for the expanding population of Germany.

This basic foreign policy explains Hitler's reluctance to press on with Operation Sea Lion against Great Britain in August and September of 1940. As he put it during a staff conference, the German people did not need Great Britain. Why this substantial effort and the possible costs to the German armed forces? For what purpose? Germans don't want the place. Only an Englishman would want to live in England. Conquering and occupying Great Britain would amount to an empty gesture. So he called off Sea Lion in September 1940 and turned his undivided attention to the next element of his foreign policy—the acquisition of land in Eastern Europe.

Hitler's policies brought on World War II as well as the demise of six million Jews in Polish extermination camps. The enormity of this crime against a homeless people aroused so much worldwide sympathy that in 1948 the United Nations was able to turn over the western part of Palestine to the Jewish people, permitting them to reoccupy their ancient homeland of Israel. And so, at a cost of six million casualties during Hitler's pogrom of 1933-45, the Jewish people won the right to return to Jerusalem after nineteen hundred years of exile. The Arab states in the area attacked the Israelis in three wars with the objective of driving them out again, but failed, and today Israel appears to be on the brink of peace and security in the Middle East.

Hitler's desire for fresh German territory at the expense of countries to the east resulted in a devastation of Germany comparable to that of the Thirty Years War. It was followed, however, by a remarkable political, economic, and cultural recovery that came to a climax in 1990 with the reunification of the western and eastern sections of the country. One notices, too, that Hitler's war put an end to the British, French, Belgian, and Dutch overseas empires, thus paving the way for the formation of the United Nations. Today the United Nations is embroiled in many frustrating conflicts in Africa, the former Yugoslavia, Arabia, Turkey, Cambodia, and elsewhere, but the concept of world collective action against an aggressor finally has been established as a universal principle of conduct.

Hitler in Landsberg

A Play in Two Acts

TIME: Spring, summer, and fall of 1924
PLACE: Landsberg Prison, Bavaria
CHARACTERS:
Adolf Hitler, at ages thirty-four and thirty-five
Otto, an elderly jailer
Ulrich Schwarz, a young man in his twenties
Poldi, a friend in Linz
Klara, Hitler's mother
Erika Wendt, Ulrich's fiancée
Fritz Beck, a World War I dispatch runner
Rudi Kertz, a novelist
A waiter
Bert, a playwright
Three judges at the trial
Two lawyers at the trial
Warden Leybold
Three National Socialist prisoners
Members of the prison staff
SYNOPSIS OF SCENES:
Act I, scene 1: The prison cell, a spring morning, 1924
Act I, scene 2: A few days later
Act I, scene 3: A month later

Act II, scene 1: A few months later, summer
Act II, scene 2: Some weeks later, fall
Act II, scene 3: December 1924

STAGE SETTING:

The stage is divided in half throughout the play. The stage right area represents a small jail cell in Landsberg Prison in Bavaria, Germany.

Down right is the door to the corridor outside. The door is reinforced and has a heavy metal lock-and-bar arrangement on the corridor side. There is a small barred window in it.

Along the right wall are a dresser and a large wardrobe. Above these is the toilet, in the corner.

Along the back wall are a washbasin and a cabinet for personal utensils. Above the washbasin is a large barred window that looks out to the north. Beyond the window is a walled courtyard.

In the up left corner of the cutaway left wall is a small night table. The wide single cot extends from upstage to downstage along the cutaway left wall.

Upstage and in the middle of the cell area is a large worktable. It has drawers and can be used as a writing desk. A number of books and papers are kept on it throughout the play until the last scene.

The jail cell is always neat and clean. Clothes are kept in the wardrobe.

The stage left area is used to represent various locales from Hitler's past life. He walks from the cell right to the left area during a lighting cross-fade from right to left. The area is set at the beginning of each scene in the dark.

The following settings are required stage left: Act I, scene 1: a hill overlooking the city of Linz, a moonlit night with moving clouds, spring, 1906; scene 2: the kitchen in the small house in which Hitler lived with his mother, Linz, a night in December 1907; scene 3: a World War I battlefield, October 13, 1918; Act II, scene 1: interior of a beer hall in Munich, November 1923; scene 2: a courtroom in Munich, March 27, 1924; scene 3: the reception room in Landsberg Prison, December 20, 1924.

ACT I

SCENE 1: *A morning in early spring of 1924.*

Stage left, various platforms are arranged to suggest a series of hills overlooking a city. A cyclorama extends from down left to up right, and on it are projected a moon and moving clouds when the memory scene begins. There are various rocks scattered about on which **Hitler** *and* **Poldi** *can sit. There is no light stage left when the scene begins.*

Stage right, the jail cell is brightly lit. The sun comes in the upstage window from stage left to stage right, suggesting morning light.

AT RISE: Hitler *is sitting at the table, reading. There are books and writing materials on the table. He is dressed in comfortable civilian clothing.*

Hitler *is still badly shaken by the failure of the Munich Putsch of November, 1923, his trial, and his sentence to five years in prison, with parole possible after six months.*

His dislocated shoulder has healed, but his mind is still in considerable torment. During the course of the play, as he recounts his past experiences and formulates his political aims to his secretary, **Ulrich Schwarz**—*who writes them down and makes them part of* Mein Kampf—*Hitler gradually recovers his nerve.*

As he does so, we see **Ulrich Schwarz,** *a typical, not unintelligent German of the period, slowly entering into a kind of communion with* **Hitler,** *a communion he doesn't understand at the time and was never able to explain afterward.*

After some moments of silence, the sound is heard of the bolt on the door down right being slid back, the door opens, and **Otto, Hitler's** *jailer, brings in a young man in his twenties.*

Otto: Someone to see you, Herr Hitler. (**Hitler** *rises as they enter his cell.*)

Ulrich: Ulrich Schwarz, Herr Hitler. I was sent by the Party.

Hitler: Please come in. Thank you, Otto. (**Otto** nods politely and exits down right, closing and locking the door after him.)

Ulrich: I was hired as your secretary, sir.

Hitler: Who hired you?

Ulrich: Herr Ernst Hanfstaengl. He told me he is now the treasurer of the National Socialist Party.

Hitler: Are you a member of the Party?

21

Hitler: No—no. I only need a secretary.

Ulrich: Well, I've just finished my training at a secretarial school in Munich. I heard about this job and went to see Herr Hanfstaengl.

Hitler: What did he say?

Ulrich: He said it was for a male secretary and the work would be of a confidential nature.

Hitler: Sit down.

(*They sit at the table.*)

Ulrich: Thank you.

Hitler: What else did he tell you about the job?

Ulrich: Only that I would have to live here in Landsberg, and that I would take my instructions from you.

Hitler: Have you heard of me, then?

Ulrich: Yes, of course. Everyone has heard of you.

Hitler (*pleased*): Well . . . not everyone.

Ulrich: I followed your trial in the newspapers every day.

Hitler: I received shabby treatment at that trial.

Ulrich: I thought so, sir.

Hitler: But there will be a reckoning . . . a day will come. . . . (*He pauses, thinking over an idea. Meanwhile, he stares at* **Ulrich** *with a sharp, penetrating gaze. After a moment,* **Ulrich** *looks away.*)

Ulrich (*somewhat defensively*): I can type and take shorthand—

Hitler (*suddenly rising from his chair*): I will call my book *A Reckoning.* And as a subtitle . . . (*He paces slowly about the room.*)

Ulrich: Shall I write this down, sir?

Hitler: Yes. Write down everything. We will condense it later. (**Ulrich** *writes on a notebook in shorthand through the following.*) And as a subtitle: *Four-and-a-Half Years of Struggle against Lies, Stupidity and Cowardice.* (**Hitler** *crosses to the right side of the window and stares out, gathering his thoughts.*) A pleasant spring day in Bavaria . . . sunlight . . . I always feel better in the springtime. (*He turns, facing downstage, and leans against the window casement. The sun, coming in the window from stage left, catches his features from the side.* **Ulrich***, at the table, is in a shadowy part of the room.*) My worst experiences have been in winter . . . my mother's death . . . Vienna . . . my blinding by poison gas during the war . . . the Putsch last November. . . . (*He sighs deeply.*) I hate winter. Don't you?

Ulrich: Yes, sir. I prefer the spring and summer.

Hitler: Winter confines one. Like a prison. . . .

Ulrich: Shall I note this down, too?

Hitler: I hate confinement. Freedom is everything. (**Ulrich** *writes this down.*) Today, it seems to me fortunate—or providential—that Fate chose the town of Braunau am Inn as the place of my birth in 1889. (*He pauses to see if* **Ulrich** *is writing down what he says.*)

Ulrich: You may go faster if you wish, sir.

Hitler: Thank you. (*He paces down center and stares out at the audience, arms folded over his chest. His thinking becomes more concentrated.*) On April 20, to be precise. Braunau is a small town, but it has an interesting location. It is situated on the Inn River, a stream that separates two German states that ought to be one state—Germany and Austria. (*His tone becomes menacing.*) All the German states should be united into one state.

Ulrich: I have often wondered why we are . . . separated. . . .

Hitler: We should be united. We shall be united! I tell you, Herr Schwarz (*He suddenly advances threateningly on* **Ulrich**, *who watches him in amazement,*) it is the dog Clemenceau—the self-styled Tiger of France (*he points a threatening finger at* **Ulrich** *whom I call the poodle dog of France—who is responsible for this miserable state of affairs. (He pauses as* **Ulrich** *writes down what he has said.*) Austria asked to join Germany after 1918 . . . after she lost her empire. And what did the poodle dog of France reply? (*He mimics Clemenceau in a high-pitched, squeaky voice.*) "I did not fight the Germans for four years to make Germany stronger." (*He rages about the cell.*) He will pay—he will *pay* for this vicious and stupid statement. I will make him repeat it while he is being strangled with a steel wire! (*He pauses, breathing heavily.* **Ulrich** *stares at him in fascination.*)

Ulrich: Shall I include the last sentence?

Hitler: No . . . no. (*He becomes calmer.*) Well, as I was saying . . . this little town of Braunau lies on the boundary between two German countries. These countries must be reunited. Austria must return to the mother country. And not only for reasons of economics, but for a higher reason: One blood demands one *Reich*! (*His excitement returns.*) One community of people, welded together in a common purpose . . . disciplined . . . orderly . . . a people guided by the example of Frederick the Great, who said . . . (*He walks over to the table.*) My yellow pad. . . .

Ulrich: Is this it? (*He hands* **Hitler** *a yellow notebook.*)

Hitler: He said, "Discipline is based on obedience and order. It begins with the general and ends with the private. Its foundation is *submission.* No subordinate has the right to make objections." (*He drops the book on the table and resumes his pacing, arms folded.*) And this people, this disciplined people, will be led by one man. And that man is I—I myself, Adolf Hitler.

Ulrich: Bravo!

Hitler (*remembering the Putsch of November 9, 1923*): I will lead the German people as I led our brave storm troopers last November against the criminal government of Bavaria. (*Standing down center. he marches in place, suiting his speech to the rhythm of his tramping feet.*) We marched from the Bürgerbräukeller, 3,000 of us, step by step . . . twelve abreast . . . arms locked in comradeship and determination. . . . (*A snare drum is heard, marking the rhythmic progression of the marchers.*) Ludendorf and I at the head of the column . . . then came Richter, Feder, Kriebel, Rosenberg, Göring. . . . (*His recitation becomes more mesmerizing, more excited.*) We crossed the Ludwigsbrücke and marched to the Marienplatz . . . the Green police tried to stop us, but Göring's men arrested them and sent them to the rear. . . . (*The drum gets louder.*) The people filled the square. They cheered us on and sang "Deutschland hoch in Ehren". We turned up Residenzstraße and marched steadily toward the Odeonsplatz . . . steadily . . . firmly . . . one people united behind one leader. . . . (*He suddenly stops his in-place marching.*) Then—there in front of us—the Green police— (*A series of rifle and pistol shots is heard over the speaker system.* **Hitler** *screams and falls to the floor. He rolls about, apparently in pain, clutching his left shoulder. Then he faints. The drum stops.*)

Ulrich: God in heaven! (*He hurries to* **Hitler's** *side and drags him to the bed left. He gets* **Hitler** *into bed and brings him a glass of water from the washbasin. After a moment,* **Hitler** *revives and sips the water.*) Shall I call for a doctor?

Hitler: What happened?

Ulrich: You were overcome. You fainted. I'll call the jailer.

Hitler: Don't leave me. Stay here!

Ulrich: Yes, sir. I'll stay right here.

Hitler: Sometimes being alone frightens me.

Ulrich: We all know that feeling. (*Lighting begins to fade down on the right*

side of the stage and to brighten a little, left. The horizon comes up first, slowly, then the moving clouds.)

Hitler: Sit here by the bed. (**Ulrich** *moves his chair to the right of* **Hitler's** *bed. During the following, he resumes his task of writing down* **Hitler's** *rambling, sometimes incoherent reminiscences.*) These spells come and go. I think I am getting better. I *must* get better!

Ulrich: If you would like to sleep, I can come back later.

Hitler (*holding* **Ulrich's** *arm*): No! Stay here. I am wide awake . . . merely a little weak. . . . (*He props his head up with a pillow.*) Have you ever been to Linz?

Ulrich: Just once, on a trip to Vienna.

Hitler: I spent some time there . . . finished school . . . studied for the exams at the Vienna Academy of Fine Arts. . . . I had plans to become an architect. . . . I used to wander around the town with a chap named Poldi. . . . (*Lighting fades down stage right, leaving only a dim head spot on* **Ulrich** *as he writes.*) I remember a moonlit night in early spring . . . we had been to the Linzer Opernhaus to see Wagner's *Rienzi*. . . .

(*Over the house sound system is heard the overture to Wagner's early opera* Rienzi. *In the darkness right,* **Hitler** *leaves the bed and exits in back of a curtain. He crosses behind the cyclorama to offstage left, and puts on a coat and a student-style cap. Stage left, the lighting comes up full to disclose a hilltop that overlooks the city of Linz in the distance. Bright clouds move rapidly across the sky. The music continues for a time; then* **Hitler**, *aged sixteen, and his friend,* **Poldi**, *a music student who is also sixteen, enter quickly down left.*)

Poldi: Wait a minute. . . . Why so fast? (**Hitler** *hurries on to the highest part of the setting, then pauses to look about.*)

Hitler: Because . . . because . . .

Poldi (*joining him*): Because why?

Hitler: Because we are at the top of the Freinberg. Think of it!

Poldi: What of it?

Hitler (*facing the audience*): Ah—mountaintop! Ah—dizzy heights! How I long to leap into eternity! (*He "dives" swanlike down to the next level.* **Poldi** *laughs.*)

Poldi: You do *not* look like the dying swan.

Hitler (*looking below*): We are at the top of the world.

Poldi: We're not very high, really. (*The* Rienzi *music has faded out.*)

25

Hitler: Yes, we are. Look—far below—the Danube . . . the lights of the ancient city of Linz . . .

Poldi: Linz isn't very old.

Hitler: The dark horizon in the distance . . . clouds racing . . . the moon . . . Ah! Ecstasy!

Poldi (*sitting on a rock*): I've never been up here before.

Hitler: I have. Many times. I like to look down on the world below me.

Poldi: It looks about the same.

Hitler: And tonight—what a performance!

Poldi: Yes, rather good. The violins had some intonation problems and some of the tempos were wrong, but on the whole . . .

Hitler: I feel like Rienzi . . . the Roman tribune. . . . (*He addresses an imaginary mob below him.*) Citizens of Rome! My fellow workers and artisans. My comrades. I, Cola da Rienzi, the people's tribune, will lead you to freedom . . . (*He hears applause from below.*) Follow *me* to freedom! (*Applause and cheering from below.*) The nobles of the city of Rome tighten their oppressive grip. The people cry for help. The people beg on their knees for mercy. Come! Turn to me—Rienzi—and I will lead you out of the depths of fear and poverty to the heights of freedom and glory! (*More applause from below.* **Hitler** *becomes ever more excited.*) Your destiny is my destiny! Your hopes are my hopes! Your pride is my pride! Follow me to a new day—a new rejoicing—a new Rome! Mightier than the old! Greater than any power on earth! Arise—crush the tyrants— exterminate the enemies of Rome! Kill them all! Burn them! (*Tremendous applause and shouting from the "masses" below.* **Hitler** *stares transfixed into the distance. Gradually, the shouting dies down.* **Poldi** *has been watching his friend in an indulgent manner.*)

Poldi (*clapping his hands lightly*): Bravo. (**Hitler** *sits on a rock nearby.*)

Hitler: Sometimes, I think I could do anything . . . anything at all.

Poldi: And at other times?

Hitler: I wonder if I can even earn a living.

Poldi: Me, too.

Hitler: Poldi, we must write an opera. I'll supply you a superb libretto on a classical subject, give you my ideas for the chief themes . . . then you compose the music, and I'll help you with the orchestration.

Poldi: Do you really need me at all?

26

Hitler: Then we'll submit it here to the Linz Opera, let them try it out, make revisions, and then submit it to Vienna.

Poldi: Just like that . . .

Hitler (*pacing about again*): What a performance tonight! You know, the Linz Opera must be—after Vienna—the finest opera company in Austria. Who else could do *Rienzi* so well?

Poldi: Adolf, you're just carried away by Wagner's music and by the subject matter. The performance itself . . . well . . .

Hitler: No—no! It was superb. I've never been so carried away. I'm beside myself—outside myself—up there (*he motions toward the sky*) looking down on all below. (*He turns suddenly, pointing his finger as he did to* **Ulrich** *earlier and advances on his friend.*) I tell you, Poldi, when Rienzi stood there on that burning balcony and cursed the Roman people because they didn't deserve the freedom he had won them—ahhh!

Poldi: I wish you wouldn't point your finger at me.

Hitler: I can understand such a man. Alone . . . solitary in his will . . . giving freedom and greatness to others . . . but chained, a man in the grip of a destiny he can do nothing about . . . a destiny that sweeps him to the highest power, and then casts him down to be stoned and burned by the mob . . . by the very people who owe him the most. . . . Yes! Such a man I can easily understand.

Poldi: But he exists only in an opera house.

Hitler: Poldi, I can become such a man. The spirit of Rienzi is *my* spirit. Reborn! Reincarnated! I will lead the Germanic peoples to glory, to world power, to greatness! I will unite Germany and Austria! I will make the German *Reich* the greatest power on earth!

Poldi (*after a moment*): I thought you wanted to be an architect. (**Hitler** *sits listlessly on a rock. The spell is broken.*)

Hitler: I do.

Poldi: You have a better chance at that than becoming a latter-day Roman tribune.

Hitler: German tribune.

Poldi: Austrian tribune.

Hitler: Huh—Austria! . . . You know, I don't have much chance of getting accepted at the Academy of Fine Arts in Vienna.

Poldi: You can draw.

Hitler: They'll trip me up on some technicality or other. When was Vitruvius born?

Poldi: Why talk like that? Take an optimistic view of things.

Hitler: I hate optimism. Stupid . . . provincial . . .

Poldi: A person can't live without a little optimism.

Hitler: I define an optimist as a person who can successfully conceal from himself the utter futility of life. The pessimist—the realist—sees through this charade and looks truth in the eye.

Poldi: You know, Adolf, you have a unique way of seeing clearly out of one eye and being blind in the other.

Hitler: Better to see a little something out of one eye than to go through life like most people do, seeing nothing out of either one.

Poldi: No, no—I mean, you look at something with both eyes, but . . . you see one thing with one eye and something entirely different with the other.

Hitler: That's impossible. I see what I see.

Poldi: Like with Stephanie. With one eye you see a simple, thin, slightly pretty girl who is devoted to going to church and being with her mother . . . and with the other you see her as Elsa, waiting for her Lohengrin to come and save her.

Hitler: I don't see any contradiction in that.

Poldi: I know you don't.

Hitler: If you look closely at the score, Elsa was a plain, rather naive girl who fell into a wonderful chance to marry a great knight, the very embodiment of the spirit of medieval Germany. . . . (*He rises, again gripped by enthusiasm.*) Lohengrin the Pure! Son of Parsifal, knight of the Holy Grail! (*He stares down at the Danube, looking for Lohengrin.*) Sailing down the Rhine in a boat pulled by a swan . . . (*Music fills the air, from* Lohengrin, Act 1, *as the boat appears in the distance.*) A lofty figure . . . far above poor Elsa. He fights for her honor. He wins. He will marry her on one condition . . . (*from below is heard the motif of the "Forbidden Question"*) . . . that she never ask his name . . . but . . . (*He shrugs his shoulders contemptuously. The music stops.*) She is a mere woman, consumed by female curiosity. She asks his name, and he leaves her forever.

Poldi: It must be hard to be a woman. Eurydice faced the same test, and failed it.

Hitler: Women are like wasps: stupid, but they can sting. (*The scene begins to darken. There is a flash of lightning, followed by thunder.*)

Poldi: Let's go. It's going to storm.

Hitler: No. We will stay and overcome the elements.

Poldi: Sapperment!

Hitler: We will pacify the elements by an act of will!

Poldi: You are insane. (*More lightning and thunder. The scene continues to darken.*)

Hitler (*as though transfixed*): I celebrate the Will to Power.

> I will conquer first myself, then others.
> I suppress all that can block my way to power.
> I suppress my desire for money . . . travel . . . entertainment.
> I suppress my desire for food and wine.
> I suppress my desire for women.
> I will my triumph over adversity.
> I will my ascent to the mountaintop.
> I will the subjection of all wills to my will.
> I reject petty victories.
> Victories of the marketplace, of the bedroom, of the tea table.
These I reject.
> I hail only the final conquest.
> Power!
> I call to thee!
> Come! (*He wraps his coat about himself and strikes a Byronic pose as the wind increases, followed by more lightning and thunder.*)

Poldi: I repeat: You are insane.

Hitler: I agree. Commit me. Send me somewhere.

Poldi: Where?

Hitler: Where I'm supposed to go.

Poldi: Where is that?

Hitler: I don't know.

Poldi: Let's go. It's cold up here and it'll rain any minute.

Hitler: Go ahead. I'll stay a while longer. (*More wind, lightning, and thunder.*)

Poldi (*after a moment*): If you stay, I'll stay. . . . (*The sound of a cat meowing off left is heard.*)

Hitler: Look—a cat. A black cat.

Poldi: He's hurt his leg.

Hitler: He crawled up here to die. To die on top of the mountain. (**Hitler** *goes off left to get the cat.*)

Poldi: Leave him alone.

Hitler (*off left*): His leg is broken. (*He returns with the cat.*) He crawled all the way up here to die.

Poldi: Maybe he was just looking for a saucer of milk.

Hitler: No. A place to die. All cats know when they are about to die and make their preparations. This cat has will power. This is a cat hero.

Poldi: Will power, that's all you think about.

Hitler: What else is there?

Poldi: Art . . . beauty . . . Wagner. . . .

Hitler: Wagner is worth a thought or two, but one always comes back to the fundamental question of human will power. Will power is divine power. God speaks through man's will.

Poldi: You said God is dead.

Hitler: Nietzsche says this and I agree. God is dead except during uncanny moments. . . . He returns to life once in a great while in the form of will power. You know, Poldi . . . most people don't have any will power. They eat, drink, shit, screw, and sleep. Will power has vanished.

Poldi: True.

Hitler: But it is reborn in me.

Poldi: How do you know?

Hitler: I'll prove it to you. I shall kill this cat.

Poldi: Why?

Hitler: That's the point. For no reason. An act of will.

Poldi: Oh—let the poor beast go. (**Hitler** *walks down left.*)

Hitler: An act or pure will power.

Poldi: Sadism.

Hitler (*solemnly*): Cat hero! I announce to you your approaching death! (*"The Annunciation of Death" from* Die Walküre *is heard over the speakers.*) You shall ascend to Valhalla and join your brethren, the other cat heroes who have died before you in mortal combat. There you shall defend cat Wotan, your king.

Poldi: Adolf. Come to your senses. (**Hitler** *gazes sternly into the cat's eyes. Then, with a twist of his hands, he breaks the cat's neck.*)

Hitler: Die cat hero. Die with honor. Join your brethren in cat heaven. Take them greetings from Adolf Hitler the Invincible! (*He flings the cat into the void off left.* **Poldi** *and* **Hitler** *watch the falling cat as the lighting*

30

fades out to end Scene 1. The scene change stage left is covered by music from the end of Act 2 of Die Walküre*).*

ACT I

SCENE 2: A few days later.

AT RISE: *Stage right, the scene is the same. Stage left, the scene represents a kitchen in a modest Bavarian house of the early years of the twentieth century. In addition to the table and stove, there is a bed next to the stove. A small Christmas tree sits on a table in the corner. This tree is lighted when the flashback scene begins. On the side wall is a large photograph of a painting of Jesus Christ. There is no light stage left.*

Stage right, the sun comes in the upstage window from right to left, suggesting early afternoon. Hitler sits at his table, reading. He wears lederhosen, a decorated Bavarian shirt, and long white socks.

The door down right opens, and **Ulrich** *enters.* **Otto** *closes the door and locks it without entering the cell.* **Ulrich** *has his stenographer's book with him and also carries several typed sheets of manuscript in a briefcase.*

Ulrich: May I come in?

Hitler (*rising*): Of course. I am always glad to see you. (*He shakes hands with* **Ulrich** *warmly.*) I slept well last night. We shall get a lot done today.

Ulrich: I got permission from Warden Leybold to use the typewriter in the prison library.

Hitler: Good. So you have some of the material typed up?

Ulrich: Right here. (*He hands* **Hitler** *several typewritten sheets. They sit at the table.*)

Hitler: You have to help me organize all this.

Ulrich: I have . . . er . . . already tried to organize some of it, and condense it a little, but you must judge. If I have taken out something you want put back in, just say so.

Hitler (*reading the pages*): Yes . . .

Ulrich: I am trying to organize it as both a political statement and an autobiography. Is that what you intended?

Hitler (*staring intently at him*): Yes—exactly! I hadn't thought of it that way, but that is exactly right. The political statement must be rein-

31

forced by personal experiences. Then the reader will be convinced. *(He returns to his reading.)*

Ulrich: I'm glad I'm on the right track. . . . I think these ideas are very interesting . . . very compelling. . . .

Hitler (*still reading*): When we have a chapter finished, you must take it to Putzi in Munich. He will make arrangements for publication.

Ulrich: There may be some difficulty with that.

Hitler: Why?

Ulrich: They search me every evening when I leave. I'm not allowed to take anything out, not even my notebooks. I have to leave them with the guard until the next morning.

Hitler: Well . . . I expected that.

Ulrich: They know what I'm doing, and they say that all activities of the National Socialist Party are forbidden under the recent law. They cannot permit any political writings of yours to leave the prison.

Hitler (*still reading*): We will find a way to surmount this minor obstacle. . . . A courier will be found. . . .

Ulrich: I hope so. Of course, if we must smuggle it out, it would be best to send it in small parcels. . . .

Hitler: Of course. . . . (*He looks up from the manuscript.*) You know, Ulrich, that night on the hill overlooking Linz was one of the turning points of my life. It was there that I first had revealed to me a glimpse into my future. (*He nods thoughtfully as* **Ulrich** *watches him.*) Yes . . . yes . . . it all started there. (*He resumes his reading.*) I'm not too sure. . . . it needs to be in the book, however. . . .

Ulrich: If it reveals something of significance . . .

Hitler: We'll see. (*He reads a little more, then puts the manuscript down on the table, gets up, and begins pacing about with his arms folded across his chest, a habit he has gotten into when dictating.*) So! Shall we continue?

Ulrich: Certainly. (*He takes up pad and pen.*)

Hitler: I do not remember much about my early years. My father was a customs official for the Austrian government, which is why my formative years were spent in small border towns. My mother, Klara, gave all her being to the household and was devoted to us children. Never did a mother provide more warmth and loving care to her children than my dear mother, who died when she was forty-three years old . . . of

32

cancer. . . . (*He pauses, lost in thought. Then he sighs and glances at* **Ulrich** .)

Ulrich: How hard for you.

Hitler: When I was three, my rather received a promotion in the customs service and we moved to Passau. This was a city of some importance. The Prince-Bishops of Passau had once ruled over large parts of Austria and Bavaria. Also, it too had an interesting location, as it marks the confluence of the Inn and the Danube rivers . . . and therefore sits astride the border between Austria and Bavaria. . . . (*He pauses again.*) The desire to unite these two countries is thus in my blood, as well as my head. . . . And by way of a footnote—put this in or not as you wish. . . .

Ulrich: I'll take it down in any case.

Hitler: One's speech habits are formed for life at the age of three to four, and since out house was on the Bavarian side of the river when I was at this age, I have always spoken German with a Bavarian rather than an Austrian accent. (*He paces about. concentrating.*). Passau is a beautiful city, even today. The cathedral . . . the many examples of Gothic, Renaissance, and Baroque architecture . . . (*He suddenly crosses to the table and looks among the papers on it.*) Oh . . . by the way . . . I made some notes yesterday I want to put in. . . . (*He finds a sheet of paper.*) Here we are. Can you put this in another notebook?

Ulrich: Yes. (*He writes in a second notebook.*)

Hitler: Principal lesson learned from the failure of the November Putsch: Power must be grasped only by legal means. I renounce the use of force. The revolution will be accomplished within the framework of the Weimar constitution. NO LAWS WILL BE BROKEN! (*He stares fiercely at* **Ulrich**). Underline that. It's very important. No more illegal fighting. I will never again be arrested and sent to jail like a common criminal!

Ulrich: I've got it. (*He looks up, waiting for more of this, but* **Hitler** *again abruptly changes the subject.*)

Hitler: Passau . . . it was there that my youthful imagination was first excited by architecture. (**Ulrich** *goes back to his other notebook.*) The beauty of these great and fine buildings impressed itself on me and became the source of my earliest conscious ambition—to become an architect. (*He pauses, then addresses* **Ulrich**) Have you ever been to Passau?

33

Ulrich: Yes. Fine old city. (**Hitler** *sits down at the table.*)

Hitler: The customs building is on a tongue of land that separates the two rivers. I stood many times looking at this . . . the two rivers coming together and becoming one. When I became older, this turned into a symbol for me of the eventual flowing together of the peoples of Austria and Germany.

Ulrich: I only remember the cathedral. I couldn't decide whether I liked that one better or the one at Salzburg. So I sketched them both.

Hitler: Do you paint?

Ulrich: Not anymore.

Hitler: Why?

Ulrich: My father wanted me to follow in his footsteps and enter the business world.

Hitler: So you went to secretarial school.

Ulrich: I thought that might help me on my way.

Hitler: I have some friends who might help. . . . (*He rises abruptly and resumes his pacing.*) We must get on with our work. (*In the darkness stage left,* **Klara Hitler** *enters and lies down on the bed. She is forty-three and is dying of cancer of the breast.*) Without doubt, the death of my dear mother was one of the blackest moments of my early years in Austria. Her nobility . . . her kindness . . . and her terrible suffering . . . (*He pauses, in the grip of strong emotion.*) . . . the pain that kept her from sleeping at night . . . and her acceptance of her pain . . . she never complained . . . just lay there with her eyes closed . . . trying to keep me from knowing how she was suffering. . . . (*He appears overcome.*)

Ulrich: Shall we stop now? (**Hitler** *sits on the bed and sobs convulsively.* **Ulrich** *puts down his notebook and sits next to him.* **Hitler** *takes his hand.* **Ulrich** *puts his arm comfortingly about* **Hitler's** *shoulders.*

(Lighting fades out stage right, except for a pin spot on **Ulrich,** *who takes up his notebook again and writes down what he hears. He remains on the bed.* **Hitler** *rises as before, and crosses around in back of the cyclorama to down left offstage. He puts on a coat.*

Stage left, the lighting comes up slowly. It is a cold night before Christmas. The Christmas candle lighting dims on. There is also a special on the picture of Jesus on the wall left. During the lighting cross-fade, the sound of "Silent Night, Holy Night," sung in German, is heard. **Hitler,** *aged*

34

eighteen, enters slowly from down left and crosses to his mother's bed. He sees that she is asleep and adjusts the covers around her. Soon he turns away and begins to pace impatiently about the room. The singing dies away. He pauses in front of the likeness of Jesus.)

Hitler: Well—save her! Heal her! What's a case of terminal cancer to you, a man who heals lepers and raises the dead? A minor matter. Scarcely worthy of your talents. But for my mother and I, it would be a sign of your greatness. A sign from the highest power! (*He walks away, then turns back.*) Well? In honor of your birthday, coming soon. A benevolent gesture in the direction of an Austrian town filled with true believers . . . no more fanatical believers in the world than in Austria. . . . Think how you could strengthen our resolve! What better sign of your omnipotence on a cold Christmas Eve? (*He turns away and continues his monologue, partly to himself and partly to the picture.)* A man who . . . routinely . . . turns water into wine . . . such a man can easily cure a case of cancer of the breast. Why don't you . . . out of Christian charity . . . cure all the sick people in the world? Why do you pick out one or two here, two or three there, for special dispensation? Why display such random favoritism? (*He draws close to the picture again.*) Were you bribed? What does a person have to do to obtain a reliable cure from you? Believe? Believe what? Believe whom?

Klara (*groaning deeply with pain*): Oh—God! Adolf—!

Hitler: Right here, Mother. (*She stirs in the bed.*) Do you want some water?

Klara: No . . . not now. . . .

Hitler: How you suffer! Poldi will be here soon with something for the pain.

Klara: Adolf . . . pray for me. . . .

Hitler: Yes, Mother. Of course. I pray all the time. (*She becomes calmer and soon manages to go back into a light sleep.* **Hitler** *watches over her tenderly, adjusting the covers and the pillow.*) Pray . . . pray . . . the solace of the peasantry. Marx was right about religion . . . opiate of the people. Trust in God—bah! God heals nobody. (*He stares moodily at his mother.*) Sometimes a doctor stumbles on a cure for something while looking for something else . . . but not God. What does God know about bacteria, viruses, tumors? (*He crosses again to the picture of Jesus.*) Where did you study medicine, you benign fake? Creator of false hopes in the breasts of the ignorant . . . spreader of lies . . . give a sign of your healing powers—of your greatness—cure my mother! You hear me? (*He shakes his fist at the picture.*) Heal her this

35

instant or be cursed and damned as a charlatan—a quack, a contemptible fake!

Klara (*in severe pain*): Ahhhhh—! (*She half sits up in bed, then falls back again weakly.* **Hitler** *turns quickly back, sits on the bed, and takes his mother's hand in his.*)

Hitler: There . . . there . . . lie still. Mother. Be still. . . . Poldi is coming. . . .

Klara: The doctor . . . the medicine. . . .

Hitler: We've used up everything he left. He won't come back today.

Klara (*groaning*): Some medicine . . . please. . . .

Hitler: Poldi knows where he can get some cough syrup with something in it. He'll be here soon . . . I promise you. . . . (*Gradually, his mother drops off again to sleep.* **Hitler** *watches her carefully, then rises and crosses right.*) Poldi . . . what is keeping you? (*He looks back again at the picture of Jesus.*) Ever try opium on your patients? Maybe that's how you achieved your cures . . . fed your patients opium until they were convinced they were well. (*He paces about distractedly.*) Poldi! Where are you?

Klara (groaning): Please give me something. . . . It's worse than ever. . . .

Hitler: Just a little longer, Mother. Poldi will come soon.

Klara: Oh, God—let me die!

Hitler: No, Mother, no. I will save you. I will teach you how to save yourself. By an act of will. There is no limit to what can be achieved by the human will. (**Klara** *again cries out in pain and then begins to murmur The Apostles' Creed.*)

Klara: Ich glaube an Gott—den Vater, den Allmächtigen—den Schöpfer des Himmels und der Erde. . . . *

Hitler: (*to himself*): The Apostles' Creed . . . nothing changes. . . . (*He rises and paces about again.*) God the Father . . . God the creator . . . God the healer. . . .

Klara: . . . und an Jesus Christus—seinen eingeborenen Sohn, unsern Herrn—empfangen durch den Heiligen Geist . . . ** (**Poldi** *enters down left with a bottle in a sack.*)

Poldi: I've got some. A whole bottle. (**Hitler** *takes it from him quickly.*)

---

*I believe in God—the Father almighty—the creator of heaven and earth . . .

**and in Jesus Christ—the only begotten son of the Father—who was incarnate by the Holy Ghost . . .

Hitler: Thank God. I thought you'd never get here.

Poldi: How is she?

Hitler: Worse. . . .

Klara: . . . geboren von der Jungfrau Maria, gelitten unter Pontius Pilatus . . . *

Hitler: Where did you get it? (*He studies the label on the bottle.*)

Poldi: From old Schultz . . . his special brand of cough syrup. . . .

Hitler: I understand.

Poldi: But don't tell anyone. He gives it to us by the left hand. For your mother only.

Klara: . . . gekreuzigt, gestorben, und begraben . . . hinabgestiegen in das Reich des Todes . . . am dritten Tage auferstanden von den Toten . . . aufgefahren in den Himmel . . . **

Hitler: How much opium in it?

Poldi: Plenty. (**Hitler** *sits on the bed and pours the cough syrup into a large spoon.*)

Hitler: Here, Mother. Take this . . . for the pain. . . .

Klara (*her eyes tightly closed*): . . . er sitzt zur Rechten Gottes, des allmächtigen Vaters. . . .***

Hitler: Mother! Swallow this. (**Klara** *opens her eyes and looks at the syrup.*)

Klara: Did the doctor bring it?

Hitler (*He holds it to her mouth, but she turns her head.*): Here—take and drink. The blood of the Saviour.

Klara: Is it a drug?

Hitler: It will kill the pain. Drink it.

Klara: No.

Hitler: Why not?

Klara: It is God's will that I suffer.

Hitler (*furiously*): It is not God's will that you suffer. Why would he care? Think! . . . Ask yourself!

Klara: I must have sinned. . . . I must pay. . . .

Hitler: No—no!

---

*born of the Virgin Mary, suffered under Pontius Pilate . . .

**was crucified, died, and was buried . . . descended into hell . . . and on the third day, arose from the dead . . . ascended into heaven . . .

***and sitteth at the right hand of God the Father almighty . . .

Klara: . . . von dort wird er kommen, zu richten die Lebenden und die Toten.*

Hitler: Mother, please! For me!

Klara: It isn't right, Adolf. It is a drug and drugs are evil.

Hitler: Why is a drug evil? If it is used to—

Klara: Because God says so.

Hitler: That's ridiculous. There is no God—never has been, never will be!

Klara: Ich glaube an den Heiligen Geist, die heilige katholische Kirche—**

Hitler: Stop saying that nonsense.

Poldi (*drawing* **Hitler** *away*): Adolf, leave her alone a little.

Hitler: She'll have another attack soon and this will get her through it.

Poldi: Calm yourself.

Klara (*closing her eyes again*): —die Gemeinschaft der Heiligen, Vergebung der Süden, Auferstehung die toten, und das ewige Leben. Amen.***

Hitler: We must think of a way to get it inside her. (*He puts the bottle on the kitchen table.*)

Poldi: We could mix it with milk.

Hitler: The quantities would have to be so small to keep her from tasting the syrup that they wouldn't do any good.

Poldi: We could cook it into something.

Hitler: She can't eat. (*He paces furiously about.*) Gott in Himmel! To have something that would relieve her pain and then be unable to give it to her! The irony—the injustice! The vileness of religion! (*He bangs his fist against the picture of Jesus on the wall.*)

Poldi: Control yourself. This isn't the time for—(**Klara** *suddenly rises again with a loud, piercing scream of pain.*)

Klara: Ahhhhhh—! (**Hitler** *rushes to her with the bottle.*)

Hitler: Here! Drink this medicine. It is from the doctor!

Klara: No, poison—!

Hitler: It is not poison. (*He tries to get her to drink out of the bottle, but she spits out the liquid and knocks the bottle out of his hand.*) Ahh!! Look

---

* . . . from there he will come to judge both the quick and the dead.

**I believe in the Holy Ghost, the Holy Catholic church—

***—the communion of saints, the forgiveness of sins, the resurrection of the dead, and life everlasting. Amen.

38

what you've done! After all the trouble we had getting hold of this stuff.

Poldi (*recovering the bottle*): There's still some left.

Hitler: I'll hold her mouth open—you pour it down her throat.

Klara (*screaming*): No, no—! Let me alone. Let me die in peace.

Hitler: Drink this!

Poldi: Adolf! . . . Let go of her!

Klara: It is God's will. (*Reluctantly* **Hitler** *lets her lie back down on the bed.* **Poldi** *puts the bottle on the kitchen table.*)

Hitler: It is the devil's will.

Klara: Ich glaube an Gott . . . den Vater . . . den Allmächtigen. . . .* (*Her body seems to tremble. Her eyes open and close; then she seems to relax.*)

Hitler: What can we do? (*He paces about distractedly.*)

Poldi: I don't know. Wait, I guess. For the end.

Hitler: I can't stand it much longer. I shall go insane. . . . (*The room seems to grow darker.* **Hitler** *looks out a window in the upstage wall. After a few moments,* **Poldi** *crosses to* **Klara** *and takes her pulse. Then he puts her arm across her chest and turns away.*)

Poldi: Adolf . . .

Hitler (*turning slowly*): What?

Poldi: She's dead. (*Pause.* **Hitler** *tries to control himself but can't.*)

Hitler: No—no! I can't bear to lose her! (*He takes a step toward the bed, then turns suddenly and rips the picture of Jesus off the wall.*) You! Archfiend! Torturer! Devil incarnate! (*He stamps on the picture. Then he falls to his knees by the bed and buries his head on his mother's breast, sobbing uncontrollably.* **Poldi** *stands to one side, watching him sympathetically.*)

Poldi: Ehre sei dem Vater und den Sohn und den Heiligen Geist. Wie im Anfang, so auch jetzt und alle Zeit und in Ewigkeit. Amen.** (*The lighting fades down and out on Scene 2. During the change to Scene 3, the music of "Silent Night" continues until the change is complete.*)

*I believe in God the Father almighty.

**Blessed be the Father and the Son and the Holy Ghost. As it was in the beginning, is now, and ever shall be, world without end. Amen.

ACT I

SCENE 3: *A month later.*

AT RISE: *Stage left, a World War I battlefield in total darkness. Stage right is the cell as before, except that it is empty. There are many papers on the worktable and some on a side table. Books are scattered about the cell, some on the floor. The room resembles a writer's study more than a prison cell.*

 Bright sunlight comes through the window upstage from right to left, suggesting early afternoon. After a moment, the door down right opens and **Otto** *shows in* **Ulrich** *and his fiancée,* **Erika Wendt,** *a pretty girl in her twenties. She carries a large handbag.*

Otto: You can wait in here.

Ulrich: Thank you, Otto. (**Otto** *exits and locks the door after him.*)

Erika: So this is where you toil all day.

Ulrich: Yes. I sit there at the table writing while he paces around the room dictating. (*He shows her one of his books.*) Like to see my shorthand? It's improving. (*She looks at his shorthand.*)

Erika: Yes, it is. I can even read some of it.

Ulrich: Well, sometimes I have to go very fast. His mind races along from one thing to the next. . . . I've filled up five books already and we've really only gotten started.

Erika: Where is he now?

Ulrich: At lunch. Sometimes lunch lasts quite a while. He eats with the other prisoners, then, afterward, they talk politics.

Erika: Do they all listen to him?

Ulrich: Of course.

Erika: Every meal?

Ulrich: Only lunch. He takes breakfast and supper in here.

Erika: Does he do any work?

Ulrich: Work?

Erika: Hard labor . . . breaking rocks. . . .

Ulrich (*laughing*): Of course not. They consider him their most important prisoner. He has special privileges. And he bribes the guards with presents people send him.

Erika: Presents?

Ulrich: They come from all over. The typing paper I use came from Frau Winifred Wagner at Bayreuth.

Erika: And all he does is dictate his memoirs?

40

Ulrich: He does more than that. He gets up at six, bathes, and has breakfast by seven. Then, he usually takes a walk in the garden and after that he attends to his correspondence and reads over what I brought him the previous day. (*He examines a neat pile of papers on a side table.*) In fact, it looks like he has finished up quite a bit. All this stuff is marked "approved".

Erika: I don't believe this.

Ulrich: Then, about ten, he holds a meeting of the National Socialist prisoners. Sometimes he makes a speech. . . . Sometimes he reads to them what we are writing. . . .

Erika: He holds meetings in *here*?

Ulrich: No, he has the large cell next door, too. He holds meetings in there.

Erika: Really! *Two* cells!

Ulrich (*laughing again*): Actually, he has another one where he keeps his books and receives visitors. But this is his private cell. This is where we work.

Erika: He might as well be living in a hotel.

Ulrich: After the meeting comes lunch. Then he dictates to me. At night I type up everything in the prison library while he reads, has supper, takes another walk . . . then goes to bed.

Erika: You seem to admire him.

Ulrich: Yes. . . . he has such tremendous enthusiasm. And he has ideals. He sees a future for Germany and Austria that I can only dimly perceive. But I am understanding him better every day. At least . . . somewhat better. Of course, there's a dark side to him.

Erika: I think you spend too much time with him.

Ulrich: Why?

Erika: I don't know. I just feel . . . uneasy . . . worried.

Ulrich: There's nothing to worry about.

Erika: When will you finish with all this?

Ulrich: I don't know.

Erika: Won't you come back to Munich? I miss you so. And it's expensive to come here and just stay the weekend.

Ulrich: I know. (*He puts his arm around her shoulder loosely.*)

Erika: And then to have to go back to that damn office . . . with Herr Schlange pinching me all the time and looking at my legs while he dictates. . . .

Ulrich: Quit. And stay here with me.

Erika: But you don't make anything at this crazy job.

Ulrich: I get room and board. And a little extra.

Erika: Why don't you ask Hitler for a raise?

Ulrich (*amazed*): Ask him for a raise?! Why . . . well . . . Erika, you simply don't understand what kind of a person he is. I couldn't interrupt his thoughts for such a thing. We concentrate very hard on the book. And he has only so much time to dictate. Really! You must try to understand.

Erika: I'm sorry. I don't mean to upset you. . . . Why not ask the man in Munich who hired you?

Ulrich: Hanfstaengl? Maybe . . . the next time I'm in Munich.

Ulrich: When will that be, Ulrich?

Ulrich: I don't know. (*He turns away evasively.*)

Erika: You don't know . . . you aren't sure . . . everything is so vague.

Ulrich: We have to finish the book.

Erika: And then?

Ulrich: He may have some further duties for me.

Erika: *Duties?* You sound like you're in the army.

Ulrich: It's a kind of army.

Erika: And where does all this leave us? I thought we were engaged to be married.

Ulrich: We are.

Erika: Well?

Ulrich: Well what?

Erika: Oh, Ulrich! What's come over you? (*She embraces him. He kisses her in a perfunctory manner.*) You've changed since you came here.

Ulrich: Have I? (*He breaks away from her.*)

Erika: Yes!

Ulrich: We all change. No one remains the same all his life. I've come up against . . . something remarkable . . . a strange and remarkable man.

Erika: Leave him.

Ulrich: No! (*He looks defiantly at her, then looks away.*) Not only do I owe him my loyalty—at least until the book is finished—but there are other things.

Erika: What other things?

Ulrich: He is guiding my education. He has loaned me certain books to read. Books I've never seen before.

Erika (*half to herself.*): The devil's books.

Ulrich: You sound like his mother. Gripped by superstition.

Erika: Don't you talk to me like that. I have rights, too. We are engaged to be married. We—(*There is suddenly the sound of the jail door being unlocked.*)

Otto (*off right*): Herr Schwarz and a young lady are inside, sir.

Hitler: Thank you, Otto. (**Hitler,** *dressed in comfortable summer clothing, enters quickly down right. The door is closed and locked behind him.*)

Ulrich: Herr Hitler, my fiancée, Fräulein Wendt.

Hitler (*warmly*): Ah, Fräulein Wendt! How delightful to meet you at last. (*He gallantly kisses her hand.*)

Erika: Thank you, sir. It's an honor to meet you.

Hitler: Ulrich has spoken of you often. And I must say—(*He looks her over approvingly.*)—he did not in the least exaggerate your good looks.

Erika (*pleased*): Thank you for being so kind, sir.

Hitler: I believe you reside in Munich?

Erika: Yes. I have a job as a secretary in the Commerzbank.

Hitler: And when will you be married?

Erika: Well . . . (*She looks imploringly at* **Ulrich,** *who says nothing.*) That depends . . . on several things.

Ulrich: We hope to save up a little money before we get married.

Hitler: That is wise. A young couple should have something to get started on. The children will be expensive. Especially in the city.

Erika: Yes, everything costs so much these days.

Hitler: I hope I may have the privilege of attending your wedding.

Erika: Oh! Would you really come?

Hitler: I would be honored.

Erika: We'll be sure to send you an invitation. (**Hitler** *has picked up the sheaf of typed papers from the side table and is looking quickly through them.*

Hitler: Thank you, my dear. (*He turns to* **Ulrich.**) We are through with this much, aren't we?

Ulrich: Yes, sir. Unless you have further changes to make.

Hitler: I noted down a few things in the margins last night . . . but . . . basically, I believe the first chapter is complete.

Erika: I'll be going now and leave you to your work.

Hitler (*casually*): Are you returning to Munich?

Erika: Yes. My train leaves soon.

Hitler: Would you do me a great favor?

Erika: Of course.

Hitler: I see you carry a rather large handbag. May I . . . ? (*He deftly takes it from her and opens it.*)

Erika: Yes. I . . . I stay overnight when I come here. . . . (*She stops and looks embarrassedly at **Ulrich** who is watching **Hitler**.*)

Hitler: Would you find it an excessive burden to take these pages of manuscript to my agent in Munich for me?

Erika: No. (*She watches as **Hitler** puts the pages of manuscript into her purse.*)

Hitler: His name is Ernst Hanfstaengl, and he lives in the Schwabing district of Munich. Do you know where that is?

Erika: Yes, I do. (**Hitler** *smooths out her purse, closes the flap, and carefully snaps the lock shut.*)

Hitler: I will write down his address for you. (*He hands her back her purse.*) This will be . . . (*he writes down the address on a card*) . . . a most valuable service . . . for which I shall be eternally grateful to you. (*He hands her the card.*)

Erika: The pleasure is mine, sir.

Hitler: You will be careful with it, won't you? Your future husband has worked very hard on it.

Erika: I'll guard it with my life.

Hitler: And—er—please do not discuss it with anyone or show it to anybody. The material is highly confidential.

Erika: I understand.

Hitler (*at the door*): Otto!

Ulrich: Will you come next week?

Erika: I'll try. (*They kiss warmly.* **Hitler** *watches benignly.*)

Otto (*entering down right*): Did you call, sir?

Hitler: Yes. Will you please accompany Fräulein Wendt to the front gate without any unnecessary delay? She has to catch a train to Munich.

Otto: Glad to, sir. This way, Fräulein. . . .

Hitler: Farewell, my dear. (*Again, he kisses her hand.*) I look forward with great pleasure to our next meeting.

Erika: Good-bye, sir. Good-bye, Ulrich.

Ulrich: Good-bye, Erika. Have a safe journey. (**Erika** *and* **Otto** *exit down right. The door is locked again.*)

Hitler: Well, Ulrich, she is very nice. And I think our manuscript is in safe hands.

Ulrich: They'll never think to search her. That was an inspiration.

Hitler: Is she conscientious in her work? Her habits?

Ulrich: Very. She will deliver the manuscript to Putzi today without fail.

Hitler: I thought so. I can evaluate character very rapidly, and I am seldom mistaken in these judgments. (*He begins pacing about the room.*) And now, to work. (**Ulrich** *sits at the table and writes as* **Hitler** *dictates.*) We will turn now to my Vienna period, a dark five years in my life. (*He folds his arms over his chest, as before, and stares out toward the audience.*) After the death of my dear mother, I journeyed to Vienna and took employment where I could find it. I had failed a second time in my effort to be admitted to the Vienna Academy of Fine Arts and now had literally nothing to do, since . . . if I couldn't be an architect, I didn't want to be anything. (*He pauses, thinking over his years in Vienna.*) Vienna, city of music . . . of Johann Strauss and Franz Lehár. . . . (*In the distance he hears some waltz music from* The Merry Widow.) But for me, it was all just hunger and misery. I worked first as a day laborer, then as a painter of postcards that a Jewish picture dealer sold for me on a 50 percent commission. . . . (*He puts his hand over his stomach.*) Hunger was my constant companion. I never earned enough to appease my hunger. If I went to the opera, I was hungry for days afterward, as I could only go if I gave up food. . . . I managed to buy a few books . . . such as Schopenhauer's *World as Will and Representation* . . . also at a cost of extra hunger. But it was during this period of my life that I forged the foundations of an education from which I still draw intellectual nourishment today. (*To* **Ulrich.**)Too fast?

Ulrich: No.

Hitler: In fact it was during this period of my life that there emerged from the mists of despair a quite distinct philosophy, to which I still cling. All creative ideas are revealed to us in our youth . . . and in our maturity, we shape these intuitively understood concepts into the building blocks of our future. . . . Vienna provided me not only with books, the opera, beautiful buildings, and the great art museums. I learned something else, too. The city was a study in social contrasts. Side by side in the same few blocks one could see both the rich and the poor. Outside the palaces on the Ring streets were thousands of unemployed . . . beggars . . . the destitute of all nations of the Hapsburg empire. I studied these contrasts, and not from some safe perch in a library. No . . . I walked among the poor. I lived with the poor, and I know in my bones what it is like to be destitute, without hope, without spirit, without self-esteem. (*He pauses a long time.* **Ulrich** *finally looks up from his notebook.*)

Ulrich: These must have been terrible times for you.

Hitler: Words can't describe my despair in those years. (*He sits moodily at the table. During the following, as they engage in conversation,* **Ulrich** *continues to jot down short notations in his notebook.*)

Ulrich: But you must have had some friends.

Hitler: Acquaintances. No friends. You know . . . it's odd how the weather used to make a difference to me.

Ulrich: The weather?

Hitler: Yes. I seemed to feel quite confident—enthusiastic even—in the spring and summer. Then as fall turned into winter, I became depressed again, shivered with the cold, and lost my short-lived optimism.

Ulrich: But couldn't you find any work at all?

Hitler: Oh, I was all right for a time, but I ran out of money. And then I ran out of something else . . . energy . . . spirit . . . what is the right word? What keeps us going in the midst of despair?

Ulrich: The survival instinct, I suppose.

Hitler: How I survived I don't know. By my second winter in Vienna I had to seek shelter in the Vienna poorhouse. I suffered from severe mal-nutrition . . . my feet were blistered . . . my hands covered with sores . . . I had been sleeping in doorways . . . I had no coat and was in danger of dying of pneumonia, as so many poor beggars do in Vienna every winter. (*He puts his head down on his arms.* **Ulrich** *regards him with sympathy for some moments, finally putting his hand on* **Hitler's** *shoulders.*)

Ulrich: Do you want to rest?

Hitler (*slowly straightening up*): No. We have to get through this somehow. It is important that it be recorded that my political philosophy is grounded in sympathy for the poor and downtrodden of this world. . . . (*He looks a long time at* **Ulrich** *who does not look away. Finally,* **Hitler** *resumes his narrative.*) Let us continue. . . .

Ulrich: I'm ready.

Hitler: I couldn't stay at the shelter indefinitely and finally, as spring was approaching, I found a place to live, the Männerheim, a home for single men near the Leopoldstadt. Here, I finally put my life in order. (*He* *paces about again, with his arms folded.*) I had a small cubicle I could call my own, and I began to make a little money painting postcards. These were not original works. To increase my output, my habit was to trace existing postcards, then to paint them in my own style in watercolor. They were good enough to fetch small sums in the Jewish art market of Vienna.

Ulrich: Do you still have any of these postcards?

Hitler: Yes, a few. Would you like one?

Ulrich: May I purchase one?

Hitler: Of course not. But I'll show you some of them, and if you see two or three that you like they shall be yours.

Ulrich: But I couldn't accept—

Hitler: Why not? You are an excellent secretary. And we get on well together. That's very important in a close working relationship. . . .

Ulrich: Yes . . . yes. (**Hitler** *walks over to him.* **Ulrich** *watches him as though hypnotized.*)

Hitler: And so . . . (*he bends over* **Ulrich**, *his face close to him*) you must let me give you some small tokens of my admiration for you. . . . (*he kisses* **Ulrich** *warmly on the lips*) . . . from time to time. (*They look at each other for some moments; then* **Hitler** *resumes his pacing.*) I turn now to my war experiences.

Ulrich: Is this all you wish to say about Vienna?

Hitler: No. Leave some space. We'll come back to it. I'm not in the mood to discuss Vienna any more today. (**Ulrich** *selects another notebook to write in.*)

Ulrich: As you wish.

Hitler (*with animation*): As a young man, I long believed that I lived in a most uninteresting time. The great nations behaved toward each other like so many Jewish merchants, each trying to outswindle the other, stealing each other's customers and complaining loudly but harmlessly about the "hard times" they faced. . . . (*He becomes more and more excited.*) But there were a few episodes of more than passing interest to me. . . . The Boer War was a satisfying struggle of oppressed peoples against the brutal British tyranny, and the Russian-Japanese War, in which I instantly sided with the Japanese, showed that a Russian defeat could mean a loosening of the Slavic grip on the Balkan states. (*Fervently*) Then there was a ten-year period when the Balkans were shrouded in a kind of livid sultriness . . . a period of oppressive

47

heat before the storm . . . with flashes of lightning in the distance . . . brief gusts of wind that stirred the nervous European continent. . . . (*During the following, he walks over to the left side of the stage, puts on a German World War I trench coat and a helmet, and then buckles a belt with a dispatch case and a pistol around his waist. The lighting fades out stage right, but a dim spot remains on* **Ulrich** *as he continues to write. The left side of the stage now resembles a battlefield of various levels, with a suggestion of shell holes and barbed wire.*) Time lay heavy on the chests of men . . . there was an atmosphere of tropic heat during that fateful August of 1914 . . . and we were all gripped by a sense of approaching catastrophe that turned at last into a fervent desire for action, decision, and fateful confrontation. And then, the first powerful flash of lightning struck the earth, the thunder of heaven was heard, and the earthly artillery batteries roared their defiant responses.

Ulrich: I remember that August, too . . . especially the heat. (*The dark sky left is illuminated with distant flashes of artillery fire, and the reports of the guns are heard loudly in the theater. Soon the artillery effect quiets somewhat and* **Hitler** *continues his narration. He now acts out what he describes, jumping from shell hole to shell hole and reliving his memories as a dispatch runner for a German infantry regiment in France during World War I.*)

Hitler: I volunteered for duty with the List Regiment of the Sixteenth Infantry Division of the Bavarian army, was sent to France and assigned duty as a dispatch runner. (*Another soldier,* **Fritz Beck,** *about the same age as* **Hitler,** *joins him in the shell hole.* **Beck,** *too, carries a dispatch case on a heavy belt.*) We dispatch runners were usually sent out in pairs, the theory being that if one of us got killed, maybe the other would get through.

Beck: Let's rest a minute.

Hitler: We have to go on, Beck.

Beck: The barrage is too heavy. We can't get through it.

Hitler: We'll find a way. (*He looks carefully at the terrain in front of him.*)

Beck: It'll slack off soon; then we can go on.

Hitler: No! The message is marked: "Urgent."

Beck: They mark 'em all that way.

Hitler: You heard them. The general was very excited. He said the front lines have to be notified as quickly as possible.

Beck: He's always excited about something. (**Hitler** *takes the sealed message out of the dispatch case and shows it to* **Beck**.)

Hitler: You see? Marked with three *X*'s "Highest priority."

Beck: I know that. But who says it's all that important? Some fool general with his thumb up his ass—

Hitler: Don't talk like that! Suppose an attack is about to begin—and headquarters got wind of it—

Beck: Shut up, Hitler! I'm sick of you and your heroism. Your fuckin' Iron Cross! Whoever made a square meal out of an Iron Cross?

Hitler (*after a moment*): Look, Beck . . . if you'll go on with me, I'll give it to you. I don't want the damned thing.

Beck: I can't go on.

Hitler: Why?

Beck: My number's up.

Hitler: How do you know?

Beck: I can feel it.

Hitler: We've *got* to go on.

Beck (*screaming*): No! (*He lies down in the shell hole, his entire body trembling with fear.* **Hitler** *watches him for a moment, then resumes his study of the terrain ahead of them. Soon he turns back to* **Beck**.)

Hitler: I have a plan. You see that clump of trees over there? (*He points up left.* **Beck** *follows his plan listlessly.*) You go that way (*he points off left*)—get to that shell hole over there, then to those rocks, then a fast run to the trees. OK? (**Beck** *stares at the trees in the distance.*) And I'll go this way (*he points to a spot up right*)—to that little hill, then across that ditch and over that barbed wire, and then I'll make a run for the trees. And from those trees to the front lines can't be more than a hundred yards. What do you say?

Beck (*still trembling*): You go. I can't.

Hitler: Beck, I know the feeling of fear. I'm afraid, too. The barrage is very bad. They're up to something.

Beck: Then stay here with me until the barrage dies down.

Hitler: But we have our duty.

Beck: Duty be damned. The Kaiser be damned! Four years of this is too much to bear.

Hitler: Courage, Beck. You're giving way to despair.

Beck: No, not despair, Hitler. Reason. This war is wrong. Insane. You know it is.

49

Hitler: This is not the time or place for a political discussion. We are part of the German Army, and we have our duty.

Beck: The German Army is beaten. In August, we could see the Eiffel Tower from the front lines. Now we're back in Belgium again.

Hitler: I won't argue with you, Beck, even if I think you are wrong. But whatever else you say, you have to agree that you and I are not cowards. We've been at this dirty business a long time, and we'll go on with it as long as we have orders.

Beck: It's wrong. . . . The war is wrong. . . .

Hitler: Courage is above right and wrong. I tell you, Beck (*he points his finger at* **Beck** *in his threatening way*) even after a thousand years, the subject of heroism cannot and will not be discussed without reference to the German Army in the Great War. . . . (*He becomes transfixed again by one of his visions.*) From the veil . . . from the mists of the past there will emerge the strong, pure shape of the gray steel helmets . . . unwavering and unflinching . . . an immortal monument to the will power of the German soldier. (*The sound of the shelling gets louder.*)

Beck: It's getting worse.

Hitler: As long as the Germans live they will remember us. They will remember us as true and loyal sons or the German people. . . .

Beck: You actually believe all that, don't you?

Hitler: With all my soul.

Beck: You are insane.

Hitler: Maybe, maybe not. Anyway, we've got to go.

Beck: No. (**Hitler** *suddenly hits* **Beck** *in the jaw.*)

Hitler: Yes!

Beck: You bastard! (*He reaches for his pistol.*)

Hitler (*holding his arm*): Beck! Calm yourself! Steel your will! (*He stares at* **Beck**, *trying to communicate some of his own will power to his comrade. Slowly,* **Beck** *recovers his nerve. He turns apprehensively upstage.*)

Beck: All right. (*He emits a deep sigh of resignation.*) I'll go. I'll meet you in those trees in a few minutes.

Hitler: I'll be there waiting for you. (**Beck** *looks curiously at* **Hitler** *a moment, then rushes off left.*) Good luck! (**Hitler** *starts to run from the shell hole to a hill just upstage, but before he can leave, a violent explosion is heard from off left followed by a scream of pain.*) Beck—Beck! Are you hit? (*He rushes off left and soon returns*

50

dragging **Beck** *with him.* **Beck** *is bleeding from the mouth, and there are many red splotches on his legs.*)

Beck: Help—help—medic!

Hitler: Lie still. I'll tie up your wounds. They're not too bad. . . . (**Hitler** *cuts open* **Beck's** *pants leg and examines the wounds.* **Beck** *screams.*) Courage! Courage! I'll give you something for the pain, but I have to stop the bleeding first. (*He applies a tourniquet to* **Beck's** *leg. His back is turned and he does not see* **Beck** *take the dispatch from his case, open it, and read it.*)

Beck (*suppressing his pain*): Why? . . . why? For what . . . for what did I . . . (*He reads the dispatch. The bombardment suddenly stops. It becomes ominously quiet.*)

Hitler: There. That will stop the bleeding. (*He turns around and sees* **Beck** *reading the dispatch.*) Beck! You can't do that. It is forbidden to us to read the dispatches. (**Beck** *suddenly coughs up a mass of blood.*)

Beck: Hitler, read! Gas! (*He falls back, dying of his wounds.*)

Hitler: Gas? . . . (*He snatches the dispatch from his comrade's hand and reads it quickly. From the direction of the front lines upstage, a dark green cloud appears coming closer.* **Hitler** *looks behind him frantically and rushes forward to down right. Some of the gas has already caught up with him, however, as he suddenly screams and falls to the ground, his hands pressing against his eyes. The lighting gradually fades out left and comes up in the jail cell right.* **Hitler** *leaves the belt, coat, and helmet stage left as he crawls toward the right, coughing and crying out in pain.* **Ulrich** *rises and crosses to him and helps him into bed.*)

Ulrich: Quiet . . . quiet. . . . calm yourself. . . .

Hitler: I'm blind—blind!

Ulrich (*helping him into the bed*): These memories are too vivid for you . . . too painful. . . .

Hitler: Where am I?

Ulrich: Safe.

Hitler: Am I at Pasewalk—at the hospital?

Ulrich: No.

Hitler (*gripping* **Ulrich's** *arm*): Doctor, will I ever see again?

Ulrich: Yes. The blinding is temporary.

Hitler: Will I be able to draw again?

Ulrich: Yes.

Hitler: See the sky . . . the sunset . . . the lightning on the distant horizon?

Ulrich: Everything.

Hitler: The war is over, isn't it? That priest . . . he told us. The Kaiser has abdicated. . . . (*He suddenly sits up in the bed, his hands over his eyes.*) So it was all in vain! In vain all the sacrifices and losses! In vain the hunger and thirst of endless months! In vain the hours of mortal fear clutching our hearts—fear that we conquered in order to do our duty to the Fatherland. Ahhhhh! Mother! Mother! (*He falls back on the bed.* **Ulrich** *lies beside him, trying to calm him by stroking his forehead, his cheek, and his lips. Lighting fades down and out.*)

CURTAIN.

END ACT 1.

ACT II

SCENE 1: *The jail cell, a few months later. It is a hot summer day.*

AT RISE: *The stage left area is set to represent the corner of a large beer hall in Munich. Two or three tables with chairs are in evidence, and there is a newspaper rack at rear. There is no light on the left area.*

Stage right, in the cell, bright sunlight comes through the window from right to left, suggesting late afternoon. **Hitler** *is lying on the bed wearing only his shorts.* **Ulrich** *is standing by the window as he finishes dressing.*

Hitler: Ulrich, what is the most beautiful building you have ever seen?

Ulrich: Hmmmmmm. I believe the most impressive building I've seen is the Cologne Cathedral.

Hitler: Yes. Majestic. Awe-inspiring.

Ulrich: And the most charming building I know is the Karlskirche in Vienna.

Hitler: I painted that church.

Ulrich: Then, as a statement of function, I like the little Hauptwache building in Frankfurt.

Hitler: Why do you like that relic?

Ulrich: I don't know. It appeals to me.

Hitler: But the most beautiful. You keep evading the question.

Ulrich: The Munich Opera.

Hitler: Why?

Ulrich: Purity of design. The classical facade. The frieze on the pediment.

The statue of the Elector Maximilian in front, the great Residenz building to the side . . . it fits its environment. And inside, one can see the greatest masterpieces of the theater performed by superb casts, with magnificent scenic effects, brilliant playing by the orchestra in the pit, altogether a worthy tribute to the greatest genius of the German theater, Richard Wagner.

Hitler: Yes . . . yes. Four of his greatest operas were given their first performances in that theater.

Ulrich: It's a Greek temple of German art.

Hitler: Do you like it better than the Vienna Opera House?

Ulrich: It's different. The Vienna Opera is a strange mixture of styles. It upsets me. (**Hitler** *gets up and gets dressed through the following.*)

Hitler: I like that mishmash of styles. There is a functional element, after all. One can easily do operas in it from all periods of the history of music—baroque, romantic, and modern—and the audience never feels that the work is being done in the wrong place.

Ulrich: But while you're inside watching an opera, you can't see the building from the outside.

Hitler: You can remember it. (**Ulrich** *sits at the table.*)

Ulrich: Shall we do some more work this afternoon?

Hitler: Yes. (*He has finished dressing in light summer clothing.*) Did you ever hear the popular little ditty about the architects of the Vienna Opera?

Ulrich: No.

Hitler:

"Von Siccardsburg und van der Nüll,
Die haben ihren eignen Stül.
Ob griechisch, römisch, Renaissanz,
Das ist den beiden alles ans."*

Ulrich (*laughing*): I know exactly what whoever wrote that meant.

Hitler: One of the architects hanged himself.

Ulrich: Really?

*Von Siccardsburg and van der Nüll,
They have their own special style.
Whether Greek, Roman, or Renaissance,
It's all the same to them.

Hitler: And the other one died just afterward of heart disease. Neither one of them lived to see the completed building.

Ulrich: They must have been hurt by the criticism.

Hitler: The artist finds it hard to accept criticism . . . especially ignorant, peasant criticism.

Ulrich: Perhaps that's why one seldom sees an artist in political life.

Hitler: Art and politics don't mix.

Ulrich: Of course, a king can be an artist . . . Frederick the Great, Ludwig II. . . .

Hitler: But for an artist to be a king . . . catastrophe. As in Munich in 1919 when the Communists took over the government of Bavaria.

Ulrich: You mean Toller?

Hitler: Imagine! Ernst Toller—a Jewish Communist playwright—as head of the state of Bavaria. What a grand successor to the House of Wittelsbach!

Ulrich: That was a curious interlude in our history.

Hitler: Toller! And his Jewish ministers. Did you know that both Erich Muehsam and Gustav Landauer were Jews?

Ulrich: No.

Hitler: And their successor from Moscow—Leviné. Another Jew Communist. It was at this time that I first realized the close association between Marxism and international Jewry.

Ulrich: And Marx himself was a Jew.

Hitler: In Berlin, Rosa Luxemburg . . . in Budapest, Béla Kun. . . .

Ulrich: And the Russian Communist Jews—Trotsky . . . Zinoviev. . . . Kamenev. . . .

Hitler: Yes, Ulrich, I saw it all in 1919, right under my nose. (*He paces about excitedly.*) The Jewish-Communist conspiracy seized power in Bavaria and held it for months. If they had had an equal success in Berlin, Germany today would be a Jewish-Communist state.

Ulrich: Yes, it was a close call.

Hitler: And there is still danger from the Jewish-Communist world conspiracy. The Jews in Germany and Austria must be expelled to the east. . . . (*He pauses and glances at* **Ulrich**. Underline that.

Ulrich: Yes, sir.

Hitler: They must be expelled because they have formed an alliance with the Russian Communists to make themselves masters of the world. They are as dangerous to Germany as Russia is. After we have united

Germany with Austria, after we have regained the Rhine territories and the Czech territories, and Danzig, then we must turn our gaze toward the east, and confront the Jewish-Communist power bloc with stern resolution. . . . Do you have that down?

Ulrich: Yes.

Hitler: We will have to do an entire section on this problem.

Ulrich: I agree.

Hitler: Expulsion of the Jews is central to my political philosophy.

Ulrich: I have it down. . . . You were saying a moment ago that an artist could not head a state. Perhaps that might be explained a little more. . . .

Hitler (*thoughtfully*): It is a problem with the soul of the artist. The artist lives in a world of idealism. For Toller, the perfect moment of the revolution was that intoxicating instant when the old order had been swept away, but the new order had still not been established. A moment of perfect freedom!

Ulrich: As in *Faust, Part II.*

Hitler: Exactly. The revolution was a work of art to Toller.

Ulrich: Wagner must have seen revolution in the same way.

Hitler: Probably. And what happened? Did he fight to the end on the barricades?

Ulrich: He took off for Switzerland—

Hitler: —one jump ahead of the police. (*They both laugh.*) A figure not of revolution, but of comedy.

Ulrich: Toller lacked the power to act.

Hitler: The *will* to act. As an artist, he was paralyzed by two conflicting forces within himself: his sense of humanity and the plain need for vigorous—even violent—action.

Ulrich: A playwright lives in a world of words.

Hitler: Yes. He conjures up visions of an ideal order, something beyond reality, because he deals with the written word and not the spoken word. The orator can influence world history. The poet merely comments on history.

Ulrich: But great comments sometimes . . . Homer . . . Shakespeare. . . . (*Stage left,* **Rudi Kertz,** *a tall, balding man in his forties, enters the beer hall and sits at a table. He spreads some sheets of manuscript on the table and begins to write.*)

Hitler: I had an interesting discussion with one of these political playwrights on this very subject a few days before the Putsch. . . . (*He crosses toward the left. In the beer hall, a waiter brings a stein of beer to* **Rudi** *'s table. Lighting begins to brighten to the left and darken to the right.*)

Ulrich: A political playwright. Isn't that a contradiction in terms?

Hitler: He didn't think so. His name was . . . Bert something. He wrote a play called *Drums in the Streets,* or some such title. About the Communist uprising in Berlin in 1919. (*He continues left. The lighting now cross-fades as before. leaving a dim spot on* **Ulrich** *as he writes and coming up on the left playing area.*) I had gone to a Munich beer hall to meet Rudi Kertz, the novelist and an old friend. He had told me to meet him there because he had a present he wanted to give me. (**Hitler** *steps into the left area.* **Rudi** *gets up from the table.*)

Rudi: Adolf! You are here. Sit down. I am so glad to see you. I know how busy you are these days.

Hitler: I have only a few minutes, Rudi.

Rudi: I'll get the package. I checked it with my coat. (*He starts out left.* **Hitler** *sits at the table.*)

Hitler: What is it? I can't stand the suspense.

Rudi: You'll see. Waiter, a half-liter for Herr Hitler. (*He exits left. The* **Waiter** *appears.*)

Waiter: Light beer or dark?

Hitler: Dark. (*The* **Waiter** *exits left. As he does so, a tall, thin young man wearing a cap enters carrying a stein of beer. He passes* **Hitler's** *table and crosses to the newspaper rack at rear. He selects a paper and sits at the table upstage to read and drink his beer. He and* **Hitler** *exchange brief glances. After a moment,* **Rudi** *returns with a large garment box. He puts the box on another table and begins to open it.*)

Rudi: I'll just open this little box. . . . (*He sees* **Bert** *at the other table.*) Bert! How've you been?

Bert: Hello, Rudi

Rudi: Bert, meet Adolf Hitler, the next president of Bavaria.

Bert: How do you do?

Hitler: Pleased to meet you.

Rudi: Bert wrote *Drums in the Streets.*

Hitler: Did you? I saw that play.

Bert: Always glad to meet a paying customer.

56

Rudi: Bring your beer over and join us. (*He continues opening the package.*)

Bert: All right. (*He brings his beer over and sits at* **Hitler's** *table. The* **Waiter** *brings* **Hitler** *a stein of dark beer and, as he leaves, returns* **Bert's** *paper to the rack.*) How did you like it?

Hitler: I didn't understand it.

Bert: That's possible. It didn't come out the way I intended. (*He lights a cigar.*) I'm afraid the audience sees the revolution the way my hero does—romantically—and that is not what I intended.

Hitler: Are you a Communist?

Bert: Why?

Hitler: A great force is pulling us down into the depths.

Bert: Gravity?

Hitler: The Jewish-Communist world conspiracy.

Bert: Oh—*that.*

Hitler: Yes—*that.* . . . You haven't answered my question.

Bert: I still don't know why you ask it.

Hitler: Your ideas puzzle me. If you aren't a Communist, why write about the attempted Communist Putsch in Berlin? And if you are, why don't we see your man doing a little fighting? Or at least making a speech? (**Bert** *puffs thoughtfully on his cigar.*)

Rudi: Here we are! A new coat for you! (*He holds up a good-looking trench coat.*)

Hitler: I have a coat.

Rudi: Not like this. Not a trench coat. This will make you look ready for anything. Try it on.

Hitler (*dubiously*): I don't know. . . . (*He tries on the coat.* **Bert** *watches him with amusement.*)

Rudi: Now the hat. (*He hands* **Hitler** *a wide-brimmed felt hat.*)

Hitler: I don't like hats.

Rudi: You need a hat. Put it on. (**Hitler** *puts on the hat. He snaps the front brim down.*) Perfect! (*He turns to* **Bert.**) How does he look?

Bert: Like a Chicago gangster. (**Hitler** *glances at him casually, then turns away, adjusting the hat brim.*)

Rudi: You look fine. You have never paid enough attention to your appearance.

Hitler: I lead the people. I dress like the people.

Rudi: You are about to enter history. I insist that you be suitably attired.

Hitler: But I'm not used to this coat.

Rudi: It gives you the appearance of a man of action. A man of decision. It's a kind of uniform, yet it isn't.

Hitler (*looking about*): I need a mirror.

Bert: There's one in the Klo. (**Hitler** *exits quickly down left.* **Rudi** *sits at the table with* **Bert**.).

Rudi: You're a man of the theater, Bert. Isn't the effect the most important thing? What the audience sees first?

Bert: What audience? What effect?

Rudi: Well, Ludendorf will be in dress uniform—medals, sword—the works. Hitler will march in the front row beside him. So he has to be in civilian clothes, but he shouldn't look . . . sloppy—like you always do.

Bert: Are they going to a costume party?

Rudi: Haven't you heard? (*He looks about furtively and lowers his voice.*) The Putsch. The march on the government. It's set for the ninth.

Bert: (*puffing thoughtfully on his cigar*): I've heard a lot of rumors. So he's really going through with it?

Rudi: Everything's set. Why don't you join us?

Bert: I might. Where will it start?

Rudi: At the Bürgerbräukeller, on Rosenheimer Street. . . .

Bert: I know where it is. And then?

Rudi: Then down the street to the Ludwigsbrücke, across the river and on to the Marienplatz, then from there along Residenzstraþe to the Odeonsplatz. There, in front of the Feldherrenhalle, Hitler will proclaim the new government of Bavaria and all Germany.

Bert: Hmmmm. He has a good opinion of himself, doesn't he?

Rudi: Hitler will save Germany!

Bert: What about the police? Won't they stop this thing before it gets out of hand?

Rudi: They'll be totally demoralized. They won't fire a shot.

Bert: How many do you expect to march tn this procession?

Rudi: Who knows? Thousands! All of Munich! (**Hitler** *enters left still wearing the hat and coat.*)

Hitler: You're right, Rudi. I like it. Thank you.

Rudi: It will make an effect. You'll see.

Hitler: Perhaps.

Rudi: Sit down. Finish your beer.

Hitler: I can stay a minute. (*He sits at the table and sips his beer.*)

Rudi: Bert speaks English.

Hitler: Do you?

Bert: I like the English.

Hitler: I do, too. My mustache is in the English style.

Bert: You don't say.

Hitler: I've seen many Englishmen wearing mustaches like mine.

Bert: Here in Munich?

Hitler: No, in Liverpool. I lived there awhile before the war.

Bert: You were saying you didn't understand my play. . . .

Hitler: Yes. You see, Herr . . .

Bert: Just call me Bert.

Hitler: You see, Bert, what I couldn't understand was exactly where you stand, as the author. It is a political play, isn't it?

Bert: Yes.

Hitler: And shouldn't a politician take a stand on the issues of the day?

Bert: A politician, yes. But I am a poet.

Hitler: You are beyond politics.

Bert: Not entirely. I take an interest. I keep up. . . .

Rudi: Bert's a Socialist.

Hitler: That covers a lot of ground.

Bert: What in my play wasn't clear to you?

Hitler: A soldier comes back to Berlin after the war. He expects to find his fiancée waiting faithfully for him. But he has been out of touch with her. He has been in a prison camp—in Africa, wasn't it?

Bert: French Morocco.

Hitler: She has taken up with a rich profiteer and is pregnant by him. They plan to get married. Fine, so far.

Bert: You have a feeling for plot structure.

Hitler: The soldier confronts them in a nightclub during the engagement party. A good scene.

Bert: You stayed awake through the second act.

Hitler: But then, Bert, what happens? Your hero runs out into the night and joins the Communist brigands who are attacking the Berlin government. He breaks a few windows—this all happens offstage—then gets bored and takes his girl home to bed.

Bert: Important things happen offstage in Shakespeare, too. *Hamlet*—

Hitler: What conclusion am I supposed to draw from all that? Is he a

believer in revolution, or is he an amateur of some kind who thinks
    bed is more important than ideals?

Bert: He is both.

Hitler: He can't be both. Either he has convictions or he doesn't.

Bert: You didn't like my play.

Hitler: It held my interest. Those drum effects were good.

Rudi: I love the drums.

Hitler: But that's the problem. Too many drums—not enough ideas.

Bert: An idea can be expressed by a drum.

Hitler: Only a writer would say that.

Bert: Writers can have an effect. The pen is mightier than the sword.

Hitler: Nonsense. Writers can't influence events.

Bert: I think they can.

Hitler: Writers can't improve the world, Bert. They can't even make it
    worse.

Bert: And who can improve the world, Herr Hitler?

Hitler: A man of the spoken word. A man of destiny.

Bert: There isn't any such thing as destiny.

Rudi: Oh now, Bert, I don't agree with that.

Hitler: Neither do I.

Bert: Destiny, fate—is there any evidence in the real world of these childish
    ideas? Everything happens by chance. Stupid, idiotic accidents deter-
    mine our lives from start to finish.

Hitler: I reject that.

Rudi: He's just baiting you, Adolf.

Hitler (*becoming a trifle agitated*): Will power determines the outcome of
    all human activity. The power of the human will is the supreme power
    of the universe!

Bert: Did you read that in some book?

Hitler: Yes. In Schopenhauer.

Bert: I thought so.

Hitler: I have confirmed things I've read by living. By speaking in public.
    By action.

Bert: I find human actions ambiguous.

Hitler: What I read I test in the marketplace.

Bert: How?

Hitler: By speaking to the people.

Rudi: You should hear him, Bert. Spellbinding.

Bert: I'll try it sometime.

Hitler: The spoken word is what matters, Bert. The written word is of no interest except to historians and academics.

Bert: I have respect for the spoken word. Homer created his poetry by speaking it—or singing it—to his listeners. But if the Greeks hadn't learned the knack of writing down what he sang, we wouldn't have Homer's poetry today.

Hitler: Do we need Homer's poetry?

Bert: You don't. Some of the rest of us think he has enriched our lives.

Hitler: Take your poetry into the streets. Speak to the people, like I do.

Bert: I speak to the people.

Hitler: From a safe distance, Bert. The comfort of your study, or a beer hall like this one where Rudi writes his novels. But have you ever spoken your poems to a crowd of people in a beer hall knowing that there were Communist thugs present with orders to beat you up?

Bert: I have better sense than to do that.

Hitler: Have you ever felt the need to carry a pistol?

Bert: No. (**Hitler** *suddenly draws his Walther pistol from an inside pocket and points it under* **Bert**'s *nose.*)

Hitler: I do. I carry this to protect myself from Communists . . . and other riffraff. Shall I blow your head off? (*There is a tense pause.* **Bert** *keeps his nerve.*)

Bert: Why don't you?

Hitler (*smiling*): Because I *will* not to.

Bert: And why do you will this *safe* choice?

Hitler: I enjoy discussions like this once in a while.

Bert: As long as you have a pistol and I don't?

Hitler: Anyway you like! (*He slams the pistol on the table.*) Take it! (**Bert** *stares at the pistol.*) Go ahead! Pick it up. Shoot me. Exert your will. (**Bert** *looks closely at him.*)

Bert: You are insane.

Hitler: I've been told that. (*He returns the pistol to his pocket and rises.*) Come on, Rudi. Let's leave Bert here with his verses. He's a poet and a Communist, and I don't have a high opinion of either. (*He strides out left.* **Rudi** *has gathered up his manuscript and puts some money on the table.*)

Rudi: For the beer.

Bert: Thanks, Rudi. For *everything*. (**Rudi** *hastily follows* **Hitler** *out left.* **Bert** *signals the* **Waiter**.) Waiter. . . .

Waiter: Yes, sir?

Bert: Is there a phone in this place?

Waiter: I'll bring you one. You can call from your table. (*He exits left.*)

Bert (*to himself*): Will power, huh? A man of destiny, huh? (*He puffs angrily on his cigar. The* **Waiter** *returns with a telephone that he plugs into an outlet under the table.*)

Waiter: The manager put them in so people can make bets on the horses from their tables. We're the only hall in town with this service.

Bert: I will try to remember that. (*The* **Waiter** *exits, taking the empty coat and hatboxes with him.* **Bert** *picks up the phone.*) Police headquarters. . . . (*He drinks the rest of his beer.*) Yeah . . . I want the riot police division and I want to talk to Klaus. Tell him it's Bert. . . . (*Lighting begins to fade down slowly.*) Klaus? Bert. . . . Now get this down and fast. I don't want to stay here too long. . . . OK . . . Hitler and his punks are planning a Putsch. On the ninth. They're going to march on the government. . . . They say "thousands." . . . I know that, but there's liable to be two or three hundred . . . and they have guns. . . . (*He sketches something on a napkin.*) They claim Ludendorf will lead them . . . he'll be in front with Hitler. Now, here's the route: they start at the Bürgerbräukeller . . . then across the river to the Marienplatz . . . then down Residenzstraþe to the Odeonsplatz. Yeah . . . Hitler will be wearing a trench coat. (*He puts the napkin in his pocket.*) Now listen, Klaus, you can try to stop them at the bridge, but put your best men at the Odeonsplatz . . . and tell them to shoot *Hitler.* Never mind that old fool Ludendorf—tell them to kill HITLER! (*Lighting goes out on scene 1. During the change to scene 2, music from* Rienzi *is heard.*)

ACT II

SCENE 2: *Some weeks later. A day in fall. It is early afternoon. The left area represents a courtroom. Upstage is a raised table behind which are large decorated chairs for three judges A witness chair is right, and there is a table left where two of the lawyers sit. The rest of the room extends off left. Lighting stage left is out.*
   Stage right, the cell looks much as before.
AT RISE: Ulrich and **Erika** *are again waiting for Hitler to finish lunch.* **Ulrich** *sits at the table reading over some sheets of manuscript.* **Erika** *paces about nervously.*
Erika: And I'm tired of taking piles of manuscript to Putzi.
Ulrich: Why?
Erika: He tried to kiss me the last time.
Ulrich: Where was his wife?
Erika: In the kitchen.
Ulrich: Tell him to leave you alone or you'll tell Hitler.
Erika: I told him to leave me alone or I'd call the police.
Ulrich (*smiling*): What did he say?
Erika: Nothing. But he stopped.
Ulrich: He doesn't want the police coming around.
Erika: But it isn't that so much. . . .
Ulrich: What is it? (*He makes a correction on the page he is reading.*)
Erika: Ulrich! What's come over you?
Ulrich: Nothing. Nothing's come over me.
Erika: You aren't the Ulrich I used to know in Munich.
Ulrich: What's changed?
Erika: You have become a cold, calculating, dedicated, fanatical piece of National Socialist Party machinery. What kind of a grip does Hitler have on you, anyway?
Ulrich: I don't know.
Erika: You're like an extension of him. A continuance of his presence in other places.
Ulrich: I believe in him. I believe in his mission.
Erika: Sometimes when we are in bed, I almost think it's him . . . disguised as you.
Ulrich (*delightedly*): Like Siegfried disguised as Gunther while he woos Brünnhilde?

63

Erika: You find an example of everything in Wagner.

Ulrich: Hitler and I talk a lot about Wagner. I have been reading the texts of his operas.

Erika: He even controls your reading.

Ulrich (*after a moment*): I can't explain why I'm drawn to Hitler. I do things for him I wouldn't do for anyone else. It's true that I work for almost nothing. I serve him. I will fight for him if he calls on me. . . . But I believe that I still retain my own individuality.

Erika: Do you?

Ulrich: Yes.

Erika: Then prove it.

Ulrich: How?

Erika: Give him up. By an act of will.

Ulrich: Don't be sarcastic about will power. It is the greatest power on earth.

Erika: So he's told you.

Ulrich: It's true.

Erika: Then prove your individuality. Exert your will. Quit him and come back to Munich with me.

Ulrich: I can't.

Erika: Why not?

Ulrich: We aren't finished with the book, yet. (*He holds up some papers.*) These are ready to go to Munich, but we have a lot left to do.

Erika: He can get another secretary. You've worked for him now for more than six months. And what have you received besides room and board?

Ulrich: He gives me presents.

Erika: What kind of presents?

Ulrich: He gave me four of his watercolors. Someday, they'll be valuable.

Erika: Watercolors of what?

Ulrich: One of the Karlskirche in Vienna—a favorite building of mine. And three of scenes he painted on the Western Front, during the war.

Erika: He painted pictures during the war?

Ulrich: During lulls in the fighting. He loves to paint.

Erika: Has he given you anything else?

Ulrich: Some books.

Erika: Anything we could raise a little cash on?

Ulrich: Erika!

Erika: I'm sorry.

Ulrich: Look—he and I have a good working relationship. I take notes . . .

but not on everything he says. I know what is important and what is simply passing conversation. It would take a new secretary weeks to learn this.

Erika: Any new secretary has to be broken in on a job.

Ulrich: I do the typing. I sort out all the ideas and put them together. I know how to listen to him.

Erika: I still think—

Ulrich: I've joined the Party.

Erika: Another surprise.

Ulrich: I consider him my leader. That's the way things are. How it all came about I don't know. . . . I only know he is my life. And I will follow him, no matter where he leads.

Erika (*softly*): But why . . . why . . . why?

Ulrich: I can't explain something I feel in my blood. (*She crosses to him.*)

Erika: Look at me.

Ulrich: I am.

Erika (*pulling him up*): Kiss me.

Ulrich: All right. (*He kisses her warmly.*) I still love you, Erika, and I hope to marry you someday . . . but you cannot insert yourself in between my leader and me. Why can't you wait for me? What's so urgent about all this?

Erika: I'm pregnant.

Ulrich (*after a moment*): Are you sure?

Erika: I saw the doctor. He examined me—did a test of some kind. And he told me he was sure. (*She eyes him helplessly.*) In about six months we'll have a baby.

Ulrich: So you want me to marry you now?

Erika: Yes. And come to Munich. And get a paying job. And get ready to take responsibility for our child. (*He walks away from her.*)

Ulrich: I can't. We are very busy with the book. We are coming to the section on the trial in Munich, and he has many things to say about that trial.

Ulrich: Marry me, Ulrich.

Ulrich: He needs me. No one else can step into my job.

Erika: Ulrich, please marry me!

Ulrich: I help him remember things. I organize the material. I even thought of the title we are using now—*Mein Kampf.* . . . I can't leave him.

Erika: All right, Ulrich. (*She turns away from him.*) I'll go to Munich and get rid of our child.

Ulrich (*showing no emotion*): As you wish.

Erika: And I don't expect to see you again.

Ulrich: I understand. (*The cell door down right opens, and* **Hitler** *enters jauntily. He is wearing a dark blue business suit, a vest, a white shirt, and a dark tie. He also wears his Iron Cross around his neck.*)

Hitler: Ah, Erika, my dear! I have a surprise for you. (*The cell door is closed behind him and locked.* **Hitler** *crosses quickly to his dresser and takes a box from a drawer.*)

Erika: Herr Hitler—

Hitler: Now, now! I insist. It is just a trifle. A token of my enduring admiration for you. Close your eyes and bend your head. (*She does so. He puts a fine pearl necklace over her head and around her throat.*) I also mean it as a wish for a happy married life and as a mark of gratitude for all the trouble you have taken to deliver our manuscript to Putzi in Munich. (*There is a pause while she looks admiringly at the necklace.*)

Erika: I don't feel I can accept this, sir.

Hitler: Please, Erika. As a favor to me. I implore you. I *implore* you! (*Her will begins to crumble.* **Ulrich** *puts several sheets of manuscript into her purse.*)

Erika: I don't deserve it. (**Hitler** *gets a hand mirror from his dresser and holds it up for her to look into.*)

Hitler: But they are so becoming—see? They do something for you. (*She is unable to resist the pearls encircling her throat.*)

Erika: They are beautiful.

Hitler: No more than that which they show off.

Erika: I shall be always in your debt, sir.

Hitler: Never. A lovely young woman is never in debt to a male admirer. You have your independence . . . as always . . . and . . . (*he looks at* **Ulrich**) do we have a few poor sheets of manuscript for Putzi?

Ulrich: Yes. In here. (*He hands the handbag to* **Erika** *She takes it and turns away from him.*)

Hitler (*crossing to the door*): You see, Erika, it is we who are in your debt. This work you are doing for us and the Party is of the utmost importance. (*He calls through the door*) Otto!

Otto (*entering*): Did you call, sir?

Hitler: Please escort Fräulein Wendt to the front gate—(*he winks at the jailer*) without any unnecessary delay—

Otto (*grinning*): —she has to catch a train to Munich.

Hitler: Correct.

Otto: I understand, sir.

Hitler (*to* **Erika**): Goodbye, my dear. (*He kisses her hand. She withdraws it quickly.*) I look forward to our next meeting.

Erika: Goodbye, sir.

Ulrich: Goodbye, dear.

Erika: Goodbye. (*She leaves hastily.* **Otto** *follows her out and locks the door. There is a short pause.*)

Hitler: Is she upset about something?

Ulrich: Just overcome, sir. She was not expecting such a lovely gift.

Hitler: She will get used to it. Women adapt quickly to gifts of jewelry.

Ulrich: Like Gretchen. . .

Hitler: I have news, Ulrich.

Ulrich: From Munich?

Hitler: Yes. I am to be released in two weeks! In time for Christmas!

Ulrich: Thank God! (*They embrace warmly.*)

Hitler: Thank the parole board. They insisted I be set free in spite of the adverse reports by the Munich police . . . who will pay for that, one of these days.(**Ulrich** *jots this remark down.*) But now it is time for work. (*He paces about the room firmly. Toward the end of his comments, three judges take their places at the judge's table stage left, and two lawyers sit at the table down left.*) There is little left to say about a trial that has been widely reported in the press and that exonerated General Ludendorf in spite of all the evidence, and that resulted in my incarceration, along with several of my comrades, for many months. The day of reckoning will come. . . . (*He begins to pace left. Lighting begins to cross-fade as before. It comes up left on the judges, the lawyers, and the witness stand. Stage right, it slowly goes out, leaving a head spot on* **Ulrich** *as he writes.*) About the only positive thing I can say for German justice is that the custom of allowing the accused to have the last word at his trial served me rather well, as I was able to say several things that needed to be said to that court. (*He takes his seat in the witness chair. The* **Prosecutor** *rises from his table left and crosses toward him. The judges listen carefully to the testimony.*)

Prosecutor: Is it not true, Herr Hitler, that you entered into the so-called Putsch of last November entirely out of personal ambition?

Hitler: I did not.

Prosecutor: General von Lossow has testified that you did.

Hitler: General von Lossow is a liar.

Presiding Judge: I require the witness to speak with proper respect before this court.

Hitler: I withdraw that statement. General von Lossow was mistaken.

Prosecutor: He said you were consumed by ambition.

Hitler: He was mistaken.

Prosecutor: He said you only wanted to become a government minister.

Hitler: How small are the thoughts of small men! You may be sure, sir, that what I did had no relation to personal ambition on my part.

Prosecutor: You didn't want to be a minister?

Hitler: I do not have a high opinion of ministers. A man doesn't leave his mark on history by becoming a minister of culture or minister of family planning. One would run the risk of being buried next to other ministers. I would mention only Scheidemann and Wutzlhofer. Who would want to share a grave with them? (*Laughter from the crowd off left.*)

Prosecutor: I ask that that stupid remark be stricken from the record.

Presiding Judge: So ordered.

Hitler: What I had in mind from the beginning was much more than becoming a minister. I wanted to crush Marxism in Germany—and the world. Being a minister! Bah!

Prosecutor: You have strange ideas about high government officials.

Hitler: Let me put it this way: The first time I visited Bayreuth, I stood a long time by Wagner's grave. My heart was filled with pride. Here lay a great man who had refused to have inscribed on his tombstone: "Here lies Geheimrat His Excellency Baron Richard von Wagner, Musikdirektor." He handed down to posterity only his name. He didn't need a title. And neither do I.

Prosecutor: Herr Kahr has testified that he was never interested in politics until you put him up to it.

Hitler: I didn't put him up to it.

Prosecutor: Then who did?

Hitler: Sir, no one can teach politics to a person. A bird sings because it is a bird. A man who is born to politics becomes engaged in politics no matter if he is free or in prison, whether he sits on a silk chair or a bench of stone.

Prosecutor: And you are a very dangerous specimen of bird, Herr Hitler.

Hitler: I do what is necessary for the German people.

Prosecutor: Some German people consider you a menace to civilized society.

Hitler: I agree with Mussolini: I would not want to live in this world if I did not know I was surrounded by waves of love and hate.

Prosecutor: Be that as it may, you have to admit that you forced all three of these officials—Gustav von Kahr, General von Lossow, and Ritter von Seisser—at pistol point to do your bidding on the night before the Putsch.

Hitler: It was their own failure of nerve, their refusal to do something about the threat from the Communists, that required me to make the decision to act. What happened to them is their own fault.

Prosecutor: But you do admit that you should be punished for what *you* did?

Hitler: Punished? Because we failed? But we did not fail, Herr Prosecutor. Our mission was not a failure. Has a single German mother come to me and said, "Herr Hitler, my son died at your side in vain!"? No. Not one. On the contrary, thousands of new recruits have joined our ranks.

Prosecutor: You twist every fact to suit your own fantasy.

Hitler: I defend myself. . . .

Presiding Judge: Are you finished with your examination?

Prosecutor (*returning to his seat at the table*): There is no use continuing it. The state of Bavaria rests its case. (*The judges whisper among themselves a moment. The lighting begins to dim somewhat, with a lag special on* **Hitler**.)

Presiding Judge: With the consent of the other judges I offer you an opportunity to make a final statement to the court. (**Hitler** *takes out a handkerchief and carefully mops his brow.*)

Hitler (*slowly at first*): Our army of National Socialists grows larger and larger day by day, hour by hour. Soon the troops will form battalions . . . the battalions will form regiments, and the regiments will form divisions. The old flags will once again wave in front of us . . . and then a final judgement will be rendered by the Court of History. . . . No, gentlemen, judgment will not be passed by you. Accusations have been made, and a verdict will be handed down. I already know what it will be. But before that higher court, the question will be asked, "Did Adolf Hitler and his comrades commit high treason against the German people?" (*He rises from his chair.*) And no matter what you gentlemen say today, even if you find us guilty a thousand times over, the goddess of the Eternal Tribunal of History will tear up your verdict and render her own sentence: NOT GUILTY! (*There is loud applause off left that the judges make no effort to stop.* **Hitler** *remains standing center as all lighting goes out on Scene 2. During the scene shift to Scene 3, the following is heard over loudspeakers in the auditorium.*)

Voice of the Presiding Judge: The court announces the following verdict. The sentences are as follows: Hitler, Weber, Kriebel, and Pöhner, for the crime of high treason, are each sentenced to five years' imprisonment. Hitler's term will be reduced by four months and two weeks. Weber's term will be reduced by four months and three weeks. Kriebel's and Pöhner's sentences will be reduced by two months and two weeks each for time served prior to the trial. Furthermore, each defendant is fined the sum of 200 gold Marks, or another twenty days' imprisonment, respectively. . . . Ludendorf is acquitted of the crime of high treason. The convicted will be eligible for parole after having served a term of six more months . . . (*The voice dies out.*)

ACT II

SCENE 3: *Two weeks later. The day of* **Hitler's** *departure from Landsberg prison. The cell right is neat and clean. All of* **Hitler's** *belongings have been sent on ahead. It is morning.*

Stage left, the flashback area now represents a large waiting room in the prison. There are a few desks, chairs, and benches in an otherwise rather severe-looking room. A small Christmas tree sits on a table in the up left corner.

AT RISE: Hitler *is pacing about the cell. He wears his Nazi uniform with the swastika armband and his Iron Cross pinned to his left pocket.* **Ulrich** *is also in Nazi uniform. He puts some last papers in a briefcase.*

Hitler: And to combat unemployment, I thought of a plan last night.

Ulrich: I'll jot it down. (*He writes in his shorthand book.*)

Hitler: Automobiles are the machines of the future. They can help bind all the folk together by making possible quick, cheap visits from one town

70

to another. . . . (*Again he seems in the grip of a vision.*) I see a network of broad highways . . . *Autobahnen* . . . with two or more lanes in one direction and two or more in the opposite, separated by a space in between. In this way slow traffic may be conveniently passed by faster traffic. What do you think of that?

Ulrich: Imaginative. And it will put a lot of people to work.

Hitler: When I achieve power, that will be one of my first acts. *Autobahnen* to link the people. . . .

Ulrich: Between every city?

Hitler: Certainly. A network. Even wide roads that enable one to drive around a big city instead of having to crawl through it.

Ulrich: Such roads might have a military use, too.

Hitler: Of course! Tanks and trucks could go rapidly from one crisis spot to another. That would enable us to put down any counterrevolutionary activity before it could get organized.

Ulrich: Brilliant.

Hitler: And the second part: I will find an automobile designer of talent—Porsche, perhaps—who can design me a small, economical car that will be within the reach of every family in Germany. A people's car.

Ulrich: A *Volkswagen*?

Hitler: Exactly. A *Volkswagen* for every German family. A united people who follow a single leader toward their immortal destiny!

Ulrich: Let's put that in your first speech when you return to Munich.

Hitler: Ah, Ulrich, the return to Munich. I am nervous. . . .

Ulrich: It will pass. You are changed. I have seen it in the months we have worked together.

Hitler: Thank you for your confidence. I'll be all right. . . . (*He paces about some more.*) We will make a new political road now. No more mistakes. No more illegal acts. We will move carefully but firmly. (**Ulrich** *watches him closely, jotting down comments now and then.*) I was a leader in name only . . . serving a party that had been founded by others. But from now on I will be a true leader . . . shaping my own program in my own way. I will lead the people once again. . . . (*He closes his eyes and seems to see himself again at the head of his followers during his disastrous Putsch of the previous November.*) from the Bürgerbräukeller . . . three thousand of us . . . step by step . . . (*eyes closed, he again marches in place as he did in Act 1, scene 1,*

71

suiting his words to the tempo of the marching) arms locked in comradeship and determination . . . (*a snare drum is heard, growing progressively louder*) Ludendorf and I at the head of the column . . . then came Richter, Feder, Kriebel, Rosenberg, Göring. . . . (*He becomes more and more excited.*) We crossed the Ludwigsbrücke and marched to the Marienplatz. . . . The Green police tried once to stop us . . . but Göring had them arrested and sent to the rear. . . . (*The drum gets louder.*) The people filled the square. . . . They cheered us on and sang patriotic songs. . . . We turned and marched firmly toward the Odeonsplatz . . . one people united behind one leader. . . . (*He stops his in-place marching.*) Then, suddenly, in front of us—the Green police. (*The rifle and pistol shots ring out as before, but this time* **Hitler** *controls himself. He opens his eyes and puts the vision aside.*) We lost good men that day, Ulrich. But . . . we can use their memories. The martyrs of the November Putsch will do us more good dead than alive.

Ulrich (*writing*): Yes, sir. (*To the left, lighting begins to come up. Three* **National Socialist prisoners** *enter and stand at attention. Then come the* **Warden**, *an older kindly man, followed by* **Otto**. **Otto** *stands to one side as the* **Warden** *crosses right.*)

Hitler (*briskly*): Do you have everything? It's time for the warden to let us out of this sink hole.

Ulrich: I have the rest of our manuscript here, and the luggage is outside. (*The* **Warden** *crosses into the cell from stage left.*)

Warden: Herr Hitler!

Hitler: Yes, Warden?

Warden: I am pleased to inform you that your incarceration in Landsberg Prison is at an end. You have been a model prisoner, and it has been a great pleasure to come to know you so well.

Hitler: Thank you, Warden.

Warden: Your car from Munich is at the front gate. This way, please. (*The* **Warden** *leads the way to the stage left area.* **Hitler** *and* **Ulrich** *follow. Lighting fades in the cell, with only a little sunlight coming in at the window from the left. Lighting brightens on the left side. The three uniformed men stand stage left.* **Otto** *stands right, where the* **Warden** *joins him, and* **Ulrich** *holds right. A few more members of the prison staff assemble upstage.*)

Hitler (*crossing to the three Nazis*): Weber . . . Kriebel . . . Pöhner (*he shakes hands with each in turn*), you will soon be free to join me in

Munich. Have patience. (*They reply in unison, "Yes, sir!"*) I wish to thank the staff of this prison for all the courtesies you have shown me. ... (*They all applaud him.*) And I wish especially to express my gratitude to Warden Leybold, for his kindness and understanding of my difficulties. (*He shakes hands with the* **Warden** *and then embraces him. The* **Warden** *is gripped by emotion.*) And may I say further, in parting, that I do not believe this term in prison has scarred me for life. (*He stands center, addressing the audience.*) In fact, on the contrary, I believe it to have been an essential link in the chain of events that stretches from Braunau to Berlin. (*He closes his eyes a moment, then opens them.*) I do not know exactly what the future holds for us, but I can assure you, my faithful followers, that I walk out of here this day in possession of a fearless faith, an optimism and a firm conviction that Destiny will fulfill our hopes and dreams for a greater German nation than has ever been seen on earth. . . . We don't have very much right now with which to begin the struggle. But then . . . he who possesses little is so much the less possessed. (*He strides quickly out the door left.*)

All (*raising their arms*): Heil Hitler!

END ACT II.

Fate, Fortune, and Final Solutions

A Stoic Comedy

Preface: On Suicide

It has been suggested recently that the next American fad to spread to other countries—like the hippie movement of the sixties—might well be the practice of assisted suicide. One thinks about the much publicized activities of the medical pragmatist Dr. Jack Kevorkian, a retired California pathologist who, in the name of respect for humanity, has assisted several desperate human beings, suffering from painful diseases that were often terminal, to put an end to it all. The press quickly labeled him "Dr. Death" and filled many a column inch with lurid descriptions of a doctor who, contrary to tradition, hastened death instead of trying to postpone it.

Dr. Death plied his trade in Michigan, a once-enlightened state that had no law against assisted suicide until national publicity goaded the legislature into correcting this oversight. Among the doctor's patients for whom he provided a face mask through which they themselves could inhale a lethal dose of carbon monoxide were Marcella Lawrence, sixty-seven, who had heart disease, emphysema, and arthritis in her back; Marguerite Tate, who suffered from the degenerative nervous disorder amyotrophic lateral sclerosis; Jack Elmer Miller, fifty-three, who was afflicted with advanced bone cancer and was in continuous excruciating pain; Hugh Gale, seventy, a former security guard who had been disabled for more than ten years with emphysema and congestive heart disease, was in terrible pain, and was continuously on oxygen; Jonathan Grenz, forty-four, whose throat cancer had led doctors to remove his larynx and much of his tongue; Martha Ruwont, forty-one, whose duodenal cancer had spread to her ovaries; Stanley Ball, eighty-two, who was blind and suffered from pancreatic cancer and jaundice; Mary Biernat, who had breast cancer that had spread into her chest; and Elaine Goldbaum, who suffered from multiple sclerosis. Ms. Goldbaum sent Dr. Kevorkian a letter, dated December 28, 1992, in which she said she wanted to die because her disease was getting worse and she could no longer care for herself. "The loss of dignity is atrocious," she

77

wrote. "I have no control over my urination and need to wear a diaper twenty-four hours a day. I am totally confined to my wheelchair and there is no hope that I will get better—just worse. I can no longer continue living like this . . . "

Would any of these cruelly tormented human beings wish, today, to be still alive? Still suffering? Still screaming with pain? Should any person, born under an unlucky star, who suffers continuous and ever-increasing torment be reduced to the status of a cog in the universal health machine, an object of medical curiosity, to be kept alive as long as possible—regardless of the patient's physical and spiritual degradation—with the very latest instruments of death defiance?

And in the larger world of the hale and hearty, if a person in full possession of his faculties wishes—for reasons sufficient unto himself—to end his life, why shouldn't painless, civilized assistance be provided by a licensed service? Especially to those of us who lack that special brand of self-confidence needed to dive under the whirling wheels of a ten-ton truck, for instance, or to swallow a definitive dose of drain cleaner liberally laced with sulfuric acid?

Well, we have been brought up on the questionable idea of the sanctity of human life. The sacredness of the human race. The police are trained to try to prevent public suicide. If a man is standing on a ledge of a building two hundred feet above the pavement and giving plain indications that he is about to jump, the nearest police officer is expected to risk his life by crawling out on the ledge to talk to him. Engage him in communication. The fellow is crying for help. He doesn't want to die. He just wants to talk to somebody.

Superstition. If a person has a right to life, he has a right to death. Let him jump.

On the morning of November 9, 1923, Adolf Hitler led a motley collection of right-wing fanatics and Nazi thugs from the Bürgerbräukeller in Munich to the Odeonsplatz in a demonstration designed to trigger the overthrow of the government of Bavaria. At the Odeonsplatz, the Munich police fired a few shots, Hitler threw himself down hard on the pavement, dislocating his left shoulder, and the *Putsch* came to an ignominious finale. Hitler managed to escape by car to the home of Ernst ("Putzi") Hanfstaengl, a Propaganda Ministry flak, in the Munich suburb of Uffing, where Putzi's wife, Helene, hid the injured revolutionary in a small attic bedroom. After a sleepless night, in severe pain and gripped by despair, Hitler—knowing the Munich police would soon find him—drew the Walther pistol he always carried with him from his pocket and prepared to shoot himself. But Frau Hanfstaengl, a big, Valkyrie-like woman, rushed into the attic (Putzi was still in Munich), got the pistol away from Hitler, and threw it into a barrel of flour.

Why? *Why?!* If she had let him alone, the human race would have been spared World War II and the murder of six million Jews!

Nevertheless, and despite the overwhelming attractiveness of this particular "What if?", we are forced to acknowledge the existence of the powerful instinct, implanted in our genes, that tells us, as it told Helene Hanfstaengl, to prevent suicide at all costs in the name of survival of the human species. But acknowledging the existence of something and approving of it are not always the same thing.

Why *do* we believe so fervently in the importance, the value, the sanctity, the cosmic significance of human life? Why do we put off death as long as we can? Why *not* "go silent into that good night" instead of making a lot of fuss and racket? Is a life of loneliness, disappointment, inadequacy, rejection, and pain really preferable to death? Or are we simply enslaved by indifference, lassitude, ennui, a preference for what we know over what we don't know, a conviction that since pain usually accompanies death, we should put it off even though it is the pain we fear, and not death itself? If we knew we could die quickly and painlessly by firmly pressing a little bone lodged beneath the skin of our left wrist, would the suicide rate go up?

On this subject, one is reminded of the name of Derek Humphry, founder of the Hemlock society (which advocates euthanasia for the terminally ill) and author of a book on do-it-yourself suicide, *Final Exit,* that made the nonfiction bestseller lists in 1991. Buyers tended to be the elderly, people interested in health care (and its outrageous costs), and AIDS patients. The book provides reliable information on numerous suicide techniques: lethal doses for several prescription drugs (mainly painkillers and sleeping pills), how to achieve oblivion with a plastic bag, the pros and cons of the auto-exhaust method, etc. The author advises mixing sleeping pills with vanilla pudding so as not to run the risk of vomiting the pills after going to sleep (something that happened to Sylvia Plath during her first suicide attempt) and thus ruining everything.

Derek Humphry feels that a doctor aught to be empowered to help a person leave life as well as enter it; that the doctor should make death, when it is bound to come soon, more acceptable and less painful; and that he should try to attenuate the solitary nature of death. One's relatives and friends ought to be present at the end, as were those of Socrates when he drank the hemlock in 399 B.C.

Humphry also distinguishes between a "rational" suicide (like that of Socrates) and an "emotional" suicide, desired by people who are momentarily depressed—a distinction the hero of my play, Harry Murdstone, is careful to make. Harry rejects the idea of a permanent solution to a temporary problem—as do we all.

There is much discussion of suicide today. College sociology departments have begun offering courses in thanatology. Church dignitaries present seminars on coping with death. A New York entrepreneur, Roberta Holpann, offers a pamphlet on how to build your own pine burial box and how to make use of it—while waiting—as a toy chest or a coffee table. No doubt much of this concern has been stimulated by a number of recent suicides of various prominent people:

Arthur Koestler (1905–83). Zionist. Author. At nineteen, private secretary to Vladimir Jabotinsky, the firebrand Zionist (and model for Max Aruns in Arnold Schoenberg's play *Der biblische Weg*), who demanded, in the 1920s, that the new permanent home for the Jews be seized from the people of Palestine by force of arms.

In 1931, a secret member of the German Communist Party. "I went to communism as one goes to a spring of fresh water," he wrote. "I left it as one who clambers out of a poisoned river strewn with the wreckage of flooded cities and dead bodies."

In 1941, wrote *Darkness at Noon,* a vivid indictment of Stalin's purge trials of 1936–38. Especially memorable is his chilling description of how a false confession is slowly, pitilessly, scientifically drawn out of the vitals of an Old Bolshevik whom Stalin has recently pronounced ripe for the firing squad.

As he aged, Koestler began to write about death, which he compared to the flow of a river into the ocean, a river that has been freed of accumulated mud and sewage and become, once more, transparent and pure.

In March 1983, Arthur Koestler, who was suffering from Parkinson's disease, and his third wife, Cynthia, who believed she could not go on living without him, committed double suicide at their home in London, from a lethal overdose of drugs.

Sylvia Plath (1932–64). American poet. Author of *The Bell Jar,* "Daddy", "Lady Lazarus", and "The Bee Meeting". Tried to commit suicide in 1953 while a student at Smith College but failed. Went to England and married the poet Ted Hughes, who was unfaithful to her with a photographer.

She moved into a dreary apartment building in London (Yeats had lived there) with her two children but without her husband. In his book *The Savage God,* A. Alvarez describes his last meeting with Sylvia Plath at her new apartment, on Christmas Eve, 1962:

> She seemed different. Her hair, which she usually wore in a tight, school-mistressy bun, was loose. It hung straight to her waist like a tent, giving her pale face and gaunt figure a curiously desolate, rapt air, like a priestess emptied out by the rites of her cult . . . Her flat was rather beautiful in its chaste, stripped-down way, but cold, very cold, and the oddments of flimsy Christmas decoration made it seem doubly forlorn, each seeming to repeat that she and the children would be alone over Christmas. For the unhappy, Christmas is always a bad time; the terrible false jollity that comes at you from every side, braying about good will and peace and family fun, makes loneliness and depression particularly hard to bear. I had never seen her so strained. (29–30)

Mr. Alvarez describes what happened next: "When I left about eight o'clock to go to my own dinner party, I knew I had let her down in some final and unforgivable way. And I knew she knew. I never again saw her alive." (31)

In the last days of her life, Sylvia Plath wrote poems about her coming death—"Edge" and "Words"—and on the morning of February 11, 1963, she turned on the gas in her oven, stuck in her head, took a deep breath, and died.

Anne Sexton (1928–74). American poet. Wife (at nineteen) of "Kayo" Sexton, who gave her two daughters and plenty of solitude while he travelled about, selling wool. To relieve the boredom of her existence in Weston, Massachusetts, she began writing poetry. A good friend was fellow poet Sylvia Plath, with whom she exchanged views on art, illness, and ways to commit suicide. When she learned of her friend's suicide in London, she told her psychiatrist that the act disturbed her and made her want to commit suicide, too, feeling that this death, a continent away, should have been her own.

She visited many doctors and psychiatrists, all of whom tried to help her cope with hysteria, depression, anorexia, insomnia, violently fluctuating moods, vicious rages, trances, confusions, and periods of self-hate. Did her father sexually abuse her? Did her Aunt Nana arouse her sexually by rubbing her back? Sexton thought so. Surviving members of her family doubt it.

"Where others saw roses, Anne Sexton saw clots of blood," said a close relative. And, said Anne Sexton, "with used furniture he makes a tree. A writer is essentially a crook."

On October 4, 1974, Sexton poured herself a glass of vodka, went into the closed garage, got into her car, started it up, listened to the radio and sipped her drink while waiting for the exhaust fumes to do for her. Which they did.

Petra Kelly (1948–92) and her lover, General Gerd Bastian (1923–92): double suicide. On October 19, 1992, in the house they shared in Bonn, Germany, Gen. Bastian shot Ms. Kelly at close range, then shot himself.

They were depressed over recent turns of affairs in Germany. Petra Kelly, who had taken the name of her American stepfather, had gone to high school in the United States and attended the International Institute at American University in Washington, D.C. from 1966 to 1970. Back in Germany, she protested the Vietnam War, German policy toward South Africa, and violations of the environment. In 1979, she helped found the Green Party, which she eventually represented in the *Bundestag.*

Gerd Bastian, a soldier in World War II, became a career officer in the *Bundeswehr* in 1956, rose to the rank of major general, and was given command of an armored division. He was deeply alarmed at the possibility that Germany might become the theater of a nuclear conflict between NATO and the Russians and opposed the stationing on German territory of American missiles with nuclear warheads. In 1980, he requested early retirement from the *Bundeswehr* and in 1983, was elected to the *Bundestag* as a representative of the Greens.

By the early 1990s, both Petra Kelly and Gerd Bastian had lost their seats in the *Bundestag* because of declining voter support for the Greens. As they watched the rise of rightist elements, the neo-Nazis, the skin-heads attacking Turkish, Italian, Yugoslav, and other *Gastarbeiter,* the growing hostility of their countrymen toward asylum-seekers, the shouts in the streets—Again!—of "Heil Hitler!", they evidently concluded that they no longer wished to live in today's Germany, or anywhere else, and put an end to their bitter disappointment.

In addition to suicide prompted by pain and despair experienced by individual sufferers, there is the phenomenon of mass suicide based on religious conviction:

Masada, Palestine, 79 A.D.. A Roman army surrounded and laid siege to a Jewish settlement of about nine hundred souls huddled together on a hilltop. Unwilling to be taken into slavery by their violent enemies, the Jews killed themselves—men, women, and children—in protest against Rome's primary principle of conduct: "Might makes right."

Russia, seventeenth century. Over a period of many years, 20,000 members of a Russian Orthodox sect called Old Believers, persecuted by the government in Moscow for seeking a return to the fundamentalist convictions of their ancestors, convinced by charismatic leaders that the end of the world was at hand, abandoned their fields, clothed themselves in white garments, and marched into funeral pyres or buried themselves alive.

Jonestown, Guyana, 1978. Some four hundred members of the Peoples' Temple, believing that their colony, conceived in the ideals of group community and group loyalty, was about to be destroyed, affirmed their convictions by drinking poisoned Kool-Aid and dying with their revered leader and idol, the Reverend Jim Jones.

Another revered leader and idol, David Koresh, led most of his followers to a fiery death at their Branch Davidian headquarters near Waco, Texas, on the morning of April 19, 1993. But in this case, to those inside the compound the end of the world must indeed have seemed near. At dawn of the fatal day, big tanklike M728 Army Combat Engineering Vehicles that mounted battering rams and tear-gas guns attacked Ranch Apocalypse, smashing large holes in the walls and spewing tear gas inside. The cultists responded as one might expect: they set the building on fire and died together, in the not unreasonable conviction that a fiery death in the name of their religious values was preferable to life in a Texas prison.

The nineteenth-century French sociologist Emile Durkheim was among the first to explain mass suicide in terms of human altruism, the belief that the ideals of the group stand above the petty desire of the individual to preserve his life. Then a suitably charismatic leader succeeds in planting this conviction in the souls of his faithful followers, then the appearance of a real or imagined threat to the group's existence can result in mass self-destruction.

Groups capable of such behavior are often made up of persons who have rebelled against the tensions and uncertainties of the social system in which they found themselves and sought refuge in a return to the simplicities and satisfactions of early group lifestyles, in which man was able to live in harmony with nature. Descriptions of such utopias abound—in Rousseau, for instance, and in the writings of his later disciple Karl Marx.

Of course, there never were such ideal communities. The ravages of disease in such cut-off cooperatives are usually ignored by those intent on spiritual, as opposed to physical, well-being. And even if ideal conditions free of illness did exist in some remote and forgotten Garden of Eden, we can't go back to it. We can't go back to anything. We are genetically structured, like all living species, to remain where we are, conscious only of the present moment—the future unknown, the past forgotten.

To the three broadest reasons for suicide—pain, despair, and religious conviction—should be added a special category: if the would-be suicide is sure he can bring it off properly, it is possible that this act of finality can embellish one's earthly reputation with a certain gratuitous distinction. How much did Hitler enhance his place in history by killing his wife and himself before the Russians could get their hands on him? And what about *Reichsmarschall* Hermann Göring who, after he was sentenced to hang, proclaimed, "Mich hängen die nicht!" and managed to outwit the Allied prison authorities at Spandau by swallowing poison in his cell? (Next day, the New York *Times,* headlined: "Göring Beats Death by Suicide!")

General Aleksandr Vasilyevich Samsonov redeemed his reputation in the eyes of the Russian people in August 1914 by shooting himself after losing the decisive battle of Tannenberg to a German army commanded by Generals Hindenburg and Ludendorff.

Captain Hans Langsdorff salvaged something after losing his ship, the pocket battleship *Graf Spee* to three British cruisers off the east coast of

South America in December 1939. He retired to a hotel room in Buenos Aires, spread out the Imperial Ensign under which he had fought at Jutland, lay down on it, and shot himself.

Sophocles' Ajax fell on his sword rather than endure public disgrace in the midst of the Greek forces besieging Troy by sitting alone in his tent for one day of repentance.

And Brutus, after losing the battle of Philippi in 42 B.C., fell on his sword with the immortal words (by Shakespeare), "Farewell good Strato, Caesar now be still. I killed not thee with half so good a will."

Suppose poor President Nixon with the implacable shadow of impeachment darkening his opportunistic existence, had sat himself down at his big desk in the Oval Office one midnight, kicked on his tape recorder, shouted, "I cannot live with dishonor!" and shot himself, while recording it right there on the tape? By now, he would be a national hero, enjoying a moment of respectful silence at the opening of the Republican National Convention every four years.

Finally, there is the rare instance of a carefully planned act of self-destruction that makes a clear political statement of some kind. After the failure of his raid on the federal arsenal at Harper's Ferry in 1859, John Brown was tried at Charles Town, Virginia, found guilty of premeditated murder, and sentenced to be hanged. While awaiting the fatal day, he learned of plans by Northern friends and supporters to rescue him from his cell and spirit him away to safety. But Brown refused the offer, insisting that he wished to die for his anti-slavery convictions. After he was hanged, a song appeared describing how his body lay a-moldering in its grave, and the North had a genuine martyr around whom to rally during the coming showdown between the states over the issue of human slavery.

In British-ruled India, Mohandas Karamchand Gandhi rallied millions of his countrymen to violently protest the continued presence of the British Raj on their soil by nearly starving himself to death on various occasions. And after the end of World War II, the British left.

In Vietnam, during the war, a Buddhist monk sat down in a public square in Saigon, doused his body with gasoline, and set himself on fire in order to make a sensational protest against the war, duly recorded by the press photographers who had been informed where to be and when.

This political reason for suicide is the only one of the five under discussion here that can be associated in any way with a loftier vision of some kind, a way of rendering one's life meaningful by sacrificing it in the name of an ideal—peace, for instance, independence, freedom, or justice. In this condition of suicide, the doer of the deed receives none of the personal benefits that accrue from the other four. Self-destruction becomes a wholly altruistic, unselfish act and, therefore, an act that confers meaning on one's life. "He died for the cause." Ergo, he did not die in vain.

But if some people don't die in vain, does meaninglessness mark the lives and pointlessness the deaths of all the rest of us? Is there really such a thing as a "meaningful" life, the significance or which is revealed only when one dies "to free the slaves" or "to make the world safe for democracy" or whatever? Does life have meaning? Does life become meaningful through love, for instance?

But what *is* love? Evolutionary biologists maintain that the love of mother for child, child for parent, husband for wife, wife for husband, brother for sister all boil down to the effect on the human system of certain chemicals: phenylethylamine, dopamine, norepinephrine, and oxytocin. Love—a chemical reaction in the human body—has only two specific biological purposes: to spread the genes of the lovers or to protect the genes of a near-relative. The rest is poetry.

If love doesn't establish the meaning of life, what does? How can we hang on to our learned-in-childhood conviction that life *must* have meaning?

The trouble is that meaning is the legitimate offspring of logic—major premise–minor premise–conclusion. One thing leads meaningfully to the next. If the universe has meaning, then nature must be governed by immutable laws of cause and effect. And so it is, thought classical physicists. Even up to the time of Albert Einstein, the problem was simply to determine the laws of physics. Sooner or later, everything would fall logically into place.

But in 1926, with the publication of his *Principle of Uncertainty,* Werner Heisenberg proved that this comfortable view of things is false. According to Newtonian mechanics, one could predict what any material object would do if one could determine both its location and its momentum. The laws of motion could be used to predict the amount of time a falling body would require to traverse a certain distance. The orbit of the Earth around the sun could be determined precisely as could the trajectory of any object in space. But in trying to determine the exact location and momentum simultaneously of an electron, Heisenberg found to his surprise, and the surprise of the world of science, that this cannot be done. Thus the behavior of an electron is unpredictable. Since the electron is the smallest building block in the universe, it must be admitted that there is no such thing as determinism in the universe. Instead of being governed by immutable laws of cause and effect, nature is fundamentally governed by chance, and so our understanding of the physical world is merely an approximation based on the laws of probability.

Chance rules our lives. One's very birth is an accident. One's mother might have opted for an abortion. Or one might have been aborted spontaneously at the age of three weeks and flushed down the toilet. One could be born dead. One's father could always have been somebody else.

One might grow up rich, like Marcel Proust, or poor, like Tennessee Williams. One might grow up black in a white country (like the United States) or white in a black country (like South Africa). One looks forward to a bright future when young but dies in the trenches "for one's country." Or somebody else's country in the French Foreign Legion. Or in a car accident. What chance provides chance can take away.

Perhaps it is time to begin evaluating things that happen to us and our children, relatives, friends, and fellow human beings on the basis of the scientific Principle of Uncertainty. Ulrich, the hero of Robert Musil's novel *The Man without Qualities,* happened onto this guiding principle of life as a schoolboy while writing a paper on patriotism. He wrote that if one really loves his country, he should never think of it as the best country in the world. This led Ulrich to a further idea: while God was creating the universe, the thought may well have crossed his mind that, after all, the whole thing could just as well have been done some other way.

Ulrich's teachers were outraged, but because they couldn't agree on whether the paper was unpatriotic or blasphemous, they let him stay in school. Also, one must surmise, they may have seen a grain of truth in this odd logic. Is there a single event in history that couldn't have turned out some other way?

The big bang? What if it had happened a little sooner? Or later?

The meteors whose violent crash into the Earth at the end of the

Cretaceous period, about 66 million years ago, killed off the dinosaurs and thousands of other species? The meteors might have hit some other planet.

Waterloo? Napoléon might have won if the Prussian attack on his right flank had been delayed an hour or two.

Gettysburg? General Pickett's charge on Cemetery Ridge? In discussing the proposed action with General Lee, General A. P. Hill suggested that he support Pickett with five more brigades, thus sending in all thirteen brigades of his corps. Lee refused the advice, however, explaining that he needed those five brigades in reserve in case Meade launched a counterattack.

Meade! *Counterattack?!* Pickett's charge might have succeeded with the support of five more brigades. Meade's Army of the Potomac might have been routed, and America might have become two countries with a common language, like Germany and Austria.

Leyte Gulf? The biggest and most decisive naval battle of World War II? The outcome turned on a defective radio transmitter aboard Admiral Jisaburo Ozawa's flagship, the *Zuikaku.* The Japanese attacked the American landing forces at Leyte Gulf from three directions. The South Force of surface ships, commanded by Admirals Nishimura and Shima, was almost completely destroyed as it entered the Gulf through Surigao Strait the night of October 24–25, 1944, by the American Seventh Fleet under command of Admiral Thomas Kinkaid. Admiral Ozawa's Northern Force, consisting of some old carriers, a few planes, and their escort vessels, sailed down from the north of Luzon as bait to draw Admiral Halsey's Third Fleet away from Leyte Gulf, where it was protecting the invasion fleet and General MacArthur in command of the 130,000 men of the Sixth Army, which had gone ashore on October 20th. It was on this date that MacArthur staged his wading-ashore routine for the cameras.

Admiral Ozawa sent some planes south to announce his presence, and Admiral Halsey swallowed the bait hook, line, and sinker. He took off northward with all the fleet carriers, all the new fast battleships, and all the escort vessels of the Third Fleet, leaving Kinkaid's fleet and some escort carrier groups to protect General MacArthur. This was what the Japanese high command had been hoping for, because they also had a strong Central Force sailing through San Bernardino Strait under the command of Admiral Takeo Kurita, who flew his flag on the eighteen-inch-gunned *Yamato,* possibly the most dangerous battleship ever built.

Admiral Kurita, on the morning of October 25th, was surprised to find no enemy ships waiting for him as he emerged from San Bernardino Strait. He turned south, encountered some escort carriers that he brushed aside, and prepared to enter Leyte Gulf. It was at this crucial moment that Admiral Ozawa's message to the effect that he had successfully lured Halsey's Third Fleet nearly four hundred miles to the north of Leyte Gulf failed to reach the Central Force. If it had, Admiral Kurita would surely have pushed south and entered Leyte Gulf.

And what would he have found? An exhausted Seventh Fleet, low on fuel and ammunition after their night-long battle with the Japanese Southern Force, about two hundred cargo ships and tankers of the invasion fleet and, on the shore, the 132,000 men of General MacArthur's Sixth Army with 200,000 tons of supplies stacked in plain sight all over the beach.

Could Kurita have destroyed the Sixth Army? One has to wonder. The force under his command—four battleships, including *Yamato*; two heavy cruisers; two light cruisers; and eight destroyers—was capable of dealing with Kinkaid's ships, especially when they ran out of ammunition, and Kurita was equally capable of launching a devastating shore bombardment on MacArthur's troops. Such a bombardment by four battleships and four cruisers, especially if they destroyed most of the supplies, would have left the Sixth Army decimated, out of ammunition and food, with surrender to General Tomoyuki Yamashita's Army of the Philippines the likely outcome. And General MacArthur would have been either killed or captured.

The effect on the American people of such a catastrophe is hard to gauge. The loss of tens of thousands of soldiers, sailors, and marines and the knowledge that launching another attack on the Philippines would have to wait for months, even years, might have led Americans to turn against the War in the Pacific as they turned against the War in Vietnam some years later, after the big Communist success with their Tet Offensive of 1968.

Would President Roosevelt have lost the 1944 election? Would the new President have reached an accommodation with the Japanese? If so, would there have been anybody on whom to drop the atomic bombs of August 1945?

Well—! None of this happened. Not knowing where the Third Fleet was, having been under air and submarine attack for three days and nights, Admiral Kurita passed up the chance of a lifetime and, like Hannibal before the undefended gates of Rome after the Battle of Cannae, unaccountably turned away from his adversary and retired to safety.

Why? A rare display of cowardice on the part of a senior Japanese naval officer? "Those who have endured a similar ordeal may judge him," observed Sir Winston Churchill.

Since everything that *is* might have been something that *is not*, it follows that "meaning" (as applied to life) is just another poetic idea, like "love", "fate", "destiny", "heroism", "equality", or "justice". As the Irgun leader in the film *Exodus* observes, "Justice is an abstraction. It has no relation to reality."

Well, life may not have meaning. But does it have, nonetheless, a certain value? Is it a desirable condition? It would seem so. When young, we look forward to the rest of our lives with measured anticipation. Think of all the interesting things that might happen! Toward the end of our lives, we can see that the really memorable moments occupied very little time—a few spasms of ecstasy, a few experiences of beauty in the theater, the opera house, the art gallery, preceded and followed by millions of moments of stupefying routine. As Heimito von Doderer expressed it in the final couplet of his dedicatory poem to the *Strudlhof Stiege* of Vienna:

> Viel ist hingesunken uns zur Trauer,
> Und das Schöne zeigt die kleinste Dauer.
>
> [Endless sad and empty years are past,
> Only shafts of beauty hold them fast.]

And so, a little-noted rule of life: its value can be measured only in the instant of measurement. We can recall past moments of joy or aesthetic pleasure, but we can't re-experience the feelings that accompanied them. Our perception of life runs only from one instant to the next, and so our evaluation of life depends on the circumstances of the instant. If we are being tortured to death by Mexican drug dealers, we will be glad, at any given instant, to die. If we are experiencing sexual intercourse for the first time, we will wish the instant to last forever. There is no such thing as a cumulative value of life.

If life has no meaning, and only momentary rather than enduring value, can the life of the human race itself have meaning or value? If the human race became extinct tomorrow, would it matter? How could it? There would be no human being alive to whom it could matter. Dead people matter only to the still living. We mourn the demise of our children, our parents, our spouses, friends, revered political figures, important generals and admirals, movie stars, and rock singers. But when *we* go, all our mourning goes with us. When all people are gone, all mourning is gone. And God is gone, since there are no more souls to receive for judgment. Heaven, hell, and purgatory are as full as they can ever be. God's work is ended.

So, to repeat, would the demise of God and his human race matter? Would it matter to any of the surviving species? To the wasps, perhaps?

In his book, *The Diversity of Life,* Edward O. Wilson observes that although human life began on Earth less than two million years ago, insects originated nearly 400 million years ago and have dominated terrestrial and freshwater habitats ever since. They easily survived the five great extinction spasms, the last of which did for the dinosaurs, and today number about a billion billion individuals. Altogether, the insects weigh about a trillion kilograms, more than twice the weight of the whole human race. As Wilson notes, "Insects can thrive without us, but we and most other land organisms would perish without them." (211)

No, "we never will be missed." Or, "*apres moi,* the wasps."

Samuel Beckett sensed the futility of life and the unimportance of the human race. In his perceptive play *Waiting for Godot,* five allegorical figures, who seem to represent the various strata of human soci- ety—Vladimir and Estragon, two tramps at the bottom of the heap; Pozzo, who owns everything, at the top; Lucky, his hired man (who used to be a college professor), in the middle; and a Messenger, who represents Western Union—all wait for Godot who, the Messenger announces at the end of Act I, and again at the end of Act II, "isn't coming today. But he will come tomorrow." After this second disappointment, one of the tramps tries to hang himself, but his rope breaks. Godot will come when he comes.

So, Beckett seems to be saying, all of us members of the human race while away our days on earth waiting for only one event—the arrival of *der Tod* [death], expressed by the anagram *Godot.*

And the arrival of Godot for the entire human race may not be so far off. Various portents are ominously clear. The widespread acceptance of homosexuality as a way of life presages a falling off in the birth rate, since homosexuals do not reproduce.

Abortion is on the rise everywhere. A woman's right to regulate the functions of her own body takes precedence over the survival of the human race. As women achieve equal rights, the birth rate will decline.

We are slowly poisoning our environment. Edward O. Wilson believes that we are in the midst of a major extinction spasm brought on this time not by giant meteorites striking the Earth at supersonic speeds, but by our habits of polluting the atmosphere and destroying earthly ecosystems. It is these ecosystems that enrich the soil and create the very air we breathe. Without them, our remaining tenure on Earth will be nasty and brief. (347)

But the most convincing signal of the decline of the human race toward extinction is, as Schopenhauer observed in the last century, the rise of intelligence among human beings. Intelligence will eventually frustrate the will to reproduce, causing a decline in the birth rate. Already, we see this decline in western countries with highly educated populations—France, England, and Germany,* for example. The birth rate still exceeds the death rate in the United States, but only because of the millions of minority citizens living here. As they achieve education, their urge to have children will be reduced and, sooner or later, the American death rate will exceed the birth rate. In China, the intelligence of the Communist party manifests itself in the recent decree that a family may have only one child. And in India, the masses are being systematically educated in techniques of birth control.

If we can accept the extinction of the human race as a foregone conclusion, self-destruction by the individual human being becomes less reprehensible. Indeed, suicide seems to be acquiring the same respectable, rational place in the hierarchy of human activity as it used to enjoy in ancient times. In his book on suicide, Alvarez informs us that the magistrate in Athens kept a supply of hemlock ready for those who wished to die. All a person had to do was appear before the Senate and plead his case:

> Whoever no longer wishes to live shall state his reasons to the Senate and, after having received permission, shall abandon life. If your existence is hateful to you, die; if you are overwhelmed by fate, drink the hemlock . . . Let the unhappy man recount his misfortune, let the magistrate supply him with the remedy, and his wretchedness will come to an end. (59)

Should there be a county suicide service, available everywhere to anyone at a modest cost? It is hard to see why not. Should free suicide service be available at all state and federal prisons? If so, the criminal population would probably decline.

*In Germany (West and East combined) between 1990 and 1993, the number of births fell from 861,000 to 795,000.

One of the most famous of all suicides was that of the Greek philosopher Socrates, as related in the *Phaedo* by his student and colleague Plato. An enduring insight of Socrates was his observation: "The unexamined life is not worth living." As he swallowed the hemlock in his prison cell, however, it is possible that there flickered through his mind the obvious corollary of his famous thought: The examined life isn't worth living either.

Fate, Fortune, and Final Solutions

A Stoic Comedy in Two Acts

TIME: The recent past
PLACE: A basement apartment in New York City
CHARACTERS:
Harry Murdstone, proprietor of Murdstone's Suicide Service
Officer Lily Longstreet, a New York policewoman
Chip Checkers, a history professor
Swifty Kazan, a private detective
Horace Liverwright, a psychiatrist
Muggs McGrane, a college football coach
Maria Webster, an opera singer
Helga Liverwright, the psychiatrist's former wife
Gen. Robert ("Blitz") Blowgarden
Toothy, Harry's wife
Murk, from the funeral parlor
Hammerslog, also from the funeral parlor
SYNOPSIS OF SCENES: All the action takes place in Harry's basement
    apartment.
Act I: A pleasant Friday in April
Act II: Immediately afterward
STAGE SETTING:
    Living room/kitchen of a basement apartment in the Soho district of
lower Manhattan, New York.

    Down right, a door to the bathroom. Below the door, a chair. Upstage
of the door is the front door, which gives onto a hallway.

In the back wall are two windows at ceiling height that suggest the basement location of the room. People's legs can be seen walking back and forth during the play. Sometimes, a client looks furtively in a window before going on to the front door.

The back wall of the apartment is about thirty feet long. About ten feet from the up right corner, a curtained area begins. This area extends about ten feet parallel to the footlights and comes out from the back wall about ten feet. The windows are on either side of it.

This area is surrounded by black velour curtains on rings that run along three pipes. These pipes are suspended from the ceiling by wires at the ends of the pipes. The side curtains can be slid along their pipes so that people can enter the area either from up right, opposite the front door, or from up left, opposite the bedroom door in the left wall. The downstage curtain, the one parallel to the footlights, is never disturbed.

This area is called the Re-creation Area by the proprietor of the suicide service, Harry Murdstone. That is, Harry thinks of it as a place in which a client is re-created into a new being.

The audience cannot see into the Re-creation Area, even when the side curtains are open. But inside, stage right, is a large chair, firmly bolted to the floor. It is made of iron but has a couple of replaceable cushions for the comfort of the clients. Just right of the chair is a silver-dollar slot machine. Opposite the chair are six M-14 rifles mounted in a rack that is also bolted firmly to the floor. The barrels of the rifles are aimed at the heart of the person sitting in the chair. The triggers are wired, by means of pulleys, to the handle of the slot machine. When a client inserts a silver dollar and pulls the handle down, the guns fire and kill him instantly.

A closed-circuit TV camera, of the kind used in banks, is mounted on the back wall of the apartment and trained toward the chair. It is activated when someone sits on the chair and then records what happens next for posterity, and for use in a court of law in case the deceased's relatives lodge a complaint against Harry. The camera is mounted high enough on the back wall to be visible to the audience over the top of the front curtain. The stocks and framework for the M-14 rifles stick out through the left side curtains, but the audience cannot see the barrels. Also inside the area are several large green plastic bags into which Harry stuffs the bodies when it is all over.

Downstage center is a large kitchen table with chairs on both sides and upstage of it. On the table are a coffeepot and some cups and saucers as well as other eating utensils, and a stack of *Blue Books of Procedure,* pamphlets Harry gives to his clients that explain the procedure and philosophy of self-destruction. Also on the table is a record player. In a drawer that opens on the left side are many forms and documents that Harry uses in his business. Also in this drawer is a metal lock box in which he keeps his silver dollars needed to operate the slot machine.

Opposite the left curtains of the Re-creation Area is the door to the bedroom. Downstage of the bedroom door is a large industrial-type walk-in refrigerator. When Harry has put a dead body into a sack, he hauls the sack out through the left curtains, staples the ID tag on, then drags it into the refrigerator and lays it on a long, wide table. Dry-ice clouds, coming out the open door, give the impression of a freezing temperature inside.

Downstage of the industrial refrigerator are kitchen shelves, cabinets, a small refrigerator, a gas stove, and a sink, at which Harry prepares his meals.

There are two or three more chairs scattered about. There is no rug on the floor. As a former Marine Corps recruiting sergeant, Harry likes to hear the sound of his boots banging on the floor as he walks around.

Act 1: *A pleasant Friday in April.*

AT RISE: Harry, *wearing a Marine Corps fatigue jacket, sits left of the table, listening to a recording made by the rock group* **Suicide**, *perhaps "Frankie Teardrop" (Red Star Records, Inc.), sung by Allan Vega.* **Harry** *is husky, over six feet tall, about forty-five or so, and wears his hair in a Marine Corps haircut. He has read widely and thinks of himself as something of an intellectual. He operates his service out of a genuine desire to be helpful to distressed members of the human race.*

The doorbell rings. **Harry** *turns off the record player, crosses to the door up right, and opens it.*

Harry: Yes? (*A young, rather attractive policewoman stands in the doorway.*)

Lily: Officer Lily Longstreet, sir. May I come in?

Harry: Do you have a warrant?

Lily: Just a touch of curiosity.

Harry: Aren't you new on this beat?

Lily: Yes.

Harry: Please come in.

Lily: Thank you. (*She enters and closes the door behind her.* **Harry** *crosses to the kitchen table.*)

Harry: I have everything right here. (*He sits left of the table, opens the drawer, and takes out various papers.*) Sit down.

Lily: The sign outside says—

Harry: Yes. You read it correctly. (**Lily** *sits right of the table.*)

Lily: It says: "Murdstone Suicide Service."

Harry: Yes. Here you are. (*Through the following, he hands her various papers.*) My ID—driver's license, social security card . . . (**Lily** *looks at the papers as though contemplating a snake.*) New York Public Library card, passport . . .

Lily: This is . . . actually . . . a legal service?

Harry: Legal as sin. (*He hands her some more papers.*) Here's my permit to sign death certificates. . . . My notary public card . . . entitles me to notarize documents. . . .

Lily: I don't believe all this!

Harry: Everything on the level. (*He hands her more papers.*) My permit to own six M-14 automatic rifles . . . permit to buy ammunition for them . . . permit to fire them on the premises. . . .

Lily: What do the neighbors say about that?

Harry: They've gotten used to it. There's a guy on the third floor who practices his piano four hours a day. They think that's worse.

Lily (*still not convinced*): You operate a *suicide* service?

Harry: Yes. By choice. Here—read this. (*He hands her a* Blue Book of Procedure.) You may keep it, if you like.

Lily: What is it? (*She leafs suspiciously through the pamphlet.*)

Harry: It is my *Blue Book of Procedure.* Explains the whole routine. Describes my equipment, reliability factor, my philosophy of suicide.

Lily: You are a philosopher?

Harry: Only of suicide.

Lily: Is this a kind of—advertisement for your service?

Harry: Yes. I mail them out to people on magazine subscription lists that I buy. I try to reach a cross section of people in need of a quiet, reliable service.

Lily: Now wait a minute! This *has* to be against the law.

Harry: No, it turns out it isn't. (*He hands* **Lily** *more papers.*) Here's a copy of the action taken by the city to close me up. . . . Here's the decision of the Supreme Court. . . .

Lily: You took this to the Supreme Court?

Harry (*nodding*): And they decided suicide is a private matter. It's protected under the privacy concept that's inherent in the Constitution.

Lily: I don't understand.

Harry: It's simple. Laws against suicide are an invasion of privacy. So they are, by definition, unconstitutional.

Lily: They are?

Harry: Let me ask you a question. Do you think a woman has a right to an abortion?

Lily: Certainly.

Harry: And the Court agrees with you. *Roe* v. *Wade.* And, if a woman has the right to terminate the life of a child inside her body, by extension she has the right to terminate her own life. You agree?

Lily: I guess so.

Harry: And therefore men, by extension—Equal Rights Amendment—also have the right to terminate their lives. Unanimous decision. . . . (**Lily** *stares at him, thinking it over.*)

Lily: But the church! The church says suicide is a mortal sin.

Harry: Ah, yes . . . the Catholic church. They do object to suicide with considerable vigor. But . . . is there a secular, a political reason for their outrage? Does the pope, with the support of his cardinals and bishops and all, does he have an ulterior motive?

Lily: Maybe.

Harry: Is there a subtle desire here to prevent a decline in the world Catholic population?

Lily: Probably.

Harry: People usually have good reasons for their moral convictions. Solzhenitsyn tells a story somewhere . . . about a Polish countess—Zosia Zaleska was her name, if memory serves. She had devoted her entire life to Communism . . . even did some work for Soviet Intelligence in Poland. But . . . one rainy day . . . she was picked up by the NKVD . . . charged with being a spy for the capitalists . . . was tortured. She tried to commit suicide three times. Tried to hang herself—they pulled her down. She cut her veins—they closed them up. She jumped onto the sill of an open window on the seventh floor, but her interrogator managed to grab hold of her by her dress. . . . The NKVD saved her life three times. So they could shoot her. (**Lily** *stares hard at* **Harry**.) Well . . . well. Religion has its place. We all need a friendly group of some kind to belong to. (*He puts away his papers.*) Care to have a look around?

Lily: Yes. (*She gets up, putting the* Blue Book *into her uniform pocket.*)

Harry: No drugs . . . no porno movies . . . nothing even remotely illegal. (*He leads* **Lily** *to the curtained area up right.*)

Lily: We'll see. (**Harry** *pushes the up right curtain back on its pipe.*)

Harry: I call this little alcove the Re-creation Area.

Lily: Recreation?

Harry: It can be pronounced that way. Re-creation into a new and, possibly, exciting existence. As you can see (*he points to various objects that are out of the audience sightlines*) . . . the client sits in this nice armchair that is bolted to the floor. . . . The rifles are mounted on that iron rack that is also bolted to the floor. . . . The barrels point at the heart . . . a miss is impossible.

Lily: No question of that.

Harry: Quick . . . painless . . . reliable.

Lily: What's that thing by the chair?

Harry: A dollar slot machine. Accepts only silver dollars. No small-change equipment around here.

Lily: What's it for?

Harry: The triggers of the rifles are wired to the handle. When you've paid the fee and filled out the forms, I give you a silver dollar. You deposit the coin in the slot, pull the handle . . . and it's all over.

Lily (*as though hypnotized*): All over. . . .

Harry: I don't think they even hear the guns. A peaceful, dignified exit to nirvana.

Lily: Is that a closed-circuit TV camera?

Harry: Just like in a bank. It starts when a client sits down in the chair. Legal proof the client did the deed himself.

Lily: You seem to have thought of everything.

Harry: I'm never in the Re-creation Area when it happens. I like to give my client a moment of solitude before he makes his ultimate gesture of defiance.

Lily: And afterward?

Harry: Then I stuff the body into one of those plastic bags, staple on the identification tag with the name and address of next of kin, and pull it over this way.... (*He leads her toward the large industrial refrigerator left.*)

Lily: Are these tags things the client has already filled out?

Harry: Yes. (*He opens the door to the refrigerator. Clouds of condensed moisture—dry ice—come pouring out.* **Lily** *shivers from the cold.*) And then I lay the sack on the table there and the body freezes. Every afternoon a couple of guys from the Love and Robb Funeral Parlor down the street come by to pick them up.

Lily: There's somebody in there now.

Harry: Yes. Just one. (**Lily** *shivers again*). Then, the funeral parlor calls the next of kin and arranges a nice funeral. I get a cut. I also get rid of the bodies. (*He closes the refrigerator door.*)

Lily: Very efficient.

Harry: I value efficiency.

Lily: I do, too. We should have more of it. Especially on the police force.

Harry: Right. Too much indiscriminate club swinging lately.

Lily: Yeah.... (*She wanders over toward the other side of the room, away from the refrigerator, as though wishing to repress an unexpected impulse.*) But aren't you taking advantage of people?

Harry: In what way?

Lily: At the police academy, I was taught that if a person is thinking about suicide ... threatening to jump out a window or something ... it's my duty to intervene ... to try to talk him out of it.

Harry: But why? If he wants to jump, why not let him?

Lily: I never thought of it that way before.

Harry: Why not take a positive attitude toward suicide? Why not think of it as ... affirmative action?

Lily: But—really—to take advantage of people who are temporarily depressed ... disappointed over something ... that's wrong.

Harry: It has been my experience that most people live lives of almost continuous depression and disappointment . . . punctuated now and then by momentary victories, the effects of which don't last very long.

Lily: Some people are usually cheerful . . . hopeful . . . happy. Something unexpected happens, maybe—

Harry: Oh, I don't want somebody rushing in here without having thought things over.

Lily: And so?

Harry: And so, I do place some obstacles in the way. A prospective client has to first read over my *Blue Book of Procedure.* Then he has to fill out a waiver of liability—

Lily: Which says?

Harry: Which says—basically—that he's sure he's in his right mind, that I have not deprived him of his civil rights, that it is his firm intention to take his life. When he signs this, my lawyer tells me, I am legally in the clear.

Lily: Is that all?

Harry: And I require him to fill out a statement of identification and the address of his next of kin. For the body bag. . . .

Lily: Nothing else?

Harry: And he has to have fifty dollars in cash. No checks. No credit cards.

Lily: Hmmm.

Harry: By that time, if my client still wants to go through with it, he won't be acting on impulse.

Lily: Some business. Does it pay well?

Harry: I'm doing all right.

Lily: Not much expense.

Harry: Just the body bags, the ammunition for the guns, and the electric bill for the fridge.

Lily: I'd think you'd have a lot of competition.

Harry: Not everybody enjoys this line of work. (*While* **Lily** *stares at him reflectively, the front doorbell rings.*)

Lily: Sounds like you have a client.

Harry: Would you care to stay awhile?

Lily: Yes. If you don't mind.

Harry: Not at all. (**Lily** *sits on the chair down right and leafs through* **Harry's** *Blue Book.*) Make yourself at home.

Lily: Thanks. (**Harry** *crosses to the front door and opens it.*)

Harry: Yes? (*A short dark-haired man in his thirties enters quickly and looks furtively about.*) Do come in. (**Harry** *closes the door. The man, a history professor named* **Chip Checkers**, *hastily draws some bills out of his wallet.*)

Chip: Let's get on with it. Here's my fifty. (**Harry** *takes the money and puts it on the table.*)

Harry: Thank you. May I have your name for my records?

Chip: Chip Checkers.

Harry (*motioning toward the table*): Please take a seat, Mr. Checkers. There are one or two formalities before we . . . get on with it. (**Chip** *sits right of the table.*)

Chip: I'm in a hurry. (**Harry** *sits left of the table.*)

Harry: Quite. But if you don't mind . . . (*he hands* **Chip** *a* Blue Book) would you first read through my *Blue Book of Procedure*—

Chip: I've read it. Friend of mine has a copy.

Harry: Oh. Well then, kindly fill out this form. (*He hands* **Chip** *a form.*)

Chip: What's it for?

Harry: Waiver of liability. Just sign at the bottom.

Chip (*signing the form*): All right. . . .

Harry (*handing him an address label*): And now, kindly fill out this address label.

Chip: Address label?

Harry: Your next of kin. For the funeral parlor.

Chip: Oh, yes. (*He fills out the address label.*)

Harry (*glancing at* **Lily**): And I must insist on hearing your reasons. This is not a spur-of-the moment establishment.

Chip: My reasons?

Harry: For wishing to cross the Great Divide.

Chip: My God—I have hordes of reasons. Look at the world today. Look around you. Anti-abortionists!

Harry: They are busy, aren't they?

Chip: Priests sodomizing choir boys!

Harry: That's bad.

Chip: Illegal immigrants . . . gay bashers . . . skinhead Nazis. . . .

Harry: Yes. . . .

Chip: Fat tenors. Pavarotti tried to shake hands with Domingo the other day, but they couldn't reach each other. . . . And teaching no longer affords me pleasure.

Harry: You are a teacher?

Chip: Professor.

Harry: Sorry.

Chip: I'm just sick and tired of it all. Sick and tired—sick and tired.

Harry: Yes! I heard you.

Chip: The performance is over. . . . Life is a farce . . . dying a gesture . . . the funeral an advertisement.

Harry: I can see you've been through a lot.

Chip: So here I am. Ready to exit—laughing.

Harry: You are quite sure about this? (*He exchanges a quick glance with* **Lily**.) Aren't there any other reasons?

Chip: My whole life has been one stupid reason after another.

Harry: For example. . . .

Chip: Well . . . you know, I've always had faith in my students. I've often felt more like a student than a teacher.

Harry: With me, it was the other way around.

Chip: But just recently, I made a sickening discovery.

Harry: What?

Chip: They've started *buying* term papers and handing them in as their own work!

Harry: Scandalous!

Chip: Believe it or not.

Harry: Where do they get them?

Chip: From a slimy company that has the nerve to advertise in the college paper! "Over ten thousand subjects! Grade A work! Any length desired. As little as $25 for a 5-page paper." Imagine! They'd rather pay twenty-five dollars for a paper than achieve the satisfaction of writing it themselves.

Harry: Students get too much money from home, these days.

Chip: So I no longer accept student papers in my classes. And I used to enjoy reading student papers. I marked them with great care. Sometimes they came up with astonishingly original ideas. . . . You know . . . a friend of mine—history professor in a university out west—he saw through it all. Worked for years on his concordance for Spengler's *Decline of the West* . . . taught his classes conscientiously. You know what he did?

Harry: What?

Chip: One day, he put his affairs in order . . . paid all his bills . . . wrote some farewell letters, including one to me . . . then checked into a hotel in Kansas City, where he took a room on the top floor. And then . . . he just exploded. He hurled himself through the window without even bothering to open it—and crashed down on the pavement ten stories below.

Harry: Good Lord! What desperation.

Chip: And at this moment, I feel the same way.

Lily (*suddenly*): But what about . . . *love*? Family? Children?

Chip: I can't stand to be touched by a woman.

Harry: You have convinced me. (*He takes a silver dollar from the table drawer and hands it to* **Chip**.) Here is your silver dollar. This way, please. (*He leads* **Chip** *up right.*)

Chip: Is this machine safe?

Harry: You'll be dead before you know it.

Chip: I have looked forward to this moment all my life.

Harry: You will enjoy it all the more for having waited. . . . (*They shake hands, and* **Chip** *goes inside behind the curtain.*) Just sit down in that antique wrought-iron chair, put the coin in the slot, pull the handle, and it will be all over.

Chip: All over. . . . (**Harry** *pulls to the up right curtain and crosses left.* **Lily** *gazes at the curtain as though mesmerized.*)

Harry (*to* **Lily**): They usually wait a moment to think it over a bit. (*He takes a rubber chemist's apron from a hook on the wall up left and puts it on.*)

Lily: What if he changes his mind?

Harry: I refund his money, of course.

Chip (*from behind the curtain*): Night hangs upon mine eyes; my bones would rest, That have but labour'd to attain this hour.

Harry: Shakespeare. . . .

Chip: Farewell, good Strato—Caesar now be still: I kill'd not thee with half so good a will.

(*The guns fire with a roar.* **Harry** *and* **Lily** *jump.*)

Harry: Damn! I can't get used to that noise. (*He crosses into the Re-creation Area from the left.* **Lily** *crosses up right, pulls the curtain back a little, and watches.*)

Lily: He's dead.

Harry: And gone.

Lily: Just like that.

Harry: One less.

Lily: So now . . . it's just stuff him into a garbage bag. . . .

Harry: Clothes and all. I never try to salvage anything.

Lily: And then . . . into the fridge. (**Harry** *emerges through the left curtain dragging a large green garbage bag stuffed with a body. He staples* **Chip's** *ID tag to the top.*)

Harry: That's right. No empty ceremonies. (**Lily** *puts the* Blue Book *in her pocket and turns to go.*) No pious observations over the dead body.

Lily: Guess I've seen enough. Back to my beat.

Harry: Do come again.

Lily (*after a moment*): Thank you. (*She exits right and closes the door after her. After a moment, she can be seen through the upstage windows walking thoughtfully along the sidewalk to the left.*)

Harry: Music, Maestro. (*He puts the "Suicide" record on again, then drags his sack into the refrigerator. Waves of condensed moisture pour out the open door again. Soon he returns, closes the door, and takes some cleaning materials into the Re-creation Area to clean up after* **Chip.** *After a moment, the doorbell rings.* **Harry** *emerges, turns off the record player, crosses to the front door, and opens it.*)

Swifty (*off right*): Mr. Murdstone?

Harry: The same. (*A short dark-haired middle-aged man enters. He is a private detective named* **Swifty Kazan**).

Swifty: Swifty Kazan is the name. Private detective.

Harry: You are here to investigate my service?

Swifty: Nope. To use it. Tired of the private eye business. Spying on people in their bedrooms . . . following people in their cars . . . bugging telephones . . . tired. . . .

Harry: Does sound depressing.

Swifty: Got your *Blue Book* in the mail. Here's my fifty. (*He hands* **Harry** *the money, and* **Harry** *puts it on the table.*)

Harry: Thank you. Sit down. (**Swifty** *sits opposite him.*) So my book came in the mail. I use magazine subscription lists, of course. . . . Let's see . . . you must subscribe to . . . ?

Swifty: *Playboy.*

Harry: *Playboy!* Many of my clients subscribe to that magazine. Well . . . er . . . there must be something that triggered this decision . . . over and beyond life's routine repugnance. . . .

Swifty: Lately I've begun to worry about being a Jew in America. If I'm a Jew, why don't I live in Israel?

Harry: I don't know.

Swifty: I ask myself . . . am I a Jew who happens to live in America, or am I an American who happens to be Jewish?

Harry: Lao-tzu asks something like that. . . .

Swifty: Oh, I shouldn't complain. I've done all right . . . you know . . . done all right. I like America.

Harry: A poor place, but mine own.

Swifty: Only . . . when I think about Israel, I get confused. Guilty. I should share in their epic struggle. Their troubles should be my troubles.

Harry: Aren't they?

Swifty: I lay low. I'm scared to go over there.

Harry: Bit dangerous, now and then.

Swifty: Oh, they can protect themselves. They got atomic bombs, rockets, gas. . . . (*He clenches his fist threateningly.*)

Harry: Well then, not to worry.

Swifty: And they got fifty-one votes in the United States Senate.

Harry: Just enough.

Swifty: So why don't I move to Israel? With the rest of the exiles? Work for 'em? Help 'em with their epic struggle for life, liberty, and a reasonable return on loans?

Harry: Why don't you?

Swifty: I'm a coward.

Harry: You are a realist.

Swifty: In their hour of need . . . through all those wars with the Ay-rabs . . . where was Swifty Kazan? Carryin' a gun in the desert? Drivin' a tank? Even a garbage truck? Helpin' out in the hospital? I'll tell you where I was. I was sittin' in a comfy paid-for house in Bayonne, watchin' 'em on TV and yellin' 'em encouragement . . . from seven thousand miles away.

Harry: Maybe they heard you. In spirit.

Swifty: I hate myself.

Harry: Leave that to your friends.

Swifty: I sent 'em some money.

Harry: Good fellow!

Swifty: But they needed hands! Hearts! Fighters! And I watched 'em on TV.

107

Harry: At least you showed some interest. . . .

Swifty: And I get awful mad when I see these war protesters . . . these draft dodgers . . . yellow-bellies. Last week on TV I saw one of 'em in a parade carryin' a sign that said: "Nothing Is Worth Fighting For."

Harry: A theme for our times, Swifty.

Swifty: Bad times, Harry.

Harry: I ran into that kind of thing often a few years ago. I was a recruiting sergeant in the Marine Corps, and one time my buddy and I were trying to set up a table in the student union at the University of Texas, just to hand out pamphlets and answer questions.

Swifty: And they jumped you.

Harry: They jumped us. We couldn't even get the table set up. They threw stuff at us—eggs, tomatoes, chairs—yelled things. The women yelled even filthier things than the men.

Swifty: Women like a chance to yell at men.

Harry: So we conducted a strategic withdrawal. . . .

Swifty: Like in Vietnam.

Harry: And while I was driving home to Schulenberg, I made up my mind to quit the Marine Corps as soon as I could.

Swifty (*suddenly interested in* **Harry**): Where? Where did you drive home to?

Harry: I lived in Schulenberg with my wife and kids.

Swifty: How many kids?

Harry: Five.

Swifty: Uh.

Harry: So when my enlistment was up I quit. Got a job . . . and spent a lot of time thinking about America . . . American kids . . . like my kids . . . and I got very discouraged, Swifty.

Swifty: So what did you do, Harry?

Harry: Came up north here to get away from things . . . got a job with a funeral parlor down the street. . . . It seemed like the kind of work I wanted to do. Then I started a service of my own. But I'm still with the funeral parlor. I work for them on commission. (**Harry** *rises and paces about the room.*)

Swifty: You work for a funeral parlor on commission?

Harry: I like my independence.

Swifty: Oh. Well . . . so the result of your thinking about America and all was that suicide fits into our way of looking at things. Is that right?

Harry: Something like that.

Swifty: I agree that if there is nothing really worth fighting for, we might as well all get it over with. (*As* **Harry** *gazes reflectively at his refrigerator,* **Swifty** *pulls out a group of pictures from an inside pocket, looks through them, selects one, and puts the others back. He compares the picture with* **Harry**.)

Harry: The more I think about suicide, the clearer I see it as the only really positive action we can take. In life, everything happens to us by chance ... by accident. When we are born, the color of our skin is already determined. The country we grow up in, our religion, our family financial circumstances, the shape of our eyes ... all settled when the sperm meets the egg.

Swifty: That's the crucial moment.

Harry: Yes. After that, call it fate, fortune, chance ... suicide is a man's only personal, final decision. It's the one thing not controlled by chance.

Swifty: You've thought a lot about this, Harry. (**Harry** *turns and again adopts his usual brisk manner.*)

Harry: Well ... so you're ready to go. Is it just conditions in general? No personal reasons?

Swifty: My wife left me. For an Ay-rab.

Harry: Insensitive.

Swifty (*waving his fists in the air*): May she lose all her teeth! Except one. So she can have a toothache!

Harry: You've convinced me. Just sign those two forms there. . . .

Swifty: Can I see your contraption first?

Harry: Certainly. (*They cross up left together.*)

Swifty: Is it reliable?

Harry: Surefire.

Swifty (*looking at the rifles*): I see what you mean. . . . (*They stand up left between the rifle rack and the bedroom door.*)

Harry: The triggers of the rifles are wired to the handle of the slot machine, over those pulleys there. . . .

Swifty: I pull the handle of the slot machine down . . .

Harry: And the guns fire. . . .

Swifty: Life is a slot machine, Harry.

Harry: That's right, Swifty. . . . Then, the body goes into one of those bags there. . . .

Swifty: Garbage to garbage. . . .

Harry (*turning toward the refrigerator*): And into the refrigerator until the fellows from the funeral parlor come. (*He opens the door. Clouds of condensed vapor pour out.*)

Swifty: Two frozen asses lying on a table . . . who were they?

Harry: The nearest one was a history professor.

Swifty: Those guys got it good.

Harry: Not this one.

Swifty: Why not?

Harry: His students were buying their term papers.

Swifty: At least they'd be interesting to read.

Harry: He didn't think that was the point.

Swifty: I hated writing papers in college.

Harry: And the other one was a judge who was nominated for the Supreme Court.

Swifty: Gee! What happened?

Harry: The Senate committee found out he worked his way through Harvard Law School as a pimp. So they voted not to confirm . . . (*he closes the door of the refrigerator*) and we got it over with. (*He goes back to the table.*) As you can see, my clients are just ordinary folks, like you and me. (**Swifty** *follows him and takes a last furtive look at the photo in his pocket.*)

Swifty: Yeah. I see. (*The doorbell rings.* **Harry** *crosses up right and opens it.*)

Harry: Excuse me a moment. Yes? (*A tall, thin, youngish man enters. He is a psychiatrist named* **Horace Liverwright.**)

Horace: Mr. Murdstone?

Harry: The same.

Horace: And you offer the public a suicide service?

Harry: Yes, but I have a client ahead of you. If you would kindly take a seat here (*he motions* **Horace** *to the chair down right*) we'll just be a minute.

Horace: Thank you. (*He sits on the chair down right.* **Swifty** *crosses to* **Harry.**)

Swifty: You know, Harry, I've changed my mind.

Harry: Have you? But why?

Swifty: Well . . . maybe I'm scared of those guns. And that icebox. I just don't see myself lyin' on that table in there freezin' my balls.

Harry: You won't feel a thing.

Swifty (*shivering*): I feel it now.

Harry: As you wish. Here's your money back. (*He takes the money from the table and holds it out to his client.*)

Swifty: Oh—I don't need the money.

Harry: Please. I couldn't keep it. (**Swifty** *accepts the money and puts it in his pocket.*)

Swifty: OK. Harry, I understand. Matter of principle. (*He crosses to the door up right.*) So long, Harry.

Harry: So long, Swifty. Come back again.

Swifty: Thanks, Harry, for the kind invitation. (*He grins broadly at his new acquaintance and exits. After a moment, his legs can be seen propelling him rapidly off left.*)

Harry (*turning to* **Horace**): And whom have I the pleasure of addressing?

Horace: My name is Horace Liverwright.

Harry: And your occupation?

Horace: Psychiatrist.

Harry: Ah! Had several members of your profession as clients lately. Please sit over here at the table.

Horace: Thank you. (*He rises. crosses to the table, and sits right of it.*) Do many of your clients change their minds at the last minute?

Harry: No. When people have gotten themselves past my front door and the sign outside, they usually go through with it.

Horace: I admire firmness of decision.

Harry: A glass of wine? (*He goes to the small refrigerator down left.*)

Horace: Uhm . . . I've been on the wagon for a time . . . but—

Harry: I have a nice German Moselle here, 1942. . . .

Horace: Do you? Well, I certainly shouldn't pass up a glass of Moselle '42 before I depart this vale of tears.

Horace: Certainly not. (*He pulls the cork from a bottle of white wine and puts two glasses on the table.*) I've noticed that psychiatrists tend to like wine. . . .

Horace: I do, anyway. (**Harry** *pours the wine into the two glasses, then sits left of the table.*)

Harry: Here we are. . . .

Horace: Thank you.

Harry: No use making this into a funereal dirge of some kind . . . prosit!

Horace: Prosit! (*They lift their glasses to one another and sip the wine.*) Excellent. You have a good feeling for German wines.

Harry: I love the wine country. Bingen . . . Kesselheim . . . Bernkastel . . .

Horace: Boppard . . . Rommersdorf . . .

Harry: Have you been to Rommersdorf?

Horace: Just once. My ex-wife and I took a little motor trip along the Rhine when I was at Heidelberg.

Harry: Did you study at Heidelberg?

Horace: No, I was a psychiatrist in the army for a couple of years. We were stationed there.

Harry: I've been there. . . .

Horace (*after a sip of wine*): Well . . . I suppose you guessed why I'm here.

Harry: Yes. . . . (*He offers* **Horace** *a* Blue Book *to read.*) Would you care to look through my *Blue Book of Procedure*—or *Blue Bird of Paradise,* as I like to call it?

Horace: I've read it. My patients bring it to me.

Harry: Then you are familiar with . . . everything?

Horace: Yes. (*He takes fifty dollars from an inside pocket.*) Is the price still fifty dollars?

Harry (*taking the money*): Yes. (*He puts the money to one side on the table and pushes the forms to* **Horace***.*) Here are the forms.

Horace: Waiver of liability. Sensible precaution. . . . (*He signs it.*)

Harry: And this ID tag with address or next of kin.

Horace: Ah, yes. For the funeral parlor.

Harry: My old boss. Love and Robb. "Satisfaction guaranteed or your body back."

Horace (*filling out the tag*): My ex-wife might enjoy making the arrangements. . . .

Harry: What broke you up?

Horace: Oh, various things. She couldn't stand the thought of having children. All that pain. And what if the child were born with a disease inherited from me?

Harry: There's a lot of that kind of thing these days.

Horace: Rather a masculine type, like Hedda Gabler. She even had a pair of dueling pistols her father left her.

Harry: Dueling pistols?

Horace: A pair of matched '44s with pearl handles. Just like General Patton's.

Harry: May he rest in peace.

Horace: She also wrote things, and when a piece of sexy trash sold two million copies she didn't think she needed me anymore and flew off into the wild blue yonder.

Harry: And you don't see her anymore?

Horace: Nope. Don't even know where she lives. I'll just fill this out with her publisher's address.

Harry: That will do. They'll forward it. . . .

Horace: With her next royalty check. . . . (*He hands the card to* **Harry**, *who rather deliberately lays it on the table in front of him.*)

Harry: Thank you.

Horace: Anything else?

Harry (*dawdling over the forms*): Er . . . well . . . Mr.—

Horace: Call me Horace, please.

Harry: How about another glass of wine, Horace, before you go? (*He refills their glasses.*)

Horace: I'd just as soon get it over with.

Harry: The truth is, Horace . . . I'd like to talk you out of this. I hate to see a literate fellow . . . an admirer of German wines . . . leave us so . . . abruptly. I'm enjoying your company.

Horace: And I yours.

Harry: In my business, I don't make many enduring friendships.

Horace: I'll drink another glass with you, but no more. Don't want to sap my . . . determination.

Harry: Is your divorce the only reason? Seems a trifle thin to me.

Horace: The last straw came a few days ago. I consult for the district court. Give my professional opinion regarding whether or not a person is sane enough to stand trial for criminal actions.

Harry: That must be interesting.

Horace: It was, for a time. (**Harry** *discreetly refills* **Horace**'s *glass.*) Some years ago, a young man was booked for attacking a woman with a hammer. I examined him, concluded that he was sane, and recommended him for trial. But the jury let him go.

Harry: Why?

Horace: Two of them thought he was insane even though I testified that he was sane. They talked the others into an acquittal.

Harry: What an outrage!

Horace: A couple of years later he was back in my office in the prison again.

113

This time, the charge was serious. He had gone on a shooting spree . . . had wounded four women and fired at six others from a car. (*He pauses and sips his wine.*) I knew exactly what the trouble was. . . . He had a pathological hostility toward women. It was plainly ingrained from his earliest childhood. May even have been inherited. . . .

Harry: Can such a thing be inherited?

Horace: The sociobiology boys think so. They think criminal instincts can be passed on from one generation to the next, genetically. Like in the Mafia.

Harry: Do you agree with this?

Horace: I'm beginning to. After all, musical talent can be inherited . . . Bach . . . Mozart . . . why not a talent for crime?

Harry: I don't know.

Horace: The SOBs claim there is some kind of a biological bias in the human race that promotes self-seeking, uninhibited behavior. Part of the race survival instinct. This could explain many urges: the urge to violence, to crime . . . or an urge to murder women.

Harry: Then our worst behavior is the result of inherited impulses?

Horace: People are beginning to think so. . . . Anyway, this patient of mine clearly suffered from a fundamental character disorder. It was not a treatable mental illness. If I had again declared him sane, he surely would been found guilty this time, and sent to prison for life. . . . But . . . why? Why did I develop some kind of a perverse liking for him? Do I share his hostility, deep down?

Harry: Do you?

Horace: I don't know. . . . Anyway, for whatever reason, I declared him insane. He couldn't stand trial, of course, and they sent him to a clinic here in the city. They are strong on rehabilitation at this particular clinic. Let patients out on passes to attend computer science classes, welding schools . . . that kind of thing. (*He sips some of the wine in his glass.*) While he was out on a pass, he managed to get into a woman's home where he raped and robbed her. Later, on another pass, he threatened a woman with a knife.

Harry: Was he prosecuted?

Horace: Of course not. An insane person is considered to be incapable of defending himself in court.

Harry: But why did they keep giving him passes?

Horace: Well, they finally did put a stop to that. (*He sips some more wine.*)

Then, last year, his case came up for review. You can't keep an insane person confined indefinitely, you know.

Harry: Why not? (*He refills* **Horace**'s glass.)

Horace: Violation of his civil rights. Has to be recertified from time to time. So . . . I examined him again. He seemed calm enough. Told me he had control over himself now. I prescribed some tranquilizer pills for him, told him to take them regularly . . . and let him go.

Harry: You let him go?!

Horace (*sighing deeply*): I kept telling myself—look for something positive. Don't be such a pessimist all the time. So, I declared him cured of his insanity and hoped for the best.

Harry: And what happened?

Horace: The worst. In six months he murdered nine women. Wrapped their bodies in plastic bags and buried them in back of a house he'd rented. The police finally caught him. He confessed to all those murders . . . the police recovered the bodies . . . and then they came to me and asked me the question I couldn't answer . . . and still can't. Why did I do it? . . . I'm responsible for the deaths of nine human beings.

Harry: Not directly.

Horace: Just as surely as though I'd killed them myself.

Harry (*refilling their glasses*): Come now. Chance . . . accident. He might have behaved some other way.

Horace: I knew what he would do when I turned him loose. It's as though . . . disappointment over my marriage . . . my ambivalent feelings toward my ex-wife . . . It's as though I deliberately let loose a monster . . . who attacked only women. (*Pause. He finishes the wine in his glass.*) Well! Have you heard enough?

Harry: We still have some wine in the bottle.

Horace: No thank you. Our little talk has strengthened my resolve. Let me have that coin, please. (**Harry** *reluctantly unlocks his box, puts* **Horace**'s *fifty dollars in it, withdraws a silver dollar, and hands it to him.*)

Harry: Here you are.

Horace: Thank you. (*They cross up right and* **Horace** *enters the Re-creation Area.*)

Harry: You understand the operation of the apparatus?

Horace: I believe so. . . . I sit here?

Harry: Yes.

Horace: The coin goes in this slot?

Harry: Correct.

Horace: And then I pull the handle. I understand. Close the curtain, please. (**Harry** *does so.*) Rather like a voting booth, isn't it?

Harry: So it is. (*He paces down left nervously.*)

Horace: Thanks for the wine.

Harry: My pleasure. (*He puts on his rubber apron.*)

Horace: Remember me and keep in mind, A faithful friend is hard to find. (*The guns fire and* **Harry** *jumps at the sound.*)

Harry: Eddie Guest? (*He crosses to the table, drinks the rest of the wine, then puts on the "Suicide" recording. He goes inside the Re-creation Area and soon emerges dragging* **Horace** *in his bag. He attaches the ID card, then drags the body into the refrigerator room. Soon he comes out again, closes the door, hangs his apron on its hook, then sits at the table. He opens an account book and works on his records for the day. The doorbell rings. He closes the book, turns off the record player, and crosses to the door up right.*) Yes? (*A big, burly man with a thick neck enters the apartment. He is a football coach named* **Muggs McGrane.**)

Muggs: Is this where you catch the bus?

Harry: The bus?

Muggs (*drawing his finger across his throat*): To the sweet by-and-by?

Harry: Yes. May I have your name?

Muggs: Muggs McGrane.

Harry (*motioning toward the table*): Have a seat, Mr. McGrane.

Muggs: Thanks. (*He sits right of the table. The doorbell rings again.*)

Harry: Here's something for you to read. (*He hands* **Muggs** *a Blue Book and crosses up right to the door.*)

Muggs: OK. (**Harry** *opens the door and a well-proportioned attractive middle-aged, red-haired woman enters. She is an opera singer named* **Maria Webster.**)

Maria: Mr. Murdstone?

Harry: The same. Please come in. (**Maria** *walks further into the room and looks around apprehensively.*)

Maria: Do you provide a—er—a suicide service?

Harry: Yes, but there is a gentleman ahead of you. Please sit here. (*He motions her toward the chair down right, but she suddenly rushes up to him.*)

Maria: Please! May I go first? I'm terribly nervous. (*She puts her hand over her mouth.*)

Harry: Well, if the gentleman doesn't mind . . .

Muggs (*getting up threateningly*): The Hell with that noise! (*He crosses to her and pushes her toward the chair down right.*) I was here first. (*He shoves her again. She nearly falls.*)

Maria: All right!

Muggs: Equal rights for women! (*He shoves her onto the chair, hard.*) Understand?

Maria: Yes.

Muggs: So sit there on your ass till you hear your name called!

Harry (*to* **Maria**): I'll be with you in a moment. (*He and* **Muggs** *return to the table and sit left and right of it.*) And what is your profession, Mr. McGrane?

Muggs: Head football coach at Bare Mountain University.

Harry: Oh, yes! I've seen some of the games on TV. The Bare Mountain Gorillas!

Muggs (*pleased*): That's my team.

Harry: Please fill out these forms for me.

Muggs: Only . . . I'm finished with all that now.

Harry: And the fee is fifty dollars.

Muggs: Got the dough right here. One fifty-dollar bill. (*He hands it to* **Harry** *who puts it on the table.*)

Harry: Thank you. I don't usually give a receipt.

Muggs (*thinks it over a moment*): Don't believe I'll need one.

Harry: Er . . . the forms. . . .

Muggs: Yeah. What does this one say?

Harry: Waiver of liability. Your wife might want to sue—

Muggs: I've moved out.

Harry: Your children—

Muggs: They don't talk to me. Claim the kids at school spit on 'em 'cause the Gorillas keep losing.

Harry: Oh! That's too bad. . . . Well . . . just sign the forms anyway, please. Can't help you if you don't sign the forms.

Muggs (*signing the forms*): Uh . . . this here one . . . about the funeral. I don't want my family there. Can they just cremate me?

Harry: But they will need an address to send the ashes to.

Muggs: My ashes . . . yeah. They can send 'em to the University of Wisconsin Alumni Association.

Harry: They'll appreciate that.

Muggs (*writing on one of the forms*): Well . . . I send 'em a few dollars every year . . . and this way . . . they'll get the idea . . . no more contributions from Muggs McGrane.

Harry (*taking the forms*): Thank you. Now, I'm afraid there's one more obstacle to your departure. As a matter of policy, I always insist on knowing a client's reason for wishing to partake of my service.

Muggs: Huh?

Harry: Why do you want to kill yourself?

Muggs: Oh . . . uh . . . well . . . I had the worst losing season of my career this here . . . season. . . .

Harry: Did you say you were the head football coach?

Muggs: I was until yesterday.

Harry: What happened?

Muggs: Well . . . when I first came to Bare Mountain . . . that season I lost eight and won two. Then I did one game better the next season . . . then one game worse the next. Then I won six and lost four. That was my best season. And then . . . I started going down. And this here season . . . I lost 'em all.

Harry: Every game?

Muggs: Every game.

Harry: I can see how discouraging that could be.

Muggs: Naw . . . you couldn't see that. You couldn't know what it's like to keep losing. . . .

Harry: Yes I can.

Muggs: It gets you here. (*He puts his hand on his stomach.* **Maria** *clutches her stomach, too.*) I mean . . . you get an ulcer, see? And you can't sleep. Your wife goes to pieces . . . and your kids hate the sight of you. You got no idea what it's like.

Harry: It must be hell.

Muggs: It's worse 'n hell.

Harry: What brought on this debacle?

Muggs: Huh?

Harry: All those losses.

Muggs: Oh . . . women.

Harry: Women?

Muggs: Yeah. Women's athletics.

Harry: But . . . why?

Muggs: They passed some law somewhere . . . and the President of Bare

Mountain says that women's athletics has to get the same financial support that men's athletics gets.

Harry: And that hurt your program?

Muggs: Why, sure. They cut my football scholarships, and my recruiting program, and my coaching staff and spring practice.

Harry: An unkind cut.

Muggs: And with all the dough they saved they set up women's basketball, volleyball, and women's tennis and golf . . . and women's high jump, broad jump, and pole vault.

Harry: I didn't know they could do all that.

Muggs (*fervently*): It's women cause all the trouble in the world! *Women!* And their equal rights. I wouldn't give a woman the sweat outta my asshole! (**Maria** *goes quickly into the bathroom.*)

Harry: Well, they don't cause *all* the trouble. . . .

Muggs: Yes, they do. (**Maria** *can be heard vomiting in the bathroom.*)

Harry: Oh! She's being sick in there. (**Harry** *starts to go to her assistance, but* **Muggs** *pushes him roughly back into his chair.*)

Muggs: Stay where you're at! Equal rights for women, see? Let her puke!

Harry: You wouldn't even go to the help of a woman who is sick?

Muggs: Let some other woman help her.

Harry: There's no other woman here.

Muggs: That's *her* problem! (**Harry** *stares at him in amazement.* **Maria** *comes out of the bathroom and sits down again, a handkerchief to her lips.*)

Harry: Are you all right now, Ms., er—

Maria: Yes. I'm all right now.

Harry: Well . . . er . . . Mr. McGrane—

Muggs: Coach McGrane.

Harry: Sorry. You were saying? About your losing season?) (**Muggs** *collects his thoughts.*)

Muggs: Yeah. Well . . . uh . . . yesterday, the Athletic Director . . . he called me into his office . . . he's got a nice rug on his floor.

Harry: Has he?

Muggs: Yeah. Bearskin rug. Polar bear . . . all white . . . looks real good. (*He run his hand over his eyes.*) So . . . anyway . . . he says to me . . . he says . . . "Muggs, I think your coaching career is over." (*Pause.*) That's all he said. And then . . . it hit me what he meant. He wasn't just firing me. . . .

119

Harry: He wasn't?

Muggs: He was saying . . . nobody is gonna give me a new job. The word is out . . . Coach McGrane is a loser. Don't hire *him* as a head coach. Not even as an assistant coach . . . because any team he's with will start losing.

Harry: Oh, he probably didn't mean it quite like that.

Muggs: All my life, I've wanted to win. I've fought to win. I've played on winning teams. And now they say . . . they say . . . (*he struggles to control himself*) that Coach McGrane is a loser. (*He sobs for a moment, then pulls himself together.*) So that's why I'm here. Let's get it over with.

Harry: You've convinced me. (*He puts the fifty dollars in his strongbox and withdraws a silver dollar that he hands to* **Muggs**) You'll need this coin to operate the machine in there. (*He guides* **Muggs** *into the Re-creation Area.*) Just sit here. Insert the coin in that slot there and pull the handle. (*He comes out up right and pulls the curtain to.*)

Muggs: Pull the handle?

Harry: Yes. . . .

Muggs: Which way?

Harry: Down. (*He paces nervously left, watching the rifles.*)

Muggs: Uh . . . then what happens?

Harry: The handle of the slot machine is wired to the triggers of the M-14 rifles. (*He goes into the Re-creation Area from up left.*)

Muggs: Oh. . . .

Harry: You see? These wires go over these pulleys. . . .

Muggs: Yeah. I get the idea.

Harry: Then the rifles shoot you in the chest.

Muggs: Did you design this gizmo, Harry?

Harry: Yes, Coach, I did. (*He comes out again, closes the curtain, and waits up left for* **Muggs** *to get it over with.*)

Muggs: You got a lot of talent.

Harry: Thanks.

Muggs: You could design exercise machines.

Harry: I never thought of that. . . .

Muggs: Harry?

Harry: Yes, Coach.

Muggs: Do you think I'm a loser?

Harry: I do not. Your decision to terminate your existence displays a positive denial of the will to live. Schopenhauer would be proud of you.

Muggs: Uh . . . would he? . . .

Harry (*becoming impatient*): If you want to change your mind, Coach, just say so. I'll be glad to refund your money.

Muggs: Naw . . . I'm goin' through with it. I was just thinkin'. I sure wish I could be a winner just once more. . . . (**Harry** *paces about uneasily.* **Maria** *stares fixedly at the curtain, her hand on her stomach.*) . . . but it ain't to be . . . it ain't to be. . . . (*Another pause, then* **Muggs** *is heard singing in a strong clear voice*) "On Wisconsin, on Wisconsin, stand in dere an' fight—" (*The guns fire with a roar.* **Harry** *jumps.* **Maria** *screams, clutches her stomach, and presses her handkerchief against her mouth.*)

Harry: All right?

Maria: Yes. . . . (*There is another sound from the Re-creation Area. First some loud clicks, then the sound of many coins falling into a tin box.*)

Harry (*staring into the Re-creation Area*): Well, what do you know?

Maria: What?

Harry: He hit the jackpot! (*They hold their positions.*)

CURTAIN.

END ACT I.

ACT II: *A moment later.*

AT RISE: Harry and **Maria** *hold their positions until the curtain is part way open. Then* **Harry** *goes into the Re-creation Area from the left.*

Harry: Just imagine. . . . (*He comes out again holding a tin box full of silver coins that he shows to* **Maria**.) In the last instant of his life, he won $100!

Maria: The lucky bastard! (**Harry** *dumps the coins into his strongbox, then puts on his apron and returns with the empty box to the Re-creation Area.*)

Harry: Well . . . if you would care to fill out those forms on the table . . .

Maria: OK. (*She rises, crosses to the table, and sits.*)

Harry: As soon as I get Coach McGrane into his sack, I'll be right with you.

Maria (*apparently feeling better*): I don't see how he got to hating women so . . . just because he lost a few football games.

Harry: He said he lost because of women's athletics.

Maria (*filling out the forms*): The coaches who beat him must have had women's athletics at their places.

Harry: Probably.

Maria: He was just a simple failure . . . like most of us.

Harry: I try not to make judgments. (*He emerges up left with the sack that he drags over to the refrigerator.* **Maria** *watches him but tries to keep her mind on something else.*)

Maria: And he takes it out on women. His poor wife. . . .

Harry: As President Truman used to say, "Took it like a man. Blamed it on his wife."

Maria: And he didn't even send her his ashes.

Harry: Maybe she wouldn't want them. (*He has stapled the ID card to the sack and drags it into his refrigerator.*)

Maria: Maybe not. I wouldn't. (*She finishes with the forms.* **Harry** *comes out of the refrigerator, closes the door and hangs up his apron.*)

Harry: Neither would I.

Maria: Here's your forms. Let's go!

Harry: Just a second. . . . (**Maria** *puts fifty dollars on the table.*) I need—

Maria: I don't want to be sick again.

Harry: —a reason of some kind. Why you are doing this?

Maria: Isn't just *life* reason enough?

Harry: Some people enjoy life.

Maria: Drunks . . . idealists. . . .

Harry: I can't, in all conscience, give you your coin until—

Maria: All right. I'm an opera singer. And I'm losing my voice.

Harry (*glancing quickly at her*): I thought I'd seen you somewhere.

Maria: Really?

Harry: Did you ever sing at the Met?

Maria: A few times. Most of my career has been in Europe.

Harry: Did you sing Nedda in Pagliacci?

Maria: Yes. Some time ago.

Harry: I saw you do Nedda at the Met!

Maria (*pleased*): *Did* you?

Harry: You were wonderful!

Maria: Thank you!

Harry: In the last scene—when he stabs you—your acting was terrific!

Maria: Well . . . acting is about all I have left these days.

Harry: But why—may I call you Maria?

Maria: Sure, Harry.

Harry: Why throw in the towel, Maria?

Maria: You don't understand. For a professional singer to begin losing her voice . . .

Harry: Like a pitcher whose arm is gone?

Maria: Yeah.

Harry: Or a pool player who gets his thumbs broken.

Maria: It's like . . . losing your soul.

Harry: But you could do smaller roles. . . .

Maria Top's gone. No breath. (*She puts her hand on her diaphragm.*)

Harry: You sure had everything the night I saw you. When was that? Five years ago?

Maria: Longer than that, Harry. (*She counts on her fingers.*) More like . . . ten. Yeah . . . ten season ago. I sang six Neddas for the Met, and I covered twice.

Harry: You can teach. With all your experience—

Maria: I've had a lot of experience . . . yes. But I'm not a voice teacher.

Harry: Anyone who knows something can teach it to others.

Maria: Not me. Teaching takes talent . . . for teaching.

Harry: Hmmmm. Well, what have you been doing since those great Neddas?

Maria: Not much. Watching my career go to the dogs. Passing time. Visiting my kids.

Harry: Kids?

Maria: I have three daughters . . . by two husbands and a tenor. They married well and live in Europe. Last year, I traveled around—like King Lear—visiting my daughters and their snappy husbands . . . between performances at the Frankfurt Opera of what turned out to be my last professional engagement. . . .

Harry: What did you sing at Frankfurt?

Maria: Tosca.

Harry: Wish I'd seen it.

Maria: Well, Harry, which do you like better, art or sex?

Harry: Why do you ask that?

Maria: Did you like my Nedda because I was doing the part well or because I was playing her sexy, pulling up my skirt all the time?

Harry: I liked everything about you.

Maria: I just ask because, at Frankfurt, I played the end of the second act of *Tosca* without any clothes on.

Harry: You did?!

Maria: Yes, Harry. No clothes. Naked as a blue jay in front of 2,000 fascinated customers.

Harry: Why?

Maria: It was a new production directed by the resident terror in the staging department, Hans Sechsfels.

Harry: That's a familiar name.

Maria: He likes naked bodies on the stage.

Harry: That's him!

Maria: I went to the first stage rehearsal in all innocence and found out that he wanted me to take off all my clothes while I was singing "Vissi d'arte" on the sofa.

Harry: But—why?!

Maria: He said that Tosca has had an unconscious desire for Scarpia ever since she met him at a party in Rome one night. She didn't like him much on the surface because of his reputation as Chief of the Rome police, but she has this great *subliminal* longing to get in bed with him just once. That's why she's so nervous when she runs into him in the church in the first act.

Harry: I thought she was nervous because of Cavaradossi.

Maria: So did I, but Mr. Sechsfels said otherwise, and he was the director. So I accepted his interpretation like a good girl and tried to get used to taking my clothes off in front of everybody.

Harry: Awkward. . . .

Maria: The first general rehearsal was the hardest. I forgot my words, the Scarpia forgot his, the prompter lost his place, the orchestra got confused. . . . It was a mess.

Harry: I can see why.

Maria: But that devil Sechsfels . . . he kept telling me it was a great scene. There I am, naked before Scarpia. He grabs me in his arms, yells, "Tosca, finalmente mia!"* And I stab him in the back—!

Harry: Then what happened?

Maria: Well . . . let's see. He fell down on the floor. Mr. Sechsfels let me put my dress on—had to leave my underwear on the sofa, no time for all that—I did the candles and the crucifix business . . . just had time to say, "E avanti a lui tremava tutta Romma"*; then I grabbed the safe conduct pass out of his hand and got the hell off the stage.

Harry: How did the performance go?

Maria: Oh, Mr. Sechsfels was right about the audience. They cheered us for the Act II curtain call. I've never been so appreciated.

Harry: Wish I'd been there.

Maria: Bit hit. Whole town wanted to see it. They sold out twenty performances.

Harry: I suppose there's something about an opera singer taking off her clothes on the stage.

Maria: Yeah . . . like in that movie where Grace Moore milked a cow.

Harry: I missed that one.

Maria: Well, I signed a contract to do twenty-five more performances the next season, but that summer I thought things over and I canceled out. Why did I have to expose myself? What about Scarpia? Why not him too?

Harry: Maybe the public wouldn't be interested in seeing the baritone's member.

Maria: Anyway, I was . . . out. . . . Word went around the circuit. A couple of other things fell through. So I retired. And since I'm not the teaching type, and I'm not the solitary-walks-on-the-mountaintop type . . . (*The doorbell rings.*)

Harry: Will you excuse me a moment?

Maria: Sure. (**Harry** *goes to the front door.* **Maria** *rises and crosses toward the left.*)

Harry (*opening the door*): Yes? (*A determined looking, dark complexioned woman walks firmly in the door and closes it after her. She is a novelist and former wife of the psychiatrist* **Horace Liverwright**, *now deceased. Her first name is* **Helga**.)

Helga: Murdstone Suicide Service?

Harry: The same.

---

*"Tosca, mine at last!"
*"And before him all Rome trembled."

125

Helga: Name's Helga Liverwright.

Harry (*startled*): Is it? Any relation to Horace Liverwright, the psychiatrist?

Helga: My ex-hubby. Why?

Harry: Your ex-husband! (*He seems at a loss for words.*)

Helga: I left that bastard because I got tired of being told I should see a psychiatrist.

Harry: But your husband—

Helga: Psychiatrists never treat their own wives. Ethics of the profession.

Harry: Oh. (*He hands* **Helga** *a Blue Book.*) Would you look through this please? I have a client ahead of you.

Helga: Sure, honey. (*She sits in the chair down right and looks through her Blue Book of Procedure.*)

Maria: Well, Harry? May I have my coin?

Harry: Yes, Maria. (*He puts her money in his box and withdraws a silver dollar that he hands her.*) Here you are.

Maria: Thanks. (*She goes quickly inside the Re-creation Area and pulls the curtain.* **Harry** *puts on his apron.*)

Harry: Everything clear?

Maria: Clear as crystal. (*Long pause.*) "La commedia è finita!"* (*The guns fire.* **Harry** *goes inside to put* **Maria** *in her bag.* **Helga** *rises and crosses up right.*)

Helga: Can I look at her?

Harry: If you want to. (**Helga** *pulls back the curtain on the up-right pipe and gazes calmly at* **Maria** *'s dead body.*)

Helga: Rest . . . in . . . peace. (*She crosses to the center table. sits right of it, and puts her fifty dollars on the table.*) You . . . er . . . mentioned my husband.

Harry: Yes . . . yes, I did. Well . . . (*.He comes out of the Re-creation Area left dragging* **Maria** *in her sack behind him.*)

Helga: Did you know him?

Harry: Slightly.

Helga: I'll bet you never knew what a bastard he could be.

Harry: Well, he seemed like a nice fellow. . . . (*He staples the ID tag to the sack and drags it into the refrigerator.*)

Helga: He kept lording it over me because he had a Ph.D. in psychology and all I had was an M.A. in English.

---

*"The comedy is ended" (last line of Leoncavallo's opera *Pagliacci*).

126

Harry: An M.A. in English is a respectable achievement.

Helga: You bet your ass it is.

Harry: I wish I had earned one when I had the chance. (*He comes out of the refrigerator, closes the door, then goes into his bedroom off left to get his cleaning materials.*)

Helga: You sound like a reasonably literate fellow, Harry. Did you attend dear old Yale?

Harry: I attended the Schulenberg public schools. (*He returns and fills a bucket with tap water at the sink down left.*)

Helga: And afterward?

Harry: Two years at Del Mar Junior College in Corpus Christi.

Helga: Then?

Harry: Back to Schulenberg. Got married . . . kids . . . (*He takes the bucket, a mop, and some rags and soap into the Re-creation Area.*) And . . . to pay my bills, I joined the Marine Corps.

Helga: You were a platoon sergeant in Vietnam!

Harry: I wanted to be a combat marine, but my superiors put me into recruitment school. (*He can be heard mopping the floor.*) I've never been on the firing line anywhere.

Helga: Do you regret that, Harry?

Harry: No, Helga. (*Pause.*) But . . . about your husband . . .

Helga: Oh, he kept yelping at me about my ignorance, my stupidity, how hard it was to bring me off. . . .

Harry: So you wrote a book?

Helga: How did you know?

Harry: Oh . . . people seem to do that when they're down . . . or in jail. . . .

Helga: It sold a million copies.

Harry: Congratulations.

Helga: So I put hubby dear behind me and let out the air.

Harry: What did he do then?

Helga: Went down . . . hit the bottle . . . hard. . . . (**Harry** *comes out of the Re-creation Area, dumps the bloody water out of his bucket into the sink, and rinses out his rags.*)

Harry: And did life get better for you?

Helga: You ask that as though you know it didn't.

Harry: Not a difficult deduction.

Helga: You're a good deducer, Harry. My agent has been stealing my royalties, my girl lover has left me . . . for a man . . . and so . . . I've

127

been thinking. Here I am at the top of the tree. Why not go out strong? Why wait to hit the skids?

Harry: Those moments do come.

Helga: Why not say—now! NOW! Not tomorrow. Not the next day. NOW!!!

Harry (*after a moment*)*:* There must have been something else, Helga honey. Something more personal. Am I right?

Helga: Yes, Harry, old fruit, you are right. My daddy . . . my dear daddy was a general . . . tank man . . . fought with George Patton, Jr.

Harry: You have any brothers or sisters?

Helga: No. Why?

Harry: Go on.

Helga: General Patton was his idol and Daddy was mine. He taught me to ride and hunt and fish . . . and to stand up for myself.

Harry: Made a man of you?

Helga: What's wrong with that?

Harry: Nothing.

Helga: When he died—of syphilis—he left me his prized possessions . . . a pair of matched pearl-handled, 44-caliber dueling pistols. He told me he had killed three men who tried to flirt with Mama.

Harry: I thought dueling was against the law.

Helga: Not in Texas.

Harry: Ah, yes. Texas. . . . (*He has finished with his cleaning materials, puts them away and now sits at the table, left.*)

Helga: Harry . . . why do you bother with this boring routine? A classical pessimist like you . . . why don't you take a shiny silver dollar in there and get it over with?

Harry: I've thought of it. But . . . there's always work to do . . . loose ends.

Helga: Poses to keep up.

Harry: Doorbells to answer. . . . Well . . . and what about your dear daddy?

Helga: Yes. My sainted daddy, whom I admired more than anyone else in the world. The perfect man. Strong, fearless, a professional fighter. Left me his pistols when he died. Used to scare poor Horace with them. . . . Wonder what that bastard's doing right now?

Harry (*glancing at the refrigerator*): Repenting, probably.

Helga: You know, after I divorced him I found I kind of liked him.

Harry: Marriage has ruined many nice friendships.

Helga: Anyway . . . after my girlfriend left me I took up with a boy again.

A writer. Having a run of bad luck. Jealous of me. Hadn't had anything accepted in months.

Harry: I had a fellow like that in here last week.

Helga: Yeah? Well . . . the other day he came over to my place, showed me his latest rejection slip, and asked me to loan him one of my pistols. I could see he was ready to go. (*Pause, as she stares at* **Harry**.) Can you tell that about someone?

Harry: What?

Helga: Can you look into someone's eyes and tell . . . (*They stare into each other's eyes a moment.*)

Harry: I can tell that you're ready.

Helga: How?

Harry: There's a kind of glaze over your eyes. You seem . . . to be . . . disappointed in something. (**Helga** *puts her hand over her eyes for a moment.*) So . . . what happened next?

Helga: I gave him one of my pistols. He took it home. Got undressed. Went into the bathroom. Sat down in the tub . . . and shot himself in the neck.

Harry: In the neck?

Helga: He aimed for his temple. But he missed, and hit the back of his neck.

Harry: Well, that's close.

Helga: They rushed him to the hospital. Brilliant surgery saved his life.

Harry: They keep saving the wrong people.

Helga: The doc rushed up to me after the operation. Says to me, "I've saved his life for you. He's going to be all right. Just one problem. He's paralyzed from the neck down. He'll have to get used to that."

Harry: From his neck—!?

Helga: Down.

Harry: If I may say so, it's cases like this that demonstrate the need for a professional service.

Helga: You may say so, Harry, old sport.

Harry: Then what happened?

Helga: I went back to the hospital a few days ago. Went in to see poor Buddy. He looked up at me with his brown rabbit eyes, and he says to me, "What's the use, Helga honey? Why? Can't write . . . can't jog . . . can't screw . . . what else is there?

Harry: Meditation.

Helga: I got kind of depressed. Went home. Got out my other pistol. Put it to my temple . . . (*As though in a daze, she pantomimes the scene*

129

again. She lifts her hand to her temple.) And . . . and . . . (*Her hand trembles violently.*) And . . . (*Finally, she pantomimes putting the pistol down on the table.*) I couldn't do it. Couldn't pull the trigger. (*Pause.*) My hand shook, Harry.

Harry: It still does.

Helga: I've practiced a lot with my pistols. Took lessons. Aiming at somebody else—nothing to it. I could shoot a cockroach off the top of your head at fifty feet and you wouldn't feel a thing.

Harry: I'd like to try that sometime.

Helga: Would you, Harry? (*They stare into each other's eyes a long moment.*)

Harry: Yes. . . .

Helga: Anyway, when I aimed at my own head . . . I couldn't do it. Lost my nerve. Failed my dear daddy. Failed him! Failed him! (*She sobs for a moment, then regains control over herself.*)

Harry: We can all think of occasions when we disappointed our father.

Helga: I sat there in the bathtub thinking about Daddy. He used to tell me about the Code of Honor in the army. If an officer disgraced himself, they left him alone in his office with a loaded pistol on his desk. . . .

Harry: I saw a movie with a scene like that. . . .

Helga: The guy was supposed to shoot himself in the temple.

Harry: Who was that guy . . . ? Klaus Maria Brandauer! Big scene. Shot himself in the head.

Helga: But I couldn't do it. Disgraced my daddy. So . . . here I am. A place where your hand doesn't shake and the guns never miss.

Harry: Well put, Helga. (*He looks over her papers.*) You wish to be cremated. I need an address for the ashes. (*He puts her money in his lock box and withdraws a silver dollar.*)

Helga: Let's see . . . Mom and Dad gone—

Harry: Any kids?

Helga: No. Guess I'll send 'em to my dear ex-hubby . . . that psychological has-been . . . that shrunk. . . . (*She fills out the label.*) He can put 'em between his Jung and his Freud.

Harry: There would be an interesting significance to that.

Helga: There. All finished. (*She stands up, as does* **Harry**.) Anything else?

Harry: No. (*She starts to move closer to* **Harry** *but he merely hands her the coin.*) Your silver dollar, Ms. Liverwright.

Helga (*taking it*): Thanks, honey. (*She turns and walks firmly to the*

Re-creation Area. **Harry** *follows her. She goes in behind the curtain.*)
I sit here?

Harry: That's right. Insert the coin in that slot. . . . Pull the handle. . . . (*He closes the curtain and walks over to the up left area. Slowly, he puts on his rubber apron.*)

Helga: Still out there, Harry?

Harry: Yes, Helga. Right here.

Helga: My last view of life, Harry.

Harry: Yes, Helga. Take your time.

Helga (*after a moment*): Either this wallpaper goes, or I do! (*The guns fire with a roar. As* **Harry** *starts to go into the Re-creation Area, the doorbell rings. He goes to the front door and opens it.*)

Harry: Yes? (**Lily** *enters determinedly and closes the door after her*).

Lily: Remember me?

Harry: Officer Lily Longstreet.

Lily: I've been walking around. Sat in the park awhile. Then I went to my bank and drew out fifty dollars. (*She puts the money on the table.*) There you are.

Harry: Well! You're the first of New York's Finest to come my way.

Lily: These the forms? (*She fills them out while standing at the table.*) I want everything to be in order, Mr. Murdstone.

Harry: We New Yorkers would expect that.

Lily (*finishing the forms*): There you are. My coin, please.

Harry: I've got a body ahead of you. (*He crosses to the Re-creation Area.*)

Lily: May I be of assistance?

Harry: Delighted. (*They go inside.*)

Lily: I should think you'd get tired of this routine.

Harry: Routine is an important thing. . . .

Lily: After the first fifty dead bodies or so . . . corpse after corpse . . . creeping in this petty pace . . . (*They drag* **Helga** *out in her sack.* **Harry** *staples her ID tag to it, then pulls it into the refrigerator.*) Just haul them into the fridge to freeze . . . one after the other. . . .

Harry: Routine is the essence of life.

Lily: Routine stifles life.

Harry: That, too. (*He emerges from the refrigerator and closes the door.*)

Lily: May I have my coin now?

Harry: Certainly. (*He glances over the forms she has filled out, then gets a silver dollar from his box and hands it to her.*) Of course . . . first . . .

131

Lily: I remember. No spur-of-the-moment stuff.

Harry: Routine requirement.

Lily: Well, I've just gotten tired of the garbage I have to take all the time from "New York's Finest"—huh!! (*The bell rings.* **Harry** *crosses to the front door to open it.*)

Harry: You mean your male buddies on the force?

Lily: You hit it.

Harry (*at the door*): Please come in, sir. (*A tall four-star general enters and slams the door behind him.* **Gen. Robert ("Blitz") Blowgarden** *is in full uniform, wearing many decorations, and is anxious to get it over with.*)

Blowgarden: You operate a suicide service?

Harry: I do.

Blowgarden: Let's get at it. (*He starts for the Re-creation Area, but* **Harry** *stops him.*)

Harry: Just a minute, General, er—

Blowgarden: Blowgarden.

Harry: Blowgarden?

Blowgarden: "Blitz" Blowgarden, they call me. Got that name fighting the Krauts in '44. I blitzed through Germany like shit through a goose.

Harry: I've heard about you.

Blowgarden: And I didn't slow down any in Korea or Nam.

Harry: Well, I'm sorry to have to slow you down now, but there's a lady ahead or you.

Blowgarden (*turning around*): Oh. A cop!

Lily (*saluting*): Yes sir, General.

Blowgarden (*saluting*): At ease.

Harry: Would you kindly sit here? (**Blowgarden** *sits in the chair down right.*)

Blowgarden: Women cops! (*He eyes* **Lily** *suspiciously.*)

Harry: Something to read. (*He hands* **Blowgarden** *a Blue Book.*)

Blowgarden: Thanks. (**Harry** *and* **Lily** *play the following scene left stage.*)

Harry: Well, Officer Longstreet—

Blowgarden: Longstreet! Huh!

Lily: My great-grandfather, sir.

Blowgarden: Should have supported Pickett at Gettysburg.

Lily: I have heard discussion of that among members of my family, sir.

Harry: You were telling me about your problems. . . .

132

Lily: Well . . . I didn't mind cutting my hair.

Harry: Why did you have to cut your hair?

Lily: The male dress code—there isn't any female dress code—says how long your sideburns can be, and your mustache, and that your hair can't touch your collar. So I cut it off.

Harry: Right spirit.

Lily: Yeah, but the routine has begun to get to me. Like finding a stiff stuffed into a laundry dryer. . . . Or finding a Catholic bishop dead in a whorehouse.

Harry: What did you do?

Lily: We propped him up in his car, drove him to a parking lot, then reported that he had died reaching for his glove compartment.

Harry: Ingenious.

Lily: But the last straw was a few nights ago. I was riding with my partner—a guy I kind of liked—and a very unfortunate thing happened.

Harry: What?

Lily: There was a small riot going on outside a tavern. Lots of punks yelling and waving bottles at each other. We got out of the car, I drew my .38 and fired in the air . . . and my partner . . . (*She grips the back of a chair.*) We had to drive by his apartment so he could change his pants!

Harry: Depressing.

Lily: Then, when we got back to the station, he accused me of reckless use of my service revolver. The sergeant backed him up and reduced me from patrol cars to walking a beat.

Harry: Well, that's good exercise. . . .

Lily: Don't need any exercise. (*She goes quickly into the Re-creation Area and pulls the curtain after her.*) Just need that bastard of a sergeant to choke on his chewing tobacco. (*There is a pause.* **Harry** *is down left.*) Curses on you, Shameous O'Reagan! (**Lily** *throws her cap in the air. It sails over the top of the curtain and* **Harry** *catches it as the guns fire with a roar.* **Harry** *flinches but the general gives no sign that he has heard anything unusual.*)

Blowgarden: Why don't you get some silencers for those M-14s?

Harry: I wouldn't know where to get them. (*He goes inside the Re-creation Area to put* **Lily** *in her bag.* **Blowgarden** *rises and crosses to the table.*)

Blowgarden: You can get 'em at the Army-Navy Store on Ninth Avenue. Tell 'em Blitz Blowgarden sent you. They won't give you any static.

Harry (*behind the curtain*): Thank you, General. I'll take your advice.

Blowgarden: These the forms to fill out?

Harry: Right there on the table. (**Blowgarden** *sits at the table and fills out the forms.* **Harry** *emerges up left dragging the sack with* **Lily** *inside. He staples on the ID tag and hauls her into the refrigerator.*)

Blowgarden: This is a busy place.

Harry: Just one thing after another. (**Harry** *comes out, closes the door, and, still wearing his rubber apron. Sits at the table left.*)

Blowgarden: Fifty in cash. (*He puts the bills on the table.*) I'll take that silver dollar now.

Harry: Just a second, General. I've got to have a reason.

Blowgarden: Reason?! God damn it! Don't you read the papers?

Harry: Not every day.

Blowgarden: First we lost the war in Nam because we got stabbed in the back by a lot of war protesters.

Harry: I remember that.

Blowgarden: College students with yellow streaks up their backs a mile wide. . . .

Harry: I remember them.

Blowgarden: And those Hollywood floozies like Jane—what's her name—

Harry: I remember her. I remember them all. They attacked me when my partner and I tried to set up a recruiting desk at the University of Texas.

Blowgarden: Recruiting for what?

Harry: Marine Corps. I was a recruiting sergeant.

Blowgarden: Still in the Corps?

Harry: I quit.

Blowgarden: Then you know how I feel.

Harry: Bad enough to kill yourself?

Blowgarden: But there's so much more. Those journalist scumbags who pushed Nixon out of office—the best president we've had since General Grant . . .

Harry: And still highly regarded—in China.

Blowgarden: Things are bad at home. My principal relationship in life has degenerated into a mutual nonaggression treaty.

Harry: That describes most marriages.

Blowgarden: And now they're putting women into combat units in the army. Women!

Harry: Equal rights and all that. . . .

Blowgarden: Ever been to Fort Riley, home of the Big Red One?

Harry: No.

Blowgarden: Now it's the home of the biggest whorehouse in Kansas.

Harry: What next?

Blowgarden: I'll tell you what's next. The army of the future will be organized by race and sex.

Harry: How?

Blowgarden: By divisions of white males, black males, women, and homosexuals.

Harry: Hmmmm . . .

Blowgarden: They'll fight better if they're all together in single units.

Harry: Why?

Blowgarden: Competition. You remember a Marine Corps general called "Howlin' Mad" Smith?

Harry: Distinctly.

Blowgarden: Smith used to challenge one division to outdo another. If the First Marine Division took an island, the Second Division would try to take two. That's how we beat the Japs.

Harry: I never realized that before.

Blowgarden: You know how I'd fight the next war?

Harry: How? (**Blowgarden** *arranges various objects on the table, then moves them around during the following.*)

Blowgarden: I'm attacking this fortified position, see?

Harry: I see.

Blowgarden: First, I'd attack with my women's division . . . to trigger land mines and open up a support corridor.

Harry: How do the women trigger the land mines?

Blowgarden: By stepping on them.

Harry: Oh.

Blowgarden: Then, I'd send in my homosexual division to draw mortar and artillery fire . . . so I can locate their heavy guns.

Harry: That should work.

Blowgarden: Then I'd throw in my black division to dig the enemy out of their trenches with bayonets and razor blades. . . . (*He moves his units forward on the table.*) And finally, I'd send in my white male division—with their tanks—to consolidate our gains.

Harry: Brilliant!

Blowgarden: I think so. (*He studies his tactical position on the table.*) In addition to using each division for the job it's best suited to, my method would have another valuable effect.

Harry: What?

Blowgarden: If the war lasted long enough, we could rid this country of a hell of a lot of women, niggers, and homosexuals!

Harry (*after a moment*): Do you think we'll get into another war?

Blowgarden: I doubt it. Saw a guy carrying a sign the other day—it said: "Nothing Is Worth Fighting For."

Harry: You've answered my question.

Blowgarden: May I have my silver dollar now, Sergeant?

Harry: Yes, sir. (*He takes a silver dollar out of his strongbox and hands it to the general.*)

Blowgarden: Thank you. (*He marches stiffly into the Re-creation Area.* **Harry** *rises and crosses up left.*)

Harry: Everything clear in there, General?

Blowgarden: Perfectly clear, Sergeant. . . . Damn the torpedoes! Full speed ahead! (*The guns fire with a roar.* **Harry** *jumps, as usual. He then goes to his record player and puts on a new record, "The Stars and Stripes Forever," by John Philip Sousa. He then goes inside the Re-creation Area and emerges a moment or two later, dragging the general in his bag behind him. He staples the ID tag to the bag, opens the refrigerator door, and pulls the bag inside. The front doorbell rings.* **Harry** *comes out, closes the door, hangs up his apron, turns off the record player, and crosses to the front door, which he opens.*)

Harry: Yes? (**Swifty** *comes in quickly and crosses center.*)

Swifty: Hello, Harry. Remember me?

Harry (*his back to the door*): Mr. Swifty Kazan?

Swifty: Right on.

Harry: You've come back.

Swifty: With a client of mine.

Harry: A client?

Swifty: An old pal of yours, I believe. . . . (**Harry** *turns around as a good-looking well-developed dark-haired woman in her forties walks in and closes the door behind her. She is* **Harry** *'s wife from Texas and is called Toothy by her friends.*)

Harry (*in astonishment*): Toothy!

Toothy: Surprise!

136

Swifty: (*enjoying the reunion*): So you remember your faithful wife of yore, Harry?

Harry: How did you get here?

Toothy: I've been here quite a while, Elihu.

Swifty: Harry, is your name really Elihu Mummy?

Toothy: It most certainly is. And he called me Toothy Mummy.

Harry (*trying to grasp it all*): You came up here to New York—

Toothy: With our five kiddies, Elihu—

Harry: —to find me—

Toothy: —and collect many years of grocery money that you owe me. Not to mention my share of our savings account that you stole.

Harry: I put most of the money in that account from my Marine Corps pay. That money was mine.

Swifty: Texas is a community property state, Harry—I mean Elihu—so she owns half of everything.

Harry: Call me Harry, if you don't mind.

Toothy: He hates "Elihu"—don't you, *El-uh-hooooo*?

Harry: How did you know I was in New York?

Toothy: I didn't. I came here because they pay more welfare to a deserted wife with five screaming children than they pay in Texas.

Swifty: Texas pays AFDC $210 a month to a family of six, Harry, and New York pays $592.

Harry: But how did you two—?

Swifty: I met her in an automat on Eighth Avenue, Harry . . . and then—

Toothy (*grinning toothily*): And then, I engaged this clever and good-looking private detective, Mr. Swifty Kazan—

Swifty: We never sleep.

Toothy: —to find you, Elihu. . . .

Swifty: And you know the rest, Harry.

Toothy: Mr. Kazan is a brilliant detective—

Swifty: Call me Swifty, Ms. Mummy!

Toothy: Swifty—and you call me Toothy, hear?

Swifty: I hear.

Toothy: As you can see, Elihu, Swifty found you for me by using his awesome powers of deduction—like Sherlock Holmes.

Harry: He found me by accident.

Swifty: My fee is due, anyway.

Toothy: Elihu will be glad to pay you out of what he owes me.

137

Swifty: I'll let you off with a thousand, Harry, plus expenses.

Harry: I'm not paying you a damn cent! She hired you—she can pay you. Equal rights for women!

Toothy (*looking around*): You've got a nice little business here, Elihu.

Swifty: Nicely-nicely. Fifty bucks a body and practically no overhead. Look in here. . . . (*He opens the big refrigerator door and points inside. Clouds of dry ice pour into the room.*)

Toothy: Oh! How awful!

Swifty: They don't feel a thing, kid. Eight bodies lying on the table there, freezing their tails, times fifty bucks each. Already $400. . . .

Harry: I've got expenses. Rent, electricity, ammunition, garbage bags . . .

Toothy (*shivering*): What happens after . . . after . . . ?

Swifty: He has a deal with a funeral parlor.

Toothy: I'm cold. (*She snuggles up to* **Swifty** *, who embraces her warmly.*) Gee . . . that's better. . . . (**Harry** *sits at the table, center.*)

Harry: Shut the door! You're wasting my electricity. (**Swifty** *slams the door closed with his foot.*)

Toothy: Elihu, it does look to me like you could have sent us some grocery money. We got pretty hungry sometimes, the six of us, deep in the heart of Texas.

Harry: I was afraid you'd find me. Then I'd be back in jail again.

Toothy: I don't think our marriage was a jail.

Swifty: Where'd you two connect, anyway?

Toothy: At the famous old Oakridge smokehouse in Schulenberg one hot summer, many years ago. Him cutting up chickens and me addressing gift food parcels. Back then, he was kind of cute.

Harry: All I've ever wanted in life was freedom. Freedom from home, freedom from you and that smokehouse and that endless parade of pregnancies and howling infants. And now, I haven't got my freedom anymore.

Swifty: It says in your *Blue Book of Paradise,* Harry, that there is only one freedom left in the twentieth century—to come to terms with suicide. After which, everything is possible.

Harry: Camus said that.

Toothy: Who?

Harry: Albert Camus.

Toothy: I'll bet you made it up, Elihu. (*She turns and crosses up left.*) Is this where it happens?

Swifty: May I show you around, Toothy?

Toothy: My pleasure, Swifty. (*He leads her into the Re-creation Area.* **Harry** *sits at the table, center, gazing despondently out toward the audience.*)

Swifty: This is called the Re-creation Area. Re-creation into a new life, as Harry says.

Toothy (*giggling*): That's what I've been looking for—a new life.

Swifty: We all look for that, Toothy. (*A pause, then the sound of a kiss is heard from behind the curtain.* **Harry** *holds his hand to his mouth to keep from vomiting.*)

Toothy: That was nice, Swifty. . . .

Swifty: That's the Chair of Destiny. Six M-14 rifles aimed at it. They never miss.

Toothy: What's that slot machine for?

Swifty: The triggers of the guns are wired to the handle. Put in a sliver dollar and say good-bye. (**Harry** *opens the drawer in the table, takes a silver dollar out of his lock box, closes the box, slams the drawer shut, and puts the coin in his pocket.*) TV camera on the wall—like in banks—to record everything for the record. Over there, garbage bags for the bodies. . . . (*The front doorbell rings.* **Harry** *goes to answer it.*) He stuffs a body into its bag, then hauls it into the fridge.

Harry (*opening the door):* Oh, hello Murk. Hello, Hammerslog. *(***Murk**, *a tall, thin man with sunken eyes, enters the apartment, followed by* **Hammerslog**, *a beefy type with long arms. They are from the Love and Robb Funeral Parlor and have come for the day's bodies. They wear heavy parkas, gloves, and fur-lined boots.*)

Murk: Hello, Harry, old punk, how's business?

Harry: So-so. A few bodies in the fridge. Help yourself. (**Hammerslog** *pulls in a three-tiered steel wagon on casters on which the bodies can be strapped. The three tiers will hold three bodies each. The contraption is about seven feet long and five feet high.*)

Hammerslog: Any famous people today?

Harry: No. Just folks. Like us.

Hammerslog: Our turn will come, Harry.

Harry: That's right, Hammerslog.

Murk: Hey, Harry, I heard a good Polish joke over by the graveyard yesterday. . . (**Swifty** *and* **Toothy** *emerge from the Re-creation Area up left and stand, watching everything.*) These twelve Polish soldiers

139

was chasing a German fraulein down the street. . . . (**Hammerslog** *has dragged the body wagon from the front door area toward the refrigerator and now knocks over a chair with it.*) Hey, Hammerslog, don't beat up Harry's furniture any more than it is already.

Hammerslog (*to* **Swifty**): Get the door for me, will ya, pal?

Swifty: Sure. (*He opens the refrigerator door while* **Hammerslog** *picks up the chair. Dry ice vapor pours out into the room in thick clouds.* **Hammerslog** *pushes the wagon inside as* **Swifty** *and* **Toothy** *watch, hugging each other for warmth.*)

Murk: So . . . like I was telling you . . . these twelve Polish soldiers is chasin' this German girl down the street and she keeps yellin', "Nein—nein!"— so three of 'em went back to camp. (*He guffaws happily and follows* **Hammerslog** *into the refrigerator room.*)

Toothy (*to* **Harry**): Who are these people, Elihu?

Harry: From the funeral parlor. To get the bodies.

Swifty: So this here funeral parlor gets a bunch of bodies. They notify the next of kin and collect a tidy sum for their funeral.

Toothy: And Elihu probably gets a cut, don't you, Elihu?

Swifty: Of course he does. You've got a head for this business, Toothy, my girl.

Toothy: How much do you get, Elihu?

Harry: Ten percent.

Toothy: He sells dead bodies on ten percent commission. Think of that! (**Hammerslog** *and* **Murk** *come out with the body wagon loaded up. Three bodies are strapped to the bottom and middle shelves, and two are strapped on top. The sacks are covered with frost.*)

Swifty: I'm thinking of that. (*He closes the door to the refrigerator.*)

Murk: Got your check for last week, Harry. (*He takes off his gloves and pulls some papers from an inside pocket.*)

Harry: Is it Friday already?

Murk (*at the table*): We picked up seventy bodies. Got funerals for sixty and had to cremate ten. Net profit—$60,000. Your cut—$6,000. Sign the receipt and here's your check.

Harry (*taking the check and signing the receipt*): Thank you, Murk.

Murk: Keep up the good work, Harry. The boss likes your initiative. (**Hammerslog** *knocks over a table on his way to the front door.* **Swifty** *hurries to help him. He picks up the table and opens the front door.*)

Swifty: May I be of help, Mr. Hammerslog?

Hammerslog: Thanks, pal. Gentleman . . . (*He pushes the wagon out the front door and into the hallway.*)

Murk: Have a nice day, Harry. (*He crosses to the front door and goes out.*)

Harry: You, too, Murk . . . Hammerslog. . . . (**Swifty** *closes the door after them, then crosses slowly left to join* **Toothy** *again.*)

Swifty: Let's see . . . 6,000 bucks for the week . . . plus those fifty-dollar fees . . . maybe 3,000 bucks . . . comes to about $9,000 a week, doesn't it, Harry, old promoter?

Harry: Something like that. (*He sits listlessly at the table after putting the check in his money box in the left drawer.*)

Toothy: That's a lot of grocery money, Elihu.

Harry (*sighing deeply*): Yes, Toothy. (*There is a pause.* **Harry** *puts on his record by the Suicide ensemble. Up left,* **Toothy** *and* **Swifty** *engage in a long kiss.* **Harry** *stares out front.*

Swifty: Like to marry me?

Toothy: How can I? I'm married to *him*. . . . (*They stare at* **Harry**, *then both get the same idea simultaneously.*)

Swifty (*crossing to the table*): Hey, Harry, turn that thing off, will you?

Toothy: Yeah. We want to talk to you. (*She sits left of the table as* **Swifty** *sits right of it.* **Harry** *turns off his record player.*)

Harry: What do you want to talk about?

Toothy: Love.

Swifty: Yeah. Love, Harry. We're in love.

Toothy: We want to get married.

Swifty: And we need some freedom for the little woman.

Harry: I offered her a divorce years ago, but she wouldn't go for it.

Toothy: When I marry a man it's till death do us part. (*Pause.* **Harry** *takes the coin from his pocket and lays it on the table.*)

Swifty: How much money you got, Harry?

Harry: Thousands. Maybe a million.

Swifty: You look tired, Harry.

Harry: Do I?

Swifty: Need a change. Trip to Europe.

Harry: I've done that.

Swifty: Round-the-world cruise on a swell ship.

Harry: Done that, too.

Swifty: But, Harry, what are you going to do with all your money?

Harry: Nothing.

141

Swifty: It could help humanity. Could help the new state of Israel. Buy a few tanks. Maybe an airplane. . . .

Harry: You want me to shoot myself so you can marry my widow, who will be the sole owner of my business and my financial assets following my demise. Is that correct?

Swifty: Right on, Harry.

Toothy: Isn't it a grand idea, Elihu?

Swifty: Get used to it, Harry.

Toothy: You know, Elihu, a scorpion can kill himself with his own tail if he's surrounded by a ring of fire. (*She gazes at him encouragingly.*)

Harry: What happened to all our kids?

Toothy: Our kids. Well, I was hoping you wouldn't get into that, honey. I haven't got a lot of good news for you after all these years of growing pains, teenage problems, the draft, and not many groceries. . . . (*To* **Swifty**) We had four boys and a girl. And kids—especially boys—are hard to bring up in the city.

Swifty: She's right, Harry.

Harry: What happened to them?

Toothy: Well, Elihu Jr. and Lamar (*to* **Swifty**) our oldest boys . . . are in jail right now for blowing up a mathematics research laboratory at Columbia. Protest. You know . . .

Harry: Go on.

Toothy: And Rodrigo left the country to live in Sweden. Draft and all . . .

Harry: And?

Toothy: But I've saved some good news for last. You remember how Houston liked to crawl into Scarlett's bed?

Harry: Yes. . . .

Toothy (*with a big smile*): Well, they're happily married now and living in San Francisco.

Swifty: Don't take it hard, Harry. We all got problems with kids these days. (**Harry** *flips his coin in the air and catches it à la George Raft.*)

Harry: Will you give me a nice funeral?

Swifty: The best that money can buy.

Toothy: Fur-lined coffin . . .

Swifty: With gold-plated handles . . .

Toothy: And a full-length mirror in the lid! (**Harry** *flips the coin in the air and lets it fall on the table, covering it quickly with his hand.*)

Harry: Call it, Swifty.

Swifty: Tails. (**Harry** *removes his hand and they all stare at the coin.*)

Harry: You win. (*He looks from one to the other.*) For love!

Swifty: We'll never forget you, Harry. (*He and* **Harry** *shake hands.*)

Toothy: We'll name our first baby boy after you.

Swifty: Yeah . . . Harry Elihu Kazan. (**Harry** *crosses to the Re-creation Area and goes quickly inside. He pulls the curtain to as* **Swifty** *and* **Toothy** *cling to each other, awaiting the end.*)

Harry (*behind the curtain*): It is a far, far better thing that I do than I have ever done; it is a far, far better rest that I go to than I have ever known.

Toothy and **Swifty** (*simultaneously*): Dickens! (*The guns fire with a roar.* **Swifty** *and* **Toothy** *almost jump out of their skins.*)

Toothy (*screaming*): Ahhhhhh!!

Swifty: That noise is going to be hard to get used to. (*They go up right, pull back the curtain, and stare into the Re-creation Area.*)

Toothy: Good-bye, Elihu. It was nice while it lasted.

Swifty: We'll meet again, Harry, in a better world. (*They kiss. Then she breaks away and crosses to the record player.*)

Toothy: Do you like to dance?

Swifty: If it isn't too fast.

Toothy: He used to have some nice records. Here's one I like—"Waltz Time in Old Vienna." (*She puts the record on.*) How's this? (**Swifty** *crosses to her and takes her in his arms.*)

Swifty: Perfect. (*To the strains of "The Merry Widow Waltz" by Franz Lehár,* **Toothy** *and* **Swifty** *waltz happily about the room. The lighting fades down and out.*)

CURTAIN

END ACT II.

Note: *For the curtain call, all the dead bodies return and dance, too. Except for the icicles hanging from their ears, noses, and chins, they look quite presentable.*

The Feast of Thyestes

A Tragedy in Two Acts

Preface: On Famine

Thyestes of Mycenae and his brother, Atreus, are famous personages from the fabled times of Greek legend. As Robert Graves recounts their story in his book *The Greek Myths,* the two sons of Pelops and Hippoameia struggled with each other for many years over the rulership of the Kingdom of Mycenae. After the death of Pelops, Atreus, through a series of lucky accidents, came into possession of a horned lamb with a golden fleece (signatory emblem of kingly rights in Mycenae), and the Notables of the city elected him their King. But Thyestes, too, wanted to be King. Atreus's new wife, Aerope, had conceived a violent passion for her husband's brother, and Thyestes agreed to become her lover if she would steal the horned lamb with the golden fleece for him. This she did, and when Thyestes displayed possession of the lamb in his own house, the Notables deposed Atreus and made Thyestes their King.

Zeus looked askance at all this, however, and ordered Helius to reverse his course in the heavens. He did so and, for the first and last time in the history of the world, the sun set in the east. Thyestes was so unnerved by this ominous portent that he abdicated in favor of his brother and fled Mycenae. After he had gone, Atreus discovered his wife's adultery with his brother and was sorely vexed.

Atreus bided his time, however, while he fathered Agamemnon, Menelaus, and Anaxibia by Aerope. In due course, Atreus sent a herald to Thyestes, promised him forgiveness plus a half-share in the kingdom, and urged him to return to Mycenae. During these years in exile, Thyestes had fathered three sons by one of the Naiads—Aglaus, Orchomenus, and Callileon. Thyestes received his brother's offer of peace with joy and travelled with his offspring back to Mycenae.

After Thyestes arrived, Atreus slaughtered the three sons, hacked their limbs off, placed the limbs in a cooking pot, and then set the boiled morsels of their flesh before his brother at a grand banquet of reconciliation. After

Thyestes had eaten heartily, Atreus ordered sent in from the kitchen, upon silver platters, the severed heads of the sons in order to disclose to his brother what now resided in his stomach. After vomiting what he had eaten, Thyestes placed a monumental curse upon the head of Atreus and all his progeny.

Driven away from Mycenae once again, the desperate Thyestes consulted the Oracle at Delphi to discover how he might obtain revenge on his brother. The answer: He must violate his own daughter, Pelopia, who would give birth to an avenger. Thyestes took the Oracle's advice and lived to see the death of his hated brother at the hands of his son, Aegisthus. Thyestes again ruled Mycenae but was soon driven out for the last time by Agamemnon, who became the new King. Thyestes died and was buried beside the road that leads from Mycenae to Argos. He did not live to see the ultimate consummation of his historic curse: Upon the triumphant return of Agamemnon from his conquest of Troy, Aegisthus participated with Agamemnon's wife, Clytemnestra, in the murder of the King and was, in turn, murdered by the King's avenging son, Orestes.

This gruesome story is preserved today mainly in the *Oresteia* trilogy of Aeschylus and in the *Thyestes* of Seneca. The following play, *The Feast of Thyestes,* is a dramatization of the essence of this legend in a modern setting—the Ukrainian Republic of the Union of Soviet Socialist Republics during the time of the Stalin terror. This essence is cannibalism, and especially the partaking of the flesh of one member of a family by another. Such actions were not unknown during the terror/famine of 1932–35 in the Ukraine as Stalin tightened his mortal grip on the Russian people by means of his monstrous policy of starving to death all opponents of Communism in the rural areas of the Soviet Union.

In 1995, a Ukrainian-made film called *Famine-33* opened for a short run in a small movie house in New York City. Its subject was the "hidden Holocaust," in which, under Stalin's orders, over six million Ukrainians were murdered by starvation, preserving on film a vision of one of the monumental crimes of the twentieth century, committed by Stalin's government for the greater good of the Russian people.

This unspeakable outrage against humanity was grounded in a decree of August 7, 1932, "On the Safeguarding of State Property", drafted by Stalin and issued by the Central Committee in Moscow. It became the legal justification for the forced starvation of millions of kulaks and their families in the Ukraine, Transcaucasia, and the Kuban during 1932 and 1933. The

148

decree ordered that all farm property such as livestock, grain, and produce of any kind be regarded from that tine forward as state property, sacred and inviolable, belonging to all the people of the USSR. Anyone found guilty of trying to keep farm property for himself would be considered an "enemy of the people", subject to being shot. If there were extenuating circumstances, the criminal might be let off with ten years' imprisonment and confiscation of all personal property.

This decree sealed the rate of over six million Russian peasants. In the words of Vassily Grossman, "The decree required that the peasants of the Ukraine, the Don and the Kuban be put to death by starvation, put to death along with their little children."

Stalin had noticed that an unplanned famine in Kazakhastan that caused the loss of hundreds of thousands of lives in 1931 had seriously reduced opposition by the peasants and kulaks to the sacred ideal of universal socialism, and he may well have been using this catastrophe as a guide to his calculated policy of starvation on a much wider scale in 1932–33. In fact, one of the official aims of collectivization in the Ukraine had been the destruction of the foundation of Ukrainian nationalism—the individual landholdings.

To enforce Stalin's decree regarding the preservation of socialist property, the army and the OGPU staked out twenty-five thousand villages to ensure that the peasants could not escape to buy food in the cities or steal food from the collective farms. Watchtowers were erected in the fields all over the Ukraine, manned by armed guards who shot peasants observed stealing the people's food. Grain quotas were set so high that all the grain had to be given to the government, with none left over for the peasants working the farms.

All this was carried out unknown to the rest of the USSR and the world beyond. It has been only lately that stories in the Ukrainian press, long-suppressed government reports, and descriptions by eyewitnesses have finally made it possible to comprehend at least some of the details of this appalling tragedy. In his well-documented *The Harvest of Sorrow,* Robert Conquest recounts some episodes:

> In Kharsyn village (Poltava Province), a woman seven months pregnant was caught plucking spring wheat and was beaten to death with a board.
> Enforcers often conveyed the dying as well as the dead to the cemetery to save the extra trip. Sometimes, children and old people lay in the mass graves still alive for several days.

An enforcer remembers the children, choking, coughing with screams, the men frightened, pleading, hateful, dully impassive, nearly extinguished with despair, or flaring up with sudden, half-mad, daring ferocity.

The enforcers refused to give in to debilitating pity. They were performing their revolutionary duty. They were obtaining grain for the socialist fatherland. For the Five Year Plan.

The enforcers believed that the end justified the means; that the goal was the universal triumph of Communism; that for the sake of that goal, everything was permitted: to lie, to steal, to murder, to participate in the extermination of millions of their fellow Russians. And to express doubt about this policy was to succumb to intellectual squeamishness, to the stupid liberalism of people who couldn't see the forest for the trees.

In the spring of 1933, the enforcers saw people dying of hunger—women and children with distended bellies, turning blue, still breathing but with vacant, lifeless eyes, and corpses—corpses in ragged sheepskin coats and cheap felt boots, in their huts, in the snow, under the bridges. But the enforcers soon became accustomed to the horror—they developed an inner resistance to realities that earlier had left them limp.*

If a Ukrainian peasant managed to cross into Russia proper and buy some bread, he was arrested at the border when he tried to get back. . . .

Desperate human beings were on the move as far as their strength would take them. Villagers tried to get into the towns where food was available. Filthy crowds filled the railroad stations. Men, women and children huddled in heaps waiting for trains that they boarded and rode until they were thrown off, only to return to the next station where they waited for the next train that might enable them to find bread.

Death was everywhere. A woman died in a meadow—her remains were eaten by ravens. A man died in his hut—his remains were eaten by rats.

Starving families met their fate in their empty huts in various ways. In one hut there would be war. People would take crumbs from each ether. Wife turned on husband and husband on wife. Both turned on children. But in another hut, love would rule. A woman with four children would tell then fairy stories and legends so they would forget their hunger. Her own tongue could hardly move, but she would take then into her arms. Love lived on within her.

Some of the starving went insane. They cut up and cooked corpses. They ambushed, killed and ate the bodies of strangers. Most horrible of all, they cooked and ate the flesh of their own dead children. (226–58).

*The guards in Hitler's death camps later developed the same kind of immunity to routine horror.

150

There were people at the time who refused to believe what was happening. George Bernard Shaw visited Russia in the thirties and found no traces of hunger anywhere. "I have never eaten as well in my life as I did in Moscow," he announced. His friends and fellow parlor socialists Sydney and Beatrice Webb looked carefully for signs of famine in Russia and found nothing.

Even today, there are those believers in the ideals of socialism who refuse to accept the Stalin terror/famine of 1932–33, just as many people refuse to accept Hitler's Holocaust. "There's no convincing evidence of it," they say. Or, "who could believe such a thing?"

The Feast of Thyestes

A Tragedy in Two Acts

TIME: Fall of 1932 to spring of 1933
PLACE: The Ukraine, a small stock farm near Kiev
CHARACTERS:
Thadeus ("Thad") Nikolayevich Orlov, about fifty-five
Anna Andreyevna Orlov, his wife, about forty-five
Natasha ("Tasha") Thadeusevna Orlov, his daughter, about seventeen
Nikolai ("Niki") Thadeusovich Orlov, Thad's son, about ten
Maxim Alexseyovich Malinovsky, OGPU enforcer, about thirty
Lev Petrovich Kosarov, OGPU enforcer, about nineteen
Two more OGPU enforcers, in their twenties
Chorus of starving people in Act II
SYNOPSIS OF SCENES:
Act I, scene 1: A fall evening in 1932
Act I, scene 2: The next morning

Act II, scene 1: A spring evening in 1933
Act II, scene 2: The next day
STAGE SETTING:
    The living room and children's bedroom of the Orlov farmhouse, a rather "modern" structure for the Ukraine of the 1930s. The living room is stage right, and the children's bedroom is stage left. Beyond the children's bedroom are the bedroom of Thad and Anna and the indoor bathroom.

    The stage right room serves as a living room, dining room, and kitchen. Down right is a small table with a radio on it. Upstage of the table is a window that looks out on the front yard. Beside the window is a wall telephone.

Upstage of the window is the door to the front porch. This porch is enclosed and has a window in the porch upstage wall. Upstage of the front door in the living room is another window that looks out on the front yard. Upstage of the window is a fireplace with wood stacked nearby.

Along the back wall are three windows through which can be seen the sky and a distant wooded area. A sink, stove, and icebox are under the windows. There are also cabinets and drawers for utensils.

Before the fireplace are a sofa, a coffee table, and some chairs that form a small conversation area. To the left of the sofa are the dining room table and four chairs.

Left of the icebox is the door to the back porch. When the door is open there can be seen a large table that is used as a butcher's table when an animal is being slaughtered. Overhead left, and out of the sightlines, is a large hook from which the animal is suspended during slaughtering. In the left wall of the back porch are the back door and a small window. Off left and around the corner is the outside door to the basement. The barn and the rest of the farm are off left.

A cutaway wall separates the living room from the bedroom occupied by Tasha and Niki. The door in the wall opens into the bedroom. Upstage is a bookcase filled with books. Above it is a window. Along the side wall are two chests of drawers, a table, some chairs, and the door to Thad and Anna's bedroom. Downstage of this door are two bunk beds, one over the other. Near the table is Tasha's rabbit, Pushkin, in his rabbit cage.

The atmosphere is one of middle-class comfort, but without frills of any kind. The farm, small though it is, does provide the family a modest living as long as everybody does his share of the work. The Orlovs are hard-working, independent small landowners who have never accepted socialism, the kind of people Comrade Stalin hated the most.

ACT I

SCENE 1: *A fall evening in 1932, after supper.*
AT RISE: *Some light from the setting sun, off right, comes through the windows. During the scene, it grows darker as the sun sets and night comes on.*

A hog is being butchered on the back porch. The animal cannot be seen, as it hangs from a hook in the roof of the back porch off left, but the activities of the family make clear what is happening.

Thad Orlov, *a tall, muscular man about fifty-five wearing farm work clothing, has on a large rubber apron that is stained with blood. He uses a long butcher knife, a meat cleaver, a bone saw and a wooden mallet in his work. He cuts meat from the carcass, brings it to the butcher's table, and then dresses it. When he gets to the bones, he pounds them into small particles and puts them into a fertilizer can.*

His wife, **Anna,** *and their children,* **Natasha** *and* **Nikolai,** *help him.* **Anna,** *is also tall and rather muscular. She has a determined air about her and works quietly at her chores. She had been a teacher of history in the village school until the Central Committee of the Communist party decreed that wives of landowners were not fit to teach in the schools of the USSR.*

Tasha, *about seventeen, is a trifle thin and somewhat dreamy.* **Niki,** *about ten, is sturdy and self-reliant.*

The slaughtering process has been underway for some time. As **Thad** *chops up pieces of meat on the table,* **Anna** *wraps them in cheese cloth, after which the children put them away.*

Tasha *comes onto the back porch from off left.* **Anna** *hands her three bundles of meat.*

Anna: That's three bundles of ham. They go down in the ice chest.

Tasha: Yes, Mom. (*She takes the three bundles and exits left. After a moment,* **Niki** *enters the back porch from off left.*)

Niki: That ice chest is almost full.

Anna: Well, put this bacon in the icebox in the kitchen. (*She hands* **Niki** *three more packages.*)

Niki: OK. (*He puts the bacon in the icebox.* **Thad** *begins to pound the bones into fertilizer.* **Niki** *comes back to the porch.*) It's full, too.

Anna: All that's left are the feet. Here . . . put these in the sink. (**Niki** *takes the pig's feet to the sink and runs water over them.* **Anna** *helps* **Thad** *with the bone grinding.*)

155

Tasha (*coming in from off left*): Anything else?

Anna: Not right now.

Tasha: May I turn the radio on?

Anna: Yes. (**Thad** *and* **Anna** *work quietly through the following.* **Tasha** *turns on the radio; then she and* **Niki** *sit by it to listen.*)

Radio: Also in the news today, the question of private property came up before the Kiev Central Committee.

Niki (*starting to change the station*): Let's hear some music.

Anna: No! I want to hear this! (**Niki** *moves away.*)

Radio: Comrade Kalinov then cited the Decree of August 7, 1932, issued by the Central Committee in Moscow, to support his belief that farms in the Ukraine can no longer remain in private hands, no matter what their size. Small farms are the same as large farms, he said, and—

Thad (*entering the room*): Turn that off.

Tasha: Yes, Daddy. (*She quickly turns off the radio.* **Thad** *comes over to* **Niki**. *He holds the hog's heart in his hand.*)

Thad: Here's the heart of Old Methuselah, Niki. A present for you. (*He hands* **Niki** *the hog's heart.* **Anna** *comes into the room.*)

Niki (*taking the heart*): Thank you, Daddy.

Tasha: Let's put it in a jar of water. (*She and* **Niki** *go to the kitchen, where* **Tasha** *puts the heart in a jar, fills it with water, then puts the lid on it.*)

Anna: Take it into your room, children. (*The two children go into the left bedroom, put the jar on the table, then sit on chairs to study it.* **Tasha** *gets her biology book from the bookcase upstage.* **Thad** *returns to his work on the back porch.*)

Tasha: Gee! A real heart to study. In school all they had was a model.

Anna (*to* **Thad**): Do you mind if I listen to some more of the news?

Thad: If you want to. (**Anna** (*turns on the radio.* **Thad** *grinds bone fragments through the following.*)

Radio: In local news, the former schoolteacher Leon Alexandrovich Guryev was sentenced today to twenty years' hard labor in Siberia for making anti-Soviet statements in his classroom.

Anna (*screaming*): Ahhhhh! No! (*She holds her head in her hands.* **Thad** *comes into the room. The children stand at their bedroom door.*)

Radio: In commenting on this crime against the people of the Soviet Union, Judge Kozlov—

Thad (*turning off the radio*): What's the matter with you?

156

Anna: Lev Alexandrovich was one of the best teachers in our school. He was dedicated. He—

Thad: If you didn't keep listening to this damn radio you wouldn't have known about him.

Anna (*pacing wildly about the room*): We have a right to know what's going on. We owe it to ourselves to be informed.

Thad: The less we know, the better.

Anna: No. I don't agree with that. I don't accept that. That's the attitude of slaves. That's despair. (**Thad** *embraces her as she begins to sob.*)

Thad (*to the children*): Go back into your room. (*The children close the door and sit again at the table to study the heart in the jar.*) There . . . there . . . calm yourself. . . .

Anna: We *must* know what is happening.

Thad: Why?

Anna: We are witnesses. Someday we will tell what we saw.

Thad: Who will listen?

Anna: We will tell God if no one else will listen. (*She has regained control over herself and moves toward the sofa.*)

Thad: Sit down and rest a little. (*She sits on the sofa.* **Thad** *stands near the fireplace.*)

Tasha: It's about the same size as a human heart. (*She points to parts of the heart with a pencil.*) That's the left ventricle, that's the right ventricle . . . and those are the two auricles. . . .

Niki: How does it beat?

Tasha: It squeezes. It opens, then it squeezes, and the blood flows in and out.

Niki: How does it last so long?

Tasha: It's a muscle. Real strong . . . lasts forever.

Niki: Forever?

Tasha: Well . . . a long time. Zinaida Nikolayevna Morozov says she is 110 years old.

Niki: She looks it. (*They peer closely at the heart.*)

Thad: You're lucky you were dismissed from that school for being the wife of a landowner. That's better than chopping down trees in Siberia.

Anna: Lev will never live through that.

Thad: If he'd kept his mouth shut—!

Anna: Are we to keep our mouths shut until we're dead and buried? (*The children glance uneasily toward the front room.*)

157

Thad (*after a moment*): Yes.

Anna (*fighting an urge to cry again*): I'm sorry. . . . I'll . . . I'll be all right in a minute. (*She again controls herself.*) They said on the radio this morning there's to be a new general history book out soon.

Thad: Is there?

Anna: It's been approved by Comrade Stalin personally.

Thad: That will make it worth reading.

Tasha: It relaxes between beats. . . . That's the diastole phase. Then blood flows in. The mitral valve opens . . . there it is . . . and the tricuspid valve opens, too. . . .

Niki: Where is that?

Tasha: Well . . . I don't really see it. But it has to be there. (*She consults the pictures in her biology book.*) Because . . . when the pumping phase begins . . . the systole phase . . . then the auricles contract . . . and push blood through the valves. . . .

Niki: I don't see all this.

Tasha: I don't either. We'd have to cut it open.

Niki: No! That's *my* heart! (*He holds the jar close to his chest.*)

Tasha (*laughing*): Oh, don't be silly. I'm not going to do anything to it.

Niki: You better not! (*They laugh together and* **Niki** *puts the heart back on the table.*)

Anna: Are those people coming tonight?

Thad: The man that called said they'd be here after supper.

Anna: What do they want?

Thad: He didn't say. . . . We'll find out when they come.

Anna (*fighting back her tears*): You know what they're coming for as well as I do. (**Thad** *sits on the sofa and puts his arm around her.*)

Thad: Now, Anna . . . calm yourself. Let's don't ask for trouble. . . . Trouble will come when it's ready.

Niki: What's that little cut in the side?

Tasha: That's where the point of Daddy's knife went into his heart.

Niki: Geeee!

Tasha: Old Methuselah died very quickly. (*They continue to study the heart, turning the jar round and round.*)

Anna: They're coming to take our farm. They are going to collectivize us. (*The children listen from the other room.*)

Thad: Maybe not for a while, yet.

Anna: It's been on the radio. People talk about it in the village.

Thad: I've heard their chatter.

Anna: They're starting in the Ukraine. Then they'll collectivize all the rest. We're the first to have to go through this—this crime!

Thad: Is it a crime?

Anna: Certainly it's a crime. Lenin promised in his New Economic Policy that we can own our own land. And now . . . Stalin . . . announces *his* policy—collectivization!

Thad: Calm yourself. . . .

Anna: Collectivization! A fine-sounding word for stealing land.

Niki: What's coll—

Tasha: Col-lec-ti-vi-za-tion.

Niki: What does it mean?

Tasha: I think it means the Central Committee in Moscow owns all the land in the USSR.

Niki: Even ours?

Tasha: Even ours. . . . All the land, all the factories, all the mines, all the forests, all the oil wells . . . all belong to the Central Committee.

Niki: Why do they want everything?

Tasha: They just want it, I guess. (**Thad** *gets up from the sofa and goes back to his work on the back porch.* **Anna** *rises and paces slowly about the room. It is getting darker outside. Finally, in spite of her misgivings, she turns the radio on again.*)

Radio: Elsewhere in the news, a gang of hooligans tried to set fire to a grain storage elevator in Poltava, but State Security apprehended them. (*There is a sudden loud knocking at the front door.* **Anna** *turns off the radio. The knocking is repeated.* **Thad** *comes slowly into the room. The children listen tensely from their bedroom. There is more knocking. Finally,* **Thad** *opens the front door and goes out on the porch.*)

Thad: Who is it?

Maxim (*off right*): OGPU, sir. We've been sent by the Kiev Soviet. May we come in?

Thad: Yes. Come in. (*He unlocks the outside door, then steps back into the room. He is soon followed by two OGPU enforcers,* **Maxim** *and* **Lev**. **Maxim Alexseyevich Malinovsky** *is a tall well-built man, about thirty, who grew up on a farm.* **Lev Petrovich Kosarov** *is tall and thin, nineteen, and also grew up in the rural Ukraine. They wear pistols in shoulder holsters under their jackets but otherwise are not in uniform. They are enforcers of Central Committee decrees and, as such, are* members of a large auxiliary branch of the OGPU, headed at that time by Vyascheslav Rudolfovich Menzhinsky.)

Maxim: My name's Maxim Alexseyovich Malinovsky, and this is my partner, Lev Petrovich Kosarov. Are you Mr. Thadeus Nikolayevich Orlov?

Thad: I am.

Maxim: Pleased to meet you, sir. (*He holds out his hand, but* **Thad** *steps away from him.*)

Thad: My wife, Anna Andreyevna.

Maxim: Pleased to meet you, ma'am.

Anna: Good evening.

Lev: Didn't you teach history while I was in school here?

Anna: Yes, I did. And I remember you. (**Tasha** *and* **Niki** *have been peering through a crack between the door and the door jamb.*)

Tasha: It's Lev Petrovich!

Niki: Who's he?

Tasha: He was a year ahead of me in school.

Maxim: Been slaughtering a hog?

Thad: Yes. (*He removes his rubber apron and hangs it on a hook on the porch.*)

Anna: Will you sit down?

Maxim: Thank you, ma'am.

Lev: Thank you, ma'am. (**Maxim** *sits on the chair upstage of the fireplace.* **Lev** *sits downstage of it.*)

Maxim: Nice fireplace you have.

Thad: It keeps us warm. (*He sits on the upstage side of the sofa.* **Anna** sits on the downstage side, close to him.)

Maxim: Lev was telling me while we were driving out here that he thought he knew your daughter, Natasha Thadeusevna.

Lev: We called her Tasha.

Thad: Yes. She is my daughter. . . .

Maxim: Your given name, that's not a Russian name, is it?

Thad: My grandfather came here from Greece many years ago. I was named for him. . . .

Lev: Wasn't Tasha in the ninth grade last year?

Anna: She was in the tenth grade. And you . . . didn't you drop out of school?

Lev: Yes, ma'am. I went to Kiev to take my OGPU apprentice exam.

160

Tasha: He's in the OGPU!

Niki: Geeee.

Tasha: And he's only a little older than I am.

Anna: Do you enjoy your police work?

Lev: Yes, ma'am. I intended to finish high school. I was going to take your history class, but my family needed some help . . . so . . .

Anna: I'm not teaching history there anymore . . . since it was discovered that my husband owns a farm. . . .

Maxim: We don't make the rules, ma'am. The rules come down to us all from the Central Committee.

Thad: As from God on high, eh?

Maxim (*after a moment*): I guess that hog you slaughtered will last your family quite a time, won't it?

Thad: Nine or ten months, I suppose.

Maxim: How many hogs you got left?

Thad: Why? (**Maxim** *pulls some forms out of his pocket.*)

Maxim: Sir, we need to obtain a little information. I hope you will cooperate with us.

Anna: And if we don't? (*There is another pause.* **Lev** *shifts uneasily in his chair.*)

Thad: We have nine more hogs. Six will be ready for market, soon. (*Through the following,* **Maxim** *writes information down on his form.*)

Maxim: How big is your farm, sir?

Thad: Six hectares.

Maxim: Is that all?

Thad: That's all.

Maxim: Outbuildings?

Thad: Just the barn and the hog pens.

Maxim: Other stock?

Thad: Two cows, two horses, about forty chickens and ducks.

Maxim: Farm machinery?

Thad: A small tractor.

Maxim: What do you plant?

Thad: Five hectares are in corn for the hogs and other animals. The other one is in vegetables and fruit trees. For our own needs.

Maxim: Well . . . a nice small stock farm, as Comrade Menzhinsky would say.

Thad: Who is that?

161

Maxim: Oh, he's head of the OGPU. He grew up on a farm.

Thad: *Did* he? . . .

Maxim: Do you make a good living from your farm?

Thad: Fair. The land is paid for. (**Maxim** *finishes writing up his report. He pauses a moment, then clears his throat and begins his prepared speech.*)

Maxim: Well, sir, as you know, Comrade Stalin has said over the radio . . . (*He glances about the room.*) Do you have a radio?

Thad: Yes. (*He nods toward the table down right.*)

Maxim: Comrade Stalin has said on the radio that there must be a transition from individual capitalist farming to collective, socially correct farming.

Thad: We've heard that.

Maxim: You see, sir, small-scale farming is not productive.

Thad: Why not?

Maxim (*as though quoting something*): Sir, it can't last. History teaches us that agriculture develops either into large-scale private farms or large-scale socialist farms. And since the Revolution, private enterprise has been dying out in the Soviet Union.

Thad: Not entirely.

Maxim: Small farms like yours represent the last signs of capitalism in our country, and that is why the Central Committee in Moscow has decided on collectivization.

Thad: Are any of these decision makers in Moscow farmers themselves?

Maxim (*pause*): I believe, sir, that most members of the Central Committee were formerly factory workers.

Thad: Very likely. Well . . . where is this collectivization to begin?

Maxim: Right here, in the Ukraine, sir. The Ukraine is one of the most important parts of the Soviet Union. Where the Ukraine leads, the other states will follow.

Thad: Why not start this experiment in Siberia? Then we could all follow *their* example.

Maxim: (*smiling broadly*): I don't know, sir. I wasn't in on the decision. (*He takes some papers from an inside pocket and hands them to* **Thad**). And now, sir, if you and Mrs. Orlov will just read over these papers and sign them.

Thad (*taking the papers*): What do they say?

162

Maxim: They just say what the law is, sir. You can see for yourself. (**Thad** and **Anna** *begin to read the papers.*)

Lev: Sir, is your daughter, Tasha, at home?

Thad: Yes. She's in there. (*He nods to the left.*)

Lev (*rising*): May I say hello to her?

Thad (*after a moment*): I have no objection. (*He continues to read as* **Lev** *goes to the door of the left bedroom and knocks.*)

Lev: Can I come in?

Tasha: Yes. (*She opens the door and he goes in.*)

Lev: Remember me? Lev Petrovich? I was a grade ahead of you last year.

Tasha: Yes. I remember you. (*They shake hands.*) This is my brother, Niki.

Lev: Hello, Niki. (*They shake hands.*)

Niki: Hello.

Tasha: You were in the Komsomol, weren't you?

Lev: Yes. And after I finished my field training, I took the OGPU exam.

Tasha: You must have passed it.

Lev: That's right. Now I'm assigned to the Kiev Soviet as an enforcer. (*There is a pause.* **Lev** *sees the jar on the table.*) What's this?

Niki: That's a hog's heart. Dad gave it to me.

Tasha: We've been studying it.

Niki: We have to teach ourselves these days.

Lev: Why? Oh . . . your father. . . .

Tasha: We don't go to school any more. (*Through the following, they pantomime conversation about the heart.*)

Thad: This paper authorizes you to steal our farm.

Maxim: No, sir. With all due respect, that's no way to put it.

Thad: How would you put it?

Maxim: Your farm is being collectivized by the Kiev Soviet.

Thad: It's being stolen.

Maxim: No, sir. Collectivized. It will be combined with many small farms in this area to form one large, efficient wheat farm. (*He rises and paces about, speaking with enthusiasm.*) This whole area—hundreds of hectares—will be planted in wheat for the people of the Soviet Union!

Thad (*after a moment*): What about my livestock?

Maxim: We'll be here in the morning with trucks to take all your stock to Kiev. We've got fine up-to-date stockyards in Kiev.

Thad (*mockingly*): Up-to-date stockyards!

Maxim: Feeding is scientific. Animals are slaughtered when they reach peak weight. Not before—not after.

Thad: I do that, too.

Maxim: But in a collective stockyard the slaughtering is socially correct.

Thad: Are other people giving up their livestock?

Maxim: Yes, sir.

Thad: People around here?

Maxim: We're just getting started around here.

Thad: You think we don't hear anything? You think because there's nothing on the radio or in the paper we don't know what's happening?

Maxim: You mustn't believe idle rumors, sir.

Thad: What happened around Lvov last month?

Maxim: Some hooligans set fire to a grain elevator. They were caught and punished.

Thad: Hooligans . . . ?

Maxim: One must acknowledge criminal elements here and there. Hooliganism will be wiped out in time. Like prostitution.

Thad: And what happened in Odessa?

Maxim: More hooliganism. But you are not like those people, Comrade Orlov. You are a respected member of your community and have been for many years. (**Thad** *and* **Anna** *return to reading the papers.*)

Tasha: Would you like to see my rabbit?

Lev: Sure. (**Tasha** *pulls the cage out from under the table. They sit on the floor.*) That's a nice rabbit. What's his name?

Tasha: Pushkin.

Lev: I think Pushkin is a very good-looking rabbit.

Tasha: Thanks.

Lev: Takes after you, I'd say.

Niki: How can a rabbit take after her?

Lev: Oh, I don't know. Kind of a twinkle in his eye . . . like your sister.

Tasha: That's nutty.

Lev: No, I can see a gleam in his eye . . . just like you have.

Niki: A rabbit's not a person.

Tasha: But I love him.

Lev: Then he *is* a person.

Niki: That's dumb. (*They continue talking about the rabbit in pantomime.*)

Anna: What will happen to us? Will we have to leave our home?

Maxim: Oh, that's all taken care of, ma'am. You'll have a nice apartment in Kiev.

Anna: An apartment?

Maxim: Near the new stockyards. Your husband is an experienced stock farmer. He'll have a good job in the collective slaughterhouse.

Thad: So my future and the future of my family are all planned?

Maxim: The Central Committee has planned for everything, sir. Everyone is guaranteed a job under socialism.

Thad: And my job is butchering livestock all day?

Maxim: Oh, you won't be doing that for long, sir. Take classes at night in Marxism-Leninism, pass your examinations, and you'll be promoted to a supervisor's job in no time.

Thad: Supervisor? Of other butchers?

Maxim: Then, when you are admitted to the Party, you'll probably become a plant manager. You can shop in the Party store.

Thad: What if I don't want this job?

Maxim: But why wouldn't you? You're qualified. You just butchered a hog.

Thad: I do that kind of thing about once every nine months.

Maxim: You'll get used to it.

Thad: I won't leave my farm!

Maxim: Now, sir!

Thad: This property belongs to me. I've worked all my life to pay off the mortgage. It belongs to *me*!

Maxim: Property belongs to the people.

Thad: I'm a person.

Maxim: That's true.

Thad: If the land belongs to the people, why can't the people buy and sell it?

Maxim: Land is not for sale, sir. It is held in trust by the Central Committee for all the people of the Soviet Union. . . . Like a national park in the old days. Only now you can think of the whole country as a national park.

Anna: Or a kingdom out of the Middle Ages.

Maxim: I wouldn't know about that, ma'am. . . . (**Thad** *and* **Anna** *study the papers further.*)

Lev (*to* **Tasha**): Say, do you have a picture of yourself?

Tasha: I might have.

Lev: I'd like to have a picture of you.

Tasha: Why?

Lev: So I can look at it. (**Tasha** *gets up from the floor and goes to her chest of drawers up left.*

Tasha: Well, my yearbook picture is all I've got.

Lev (*following her*): That'll be fine. (*She hands him the picture.*) Thanks. (*He looks admiringly at the picture.*) It looks just like you.

Tasha (*laughing*): Well, I hope it does! (**Lev** *puts* **Tasha***'s picture in his pocket and comes back to* **Niki.**)

Lev: Want to learn how to trap a rabbit?

Niki: Sure.

Lev: Got some good string? And a stick?

Niki: Well . . . let's see. (*He rummages through his chest of drawers and finds a stick and some string. Through the following, Lev shows him how to make a loop, attach it to the end of the stick, and pull the loop around a rabbit's neck when he comes out of a hole in the ground.*)

Anna: How large will our apartment be?

Maxim: Well, just one room, ma'am.

Anna: One room?!

Maxim: That's the rule, ma'am. Five people or less, one room. But . . . I'll see if I can't do something about that. . . .

Anna: Will I be allowed to teach again?

Maxim: Teach again?

Anna: In the public schools.

Thad: Our land is being taken from us. I'm no longer a landowner. She's no longer the wife of a landowner. Why shouldn't she teach again if she wants to?

Maxim: Well, sir, that's not up to me to decide, of course. But . . . (*He pauses a moment, thinking it over.*)

Thad: But you could give us an opinion. . . .

Maxim: Well, sir, I hate to put it this way . . . but . . . once a landowner, always a landowner, as they say. Even if you don't own the land anymore. It's . . . the way of thinking, sir.

Thad: A leopard doesn't change his spots, eh?

Maxim: Yes, sir! That's right, sir! (*He smiles broadly at this insight while* **Thad** *and* **Anna** *stare at him.*)

Lev: So . . . this is how it works. . . . (*He holds the stick in one hand and the end of the string in the other.*) You lay this loop around his hole .

. . and you wait . . . real quiet . . . until he pokes his head out . . . and then . . . pull the string! And you've got him.

Tasha: That's cruel.

Lev: Well, if you're hungry and you want a rabbit to eat, this is one way to get one.

Tasha: We don't have to eat rabbits.

Lev: I know you don't. Not . . .

Tasha: Not what?

Lev: Not now. . . .

Niki: Well, it's a good thing to know. (*He practices with the stick and the loop.*)

Thad: Do I have any right of appeal?

Maxim: Appeal?

Thad: Against this decision.

Maxim: There is no right of appeal, sir. The Central Committee has decided that collectivization is in the best interests of the people of the Soviet Union.

Thad: So . . . collectivization is the law of the land now.

Maxim: That's right, sir.

Thad: The law is a spider's web. The bumblebee gets through it, but the fly is caught. (*He stares at the papers again.* **Maxim** *goes to the door of the bedroom and opens it.*)

Maxim: Lev, look around these rooms for firearms. If you find a pistol, we have to confiscate it.

Lev: Yes, sir. (*He begins to look around the bedroom.*)

Thad: Why just a pistol?

Maxim (*pacing nervously about*): Rifles and shotguns are needed to hunt food, but a handgun is considered a weapon against people, so we're picking up all handguns.

Niki: There's no pistol in here.

Lev: Do you know where a pistol is hidden? (**Niki** *looks at* **Tasha**, *who looks away.*)

Niki: I don't think so. (**Lev** *puts his arm around* **Niki** *and leads him down left.*)

Lev: Come on, Niki, you're a big boy now. You can talk to me. (**Niki** *again looks to his sister for guidance, but she seems confused and looks out the window in the upstage wall of their room.*) You have a duty to the Party, you know, just like the rest of us.

Niki: Well . . . come on in here. (*He leads* **Lev** *into his parents' bedroom off left.* **Tasha** *remains by the window.*)

Maxim: Well, sir, are you willing to sign these papers?

Thad: And agree to let you steal my property?

Maxim: We do not steal property. We confiscate property, but we do not steal it.

Thad: You want me to connive with you in a despicable act.

Maxim: We believe in Socialism. And if collectivizing private property is necessary to establish Socialism, so be it.

Thad: The end justifies the means.

Maxim: That's right.

Thad: The end of establishing Socialism justifies the means of taking my property from me.

Maxim: That is the considered belief of Comrade Stalin and the Central Committee.

Thad: But isn't that what any criminal believes?

Maxim (*his patience running out*): What do you mean?

Thad: The criminal needs some money, so he robs a bank. The end of obtaining money justifies the means of robbing the bank.

Maxim: Our ends are just. We seek an ideal society.

Thad: But you employ criminal means to achieve it. This turns you into a criminal by definition. (**Maxim** *turns away from him, then turns back. He becomes more determined.*)

Maxim: For the last time, will you sign those papers?

Thad: No. I'm not signing any papers. (*He throws the papers down on the coffee table.*) And we are not moving to a nice new one-room apartment in Kiev. We're staying right where we are, in our home, on our land, under God's sky!

Maxim: Now, Comrade Orlov—

Thad: Don't call me Comrade!

Maxim: Sir!

Thad: No way! It all belongs to me, and after I die it goes to my wife and my children. You can't rob me of my property! You can't do it! (*Long pause.* **Maxim** *makes an effort to control himself, as he has been trained to do.*)

Maxim (*very calmly*): Sir . . . The people own your land. The people own your house. The people own your livestock. (*He picks the papers up from the coffee table.*) And . . . although you have not signed these papers I can swear that I saw you read them. So your signature is not needed. (*He tucks the papers carefully into an inside pocket.*) The trucks will be here in the morning to take your livestock to Kiev. (*Pause.* **Thad** *stares hard at him.*)

Thad: Don't I know you?

Maxim: Well, my dad farmed near Chernigov all his life.

Thad: Alexi Alexandrovich Malinovsky?

Maxim: Yes, sir.

Thad: I knew him. . . . Is he still alive?

Maxim: No, sir. He went into debt back before the Revolution. Lost our farm to the bank. . . . He died in an insane asylum in Kiev. . . . All that turned me against the bankers when I was a kid. It . . . it hurt.

Thad: I'm sure it did. Your father was a hard worker . . . Alexi Alexandrovich. . . .

Maxim (*pacing about*): Well . . . I know how you feel. And I'm sorry. But the law's the law. They sent Lev and me out here to talk to you folks because we're from around here ourselves. I'll do anything I can for you, sir. Except break the law. . . . (*Stage left,* **Lev** *and* **Niki** *come back in from the bedroom off left.* **Lev** *is holding a pistol.*)

Lev: I want you to know, Niki, I'm going to remember this. You're a good kid. Maybe I can help you some day. (**Niki** *looks uneasily at his sister. She looks away.*) And maybe I can help your pretty sister, too. (*He puts his arm around her waist. She smiles briefly. then pulls away from him.*)

Tasha: We don't need any help, thanks. Our folks take care of us.

Lev: Sure they do. Well . . . (*He again smiles at* **Tasha**, *who smiles back*) I'll be going. See you tomorrow. (*He comes into the living room.*) There was a pistol in the back bedroom.

Maxim (*as though from memory*): Sir, we have to confiscate this hand gun. Such weapons are used in class warfare and are therefore subject to confiscation.

Thad: What class warfare?

Maxim: Well . . . you have enemies, sir. Class enemies.

Thad: Who?

Maxim: The people who work for you. They hate you for exploiting them.

Thad: I hire a few people from time to time to help me get the corn in to feed the stock. Then I pay them for their work and they leave. Why should they hate me?

169

Maxim: If they told you their real feelings about you, you wouldn't hire them.

Thad: I do most of the work on this farm myself. My wife and children help.

Maxim: There is class warfare in the cities between capital and labor, and there is class warfare in the country between farm owners and farm workers.

Thad: Where? On what farms? What are you talking about?

Maxim: The Central Committee has its information. They know what goes on out here.

Thad: *Do* they? . . .

Maxim (*writing out a receipt*): I'll give you a receipt for this pistol.

Thad: What for? You plan to steal my pistol. I make you a present of it.

Maxim (*again by rote*): Sir, you are entitled to make a request to appear before the Subcommittee on Firearms of the Kiev Soviet to explain why you need this pistol. (*He writes instructions on the receipt.*) For instance, if you have been threatened by unruly elements of the population . . . by hooligans . . . if mysterious figures have been seen lurking about the premises at night—

Thad: All right! Give me the receipt.

Maxim (*handing it to him*): There you are, sir.

Thad: Thank you.

Maxim: Everything we do is entirely legal. (*He sticks the pistol in his belt.*)

Thad: Is there a subcommittee where I can explain why I need my farm, my house, and my livestock?

Maxim (*after a moment*): No, sir.

Thad: Is there a subcommittee where I can ask compensation for my property?

Maxim: No, sir.

Thad: I say . . . shit on your legality!

Anna: Thad! Be polite to these men. They are only doing their duty.

Maxim: We'll go now. (*He and* **Lev** *stand near the front door.* **Thad** *and* **Anna** *stand by the sofa. The children watch from the left doorway.*)

Anna: What will happen to our home?

Maxim: It'll be torn down, ma'am. Basement filled with dirt. All this area is to be planted in wheat.

Lev: But you all will be in your apartment in Kiev, ma'am, safe and sound.

Thad: How much longer do we have in our home?

170

Maxim: Your apartment will be ready soon, sir. It's a brand new building.

Lev: You'll be resettled before you know it. . . . (*The Orlovs stare at the two enforcers in fear and hatred.* **Maxim** *undertakes to make his departure speech.*)

Maxim: Now, sir, and ma'am . . . and you children there . . . (*smiles at* **Tasha** *and* **Niki**), cheer up. Things aren't all that bad. Look ahead—not back. You'll be working with people like yourselves in Kiev. If you take classes in Marxism at night, you'll get a better job. If you get into the Party, you can get a larger apartment. Life will be better for everybody under socialism! I promise you!

Thad: Well . . . a one-room apartment in a brand-new building in Kiev. A job butchering livestock all day. Classes in Marxism at night. . . . But what's the real truth? Nobody's going to take me into your Communist Party. The truth is, I'm condemned to drag out the rest of my life at slave labor. . . . How can I get through the years I have left if I can only curse my work day and night? Might as well hang myself on that meathook out there. When there's no meaning to a man's work, there's no meaning to his life!

Maxim (*after a moment*): Good night, sir.

Lev: Good night, sir. (*They leave. The others are silent for a time. Finally,* **Anna** *turns to her husband and embraces him. The children run into the room and the grown-ups embrace them. too.*)

Thad: Have faith. Things will be all right.

Niki: Daddy, what's going to happen to us?

Thad: We'll get by. God will look after us.

Anna: God will look after us. . . . (*A long pause. Finally,* **Anna** *moves away from the others.*) Come children, time for your lesson. Then to bed.

Niki (*mustering his courage*): Daddy, I'm sorry about your pistol. I showed him where it was.

Thad: It's all right, Niki. As long as you always tell me the truth. (*He hugs his son.*) Now, go study your lesson.

Niki: Yes, sir. (*He and* **Tasha** *go into the left bedroom, followed by* **Anna.** **Thad** *paces restlessly about the living room, pausing now and then to look out the windows. It is now dark outside. He turns on the living room light.*)

Anna (*turning on the bedroom light*): We'll go over the history lesson tonight. (**Anna** *and the children sit at the table.* **Anna** *refers to a*

171

loose-leaf notebook in which are pages she has written out from memory.)

Niki: Mommy, why do we have to learn history?

Anna: So you will know what happened in the past.

Niki: But that man who was here tonight said to look forward, not back.

Anna: You can only make sound judgments about what you see in the present if you know what happened in the past. (*She looks over the pages in front of her.*) Now . . . to work. Last time we were talking about the early years of the Revolution. What is the date of the Revolution?

Tasha: October 27, 1917.

Anna: And what is that date today, Niki?

Niki: Uh. . . . thirteen days before.

Tasha: No! Thirteen days after.

Niki: This is my question! You keep out of it.

Anna: Tasha, let him answer.

Tasha: But he's wrong.

Anna: Niki, explain the two calendars.

Niki (*sighing deeply*): Do I have to?

Anna: Yes.

Niki (*after a moment of concentration*): I can't.

Anna: Tasha?

Tasha: Pope Gregory changed the Julian calendar because it was wrong by a few days. But we didn't adopt it because the Orthodox Church didn't recognize the Pope in Rome. So by now we've lost thirteen days. October 27 on the Julian calendar is November 9 on the Gregorian calendar.

Anna: And why are we on the Gregorian calendar now?

Tasha: Comrade Lenin wanted it that way.

Anna: And when was the change made?

Tasha: February 1, 1918.

Anna: Niki, what was the next important event in Russian history?

Niki: Uh . . . when we left the war?

Anna: Which war?

Niki: *Our* war. Against the Germans.

Anna: What was the treaty we signed?

Niki: Uh . . . I know. . . . Don't tell me . . . Brest-Litovsk!

Tasha (*proud of him*): Right!

172

Anna: Which our government signed on . . . ?

Niki (*in triumph*): March 3, 1918!

Tasha (*clapping her hands*): Bravo! (*In the living room,* **Thad** *goes to a drawer in the cabinet and takes out a long butcher knife. He sharpens it through the following.*)

Anna: You see, you can learn history if you put your mind to it.

Niki: Mama, I've got a question.

Anna: What?

Niki: Well, you and Daddy were talking about coll . . . coll . . .

Tasha: Collectivization.

Anna (*reading from her notes*): Collectivization is a return to the political system of the Middle Ages. All the land is owned the Lord of the Manor. The people work the land and give the Lord the fruits of their labor. In return, the Lord protects them from bandits. Under Marxism, the Central Committee owns all the land. The people work the land and give the Central Committee the fruits of their labor. In return, the Central Committee protects them from bandits.

Niki: Oh. (*Pause.* **Anna** *looks over her notes.*)

Anna: After we left the War, the Czar abdicated. What happened to him and his family, Tasha?

Tasha: Well . . . they were taken to Ekaterinburg in the Urals. . . .

Anna: Yes . . .

Tasha: They were confined in a house there. . . .

Anna: What were their names?

Tasha: All of them?

Niki: Czar Nicholas II—

Tasha: This is *my* question!

Niki: O.K. Sorry.

Tasha (*after a moment*): The Czar, Nicholas II; the Czarina, Alexandra Fedorovna—

Niki: She was a German.

Anna: Niki!

Tasha: —the Czarevitch, Alexis, and his sisters, Tatiana, Olga, Maria, and . . . uh . . . Anastasia!

Anna: Very good, dear. And what happened to them in Ekaterinburg?

Niki: They all got shot.

Anna: Niki!

Tasha: Oh, I don't mind if he answers some of my question.

Anna: All right. They were executed. When?

Niki: When?

Anna: When.

Niki: You mean the date?

Anna: Yes.

Niki: I don't mind if Tasha answers that part.

Tasha: July 17, 1918. New calendar.

Anna (*closing her notebook*): Well! You children know your recent history. Which is more than can be said for many your age. Time for bed.

Niki: Mommy, who shot the Czar and his family?

Anna: The head of the CHEKA in Ekaterinburg—Iakov Mikhailovich Iurovsky. A murderer whose fame has gone down in history.

Tasha: Was it wrong to kill them?

Anna: What do you think?

Niki: It was wrong.

Tasha: It was wrong.

Anna: Bedtime, children.

Tasha: Mommy, can I stay up a little while to finish a story I've been writing?

Anna: Yes, but not too long. (**Tasha** *remains at the table, takes some papers out of a drawer, and begins to work on her story. She turns on a small reading lamp that sits on the table.* **Niki** *climbs into the top bunk, left.*)

Niki: I'm ready to go to sleep, Mommy. (**Anna** *kisses her son goodnight.*)

Anna: Good night, dear Niki. Things will be better for us soon.

Niki: Sure they will, Mom. (*He turns over and is soon asleep.* **Anna** *turns out the overhead light and goes quietly into the living room, closing the bedroom door after her.* **Thad** *hides the knife and the sharpener.*)

Anna: Well, Tasha is writing a story and Niki is asleep. And tomorrow . . . (**Thad** *embraces* **Anna** *as she loses all control of herself and sobs and sobs.*)

Thad: We have to face it. . . . We have to face it. . . .

Anna: Our lives together . . . with the children . . . on our farm . . . are . . . almost over.

Thad: It's not the end of us, though. We'll hold out. And you mustn't frighten the children.

Anna (*recovering somewhat*): The children . . . yes . . . we must put on a good face for the children.

Thad: Will you read to me from the Bible, Anna?

Anna: Yes, Thad. (*She gets their family Bible from a drawer in the table down right, goes back to the dining room table, and sits down.* **Thad** *joins her at the table. She reads Psalm 137.*)

"By the rivers of Babylon, there we sat down, yea, we wept, when we remembered Zion.

"We hanged our harps upon the willows in the midst thereof.

"For there, they that carried us away captive required of us a song; and they that oppressed us required of us mirth saying, Sing us one of the songs of Zion.

"How shall we sing the Lord's song in a strange land?

"If I forget thee, O Jerusalem, let my right hand forget her cunning.

"If I do not remember thee, let my tongue cleave to the roof of my mouth; if I prefer not Jerusalem above all my joys.

"Remember, O Lord, the children of Edom who said, in the day of Jerusalem, Raze it, raze it even to the foundation thereof.

"O daughter of Babylon, thou destroyer, blessed be he who repays thee for the evil thou hast done us.

"Blessed be he that taketh and dasheth thy little ones against the stones." (*Pause, as they think over the words of the psalm. In her room,* **Tasha** *finishes a page, turns out the reading lamp, and then, after removing her outer clothing, crawls into the bottom bunk bed.*)

Thad: Well! People have gone into exile before and come out of it. If that be our fate . . .

Anna: We will endure it. (*She gets up from the table.*) I'm going to bed before I start to cry again. Coming?

Thad: In a minute. (*They embrace near the doorway.*) At least we have food for a time.

Anna: And the gold pieces. Maybe you better hide them in the basement. Those men who are coming tomorrow might steal them. In the name of the people.

Thad: I'll hide the gold pieces. And some salt. . . . Get some sleep. I'll be along.

Anna: Come soon. (*They kiss each other warmly; then* **Anna** *goes into the children's room. She makes sure they are asleep, then goes into the far bedroom, closing the door. In the living room,* **Thad** *slowly gets his knife out of the drawer and sharpens it some more. Then he puts the*

175

sharpener away, goes to the radio, turns it on, and stands listening to it far some moments as he thinks over what he intends to do.)

Radio: And now, Erich Kleiber, our guest conductor from Berlin, leads the Leningrad Philharmonic in Tchaikovsky's *Nutcracker Suite.* (*Applause: then the music begins.* **Thad** *listens a moment to the overture, then walks slowly toward the back porch. He turns out the light in the living roam and stands for a moment on the back porch silhouetted by moonlight through the window in the left wall. Then he pulls on his butcher's apron and goes outside. Only music is heard for a few moments; then, suddenly. off left, is heard the wailing scream of a dying animal. Then more animal screams are heard. The children sit up in bed, then rush to their window to look out.*)

Tasha: Oh! God! Daddy's killing them!

Niki: Oh! Oh! (**Anna** *comes through the room in her bathrobe and goes out on the back porch. The howling of the dying animals becomes louder and louder as* **Thad** *goes from one to the other with his knife.*)

Anna (*screaming*): Thad—! Thad!! Stop this madness! For God's sake, stop!! (*She watches the scene in horror for some moments, then sinks to the floor on her knees in an attitude of prayer. The screaming of the other animals is augmented by the sounds of the dying chickens and ducks.*)

Niki: He'll kill us, too! (*He takes his jar with the hog's heart inside and cowers down left in the corner.* **Tasha** *takes the cage with her rabbit and huddles beside him.*)

Anna: Oh Lord God! Help us in this awful hour. Stop this madness that has come over my beloved husband. Stop him, God, before it is too late. (*She continues to pray silently on the back porch. The screaming of the dying horses, cows, hogs, chickens and ducks rises to an ear-piercing cacophony, then begins to die down. As it subsides, the strains of the overture to Tchaikovsky's* Nutcracker Suite *can again be heard over the radio. Lighting fades down and out to end Scene 1.*)

ACT I

SCENE 2: *The next morning.*

AT RISE: *Bright sunlight comes through the back windows from off left. The family sits at the table waiting for the OGPU enforcers and their trucks to come from Kiev. A little food is on the family's plates, but no one can eat. They are red-eyed from lack of sleep.*

Anna: They will take everything. Food . . . guns to hunt with . . .

Thad: I've hidden the gold coins. We can buy food in town or in Kiev. We can trap small game in the woods. I've hidden a hundred kilos of salt in different places.

Niki: Lev taught me how to trap a rabbit.

Thad: Did he?

Tasha: Besides that, there's nuts and berries in the woods.

Niki: And we have the vegetable garden.

Tasha: And the apple and peach trees.

Thad: They'll take all that. All the fruit and vegetables belong to the "people" now. . . .

Anna: Eat something, children. We don't know what will happen next. (*The children nibble at some toast and jam. Then they stop. Another long pause.*)

Thad: Whatever happens, we'll get through it together. We're a Ukrainian family. We stick together. And the Communists can't change that.

Tasha: No, Daddy. They can't change that.

Niki: We stick together!

Anna: With God's help! . . . What's keeping them?

Thad: What's the hurry?

Anna: The waiting . . . better to get it over with.

Thad: Maybe . . . (*After a moment.* **Anna** *gets up and clears the dishes from the table. She puts leftover food in the icebox. Through the following, she washes and dries the dishes.*) Children, we face a serious threat to our way of life. The Communists are against us owning private property, and they hate the Christian religion. You must prepare yourselves.

Tasha: Yes, sir.

Niki: Yes, sir.

Thad: If they curse you, say nothing. If they call you names, just consider the source, and say nothing.

177

Niki: What does that mean—consider the source?

Thad: Just remind yourself who is calling you names. A Communist. A criminal. A person who believes it is right to rob people of their property. If you won't voluntarily give him your property, he will call you a kulak or a capitalist, or an enemy of the people. But you know that he is, himself, a criminal, so what he says doesn't matter. (*The children think this over. In the distance, off right, are heard the sounds of several heavy trucks approaching.*)

Niki: Daddy, what's that? (**Thad** *doesn't answer. The family listens in mounting fear as the trucks come near, then stop. There is silence for a few moments; then* **Maxim** *can be heard yelling, "Look at this! Look at this!" The family stiffens with apprehension. They stand close together upstage of the kitchen table. Soon there is a loud pounding on the front door.*)

Thad: Come in, gentlemen. No use locking the door, is there? (**Maxim** *and* **Lev** *burst into the room with drawn pistols. Two more OGPU enforcers, in their twenties, also with drawn pistols, follow them.*)

Maxim: You slaughtered your animals!

Thad: As you see.

Maxim: But why? Why?!

Thad: So you can't have them, that's why.

Maxim: You goddamned kulak! You dirty, criminal, capitalist kulak dog! I ought to shoot you right here and now! (**Anna** *and the children cry out in fear, but* **Thad** *doesn't move.*)

Thad: Go ahead. (**Lev** *puts his hand on* **Maxim**'s *arm.*)

Lev: Hold on, Maxim. We have orders that cover this. (**Maxim** *glares furiously at* **Lev** *then, after a moment, puts his pistol back in its holster. The other enforcers do the same.*)

Maxim: Yes, we have orders that cover this. (*He turns to the two new enforcers*). Get boxes and clean out all the food in this shithouse.

First enforcer: Yes, sir. (*He and the second enforcer go back out the front door.*)

Maxim: You'll find out what happens to kulak criminals like you!

Thad: Do your worst. (**Maxim** *goes to the front door and shouts to some of his men.*)

Maxim: Leonid! Grigori! Load all those carcasses onto the trucks. (*While* **Maxim** *is outside,* **Lev** *whispers to* **Tasha**.)

Lev: Hang on, Tasha—I'll get you out of this. (**Tasha** *turns away from him* *and remains close to her parents and brother.* **Maxim** *comes back in. During the following, men can be seen through the upstage windows going back and forth, loading the carcasses of the dead animals onto their trucks.*)

Maxim: Kulak bastards! Capitalist bloodsuckers! Enemies of the people!

Thad: Never mind the name calling. If you're going to take us to jail, let's go and be done with it.

Maxim: Jail! Feed and clothe you at the people's expense? Jail's too good for you! Too good for filth—vermin! (*He rages about the room.*) I had a *two-room* apartment for you in a new building in Kiev. Hot and cold running water. Called a good friend of mine last night and he fixed you up. And now! You do this to me!

Thad: We don't want your two-room apartment in Kiev. We want our farm—our home. We live *here*. We don't live in Kiev.

Maxim: That's right, old man! That's right, old fool! (*He stands close to* **Thad**, *almost spitting in his face as he talks.*) You live *here*. And you're going to stay here. Lev was right—we have orders for kulaks like you. You just stay right here. We take your food. And your tools. And your weapons. And we forbid you to enter any village, town, or city. Stay alive as long as you can. But sooner or later . . . you, your wife, and your children will starve to death! (*Pause.*) And good riddance to bad rubbish.

Lev: Maxim—for God's sake!

Maxim: You shut up, Lev! You hear me? (*He turns threateningly on his partner.* **Lev** *backs away from him: then he turns back to* **Thad**.) I thought you had some sense. I said to Lev last night after we left—I said, "There's a fine Ukrainian family. They've got a lot of sense. I like 'em." (*He turns to* **Lev**.) Didn't I say that, Lev?

Lev: That's right, Maxim. That's what you said.

Maxim: And now—look at you! Just like all the others.

Thad: What others?

Maxim: All the other stinking kulaks in the Ukraine that slaughtered their livestock—that's what others!

Thad: Oho! So I have some company.

Maxim: Shut up! I'm doing the talking here.

Thad: So there are others like me who won't hand over their stock to Communist thieves—(**Maxim** *hits him hard in the mouth.*)

Maxim: Shut your stupid mouth! (**Thad** *falls to the floor.* **Anna** *and the*

179

children scream in fear and kneel by **Thad.** **Lev** *rushes over to* **Maxim** *and holds onto him.*)

Lev: Maxim, lay off him! You got no orders to hit him! (*He pulls* **Maxim** *over toward the front door.* **Anna** *and the children help* **Thad** *to his feet.*)

Maxim: All right—all right! Let go of me. (**Lev** *lets go of him.*)

Lev: Just tell him his punishment and let's get out of here.

Maxim: All right! (**Lev** *moves away from him.* **Maxim** *collects his thoughts.*) All right. There's been trouble on the farms in the Ukraine.

Thad: And there'll be more!

Maxim: You shut up—you—you—

Anna: Thad, don't speak to this bully! . . .

Maxim: And so . . . in view of this *temporary* situation . . . the Central Committee in Moscow has set up guidelines for dealing with hooligan kulaks. (*He glares balefully at his victims as he paces slowly about the room.*) You're going to be cut off. Isolated. Quarantined. You hear? A state of internal exile. You damned kulaks think you're above the law. Above the will of the people. Well, you're going to find out what the people think of you. (*He spits violently on the floor.*) You're going to find out. When you're out there begging for a crust of bread and they spit on you . . . you'll see. You'll see. (*The two enforcers return through the front door with large boxes.*)

First enforcer: What shall we take?

Maxim: Take all the food in the house and the basement. Take all the tools and farm implements. Take the tractor . . . oil . . . gasoline . . . (*Through the following, the two OGPU enforcers fill their boxes with the contents of the icebox and the drawers and cabinets in the kitchen.*) Take all the weapons and all the ammunition you can find.

Thad (*holding a handkerchief to his bleeding mouth*): You are condemning us to starve to death? On our own farm?

Maxim: That's right, old man. Old fool. You and your family. That's the considered decision of the Central Committee.

Thad: The Central Committee is a stench in the nostrils of the human race!

Maxim: I'll kill you! (*He draws his pistol again.*)

Lev: Maxim, we have our orders. Put up your weapon! (*A tense pause. Finally,* **Maxim** *holsters his pistol again.*)

Maxim: You're the last of the kulaks. When you and your like are gone, capitalism will be dead and done for. You're the last of the ver-

180

min—(*The telephone rings.* **Maxim** *crosses quickly to it and tears it off the wall.*) You won't need this damn thing any longer! (*He goes out on the front porch and throws the instrument into the yard. Again, he yells at his men outside.*) Leonid! Grigori! Take that phone with you. Tear out that phone line. Cut those electricity lines. Cut the gas line and seal it off. (*The children begin to cry.*)

Lev (*again coming toward them*): Tasha! Niki! I'll help you some way. You'll get through it all.

Maxim (*still on the porch*): And get down into the cellar and clean out all the food you can find. (*Pause.*) What? (**Lev** *moves away from the children.* **Maxim** *comes back in.*) Lev, they've got a padlock on the basement doors out back. Shoot it off.

Lev: Yes, sir. (*He goes out the back door and off left. Soon a pistol shot is heard. The two enforcers have filled their boxes and now go out the front door to their trucks.*)

Maxim (*to* **Thad**): You can go into woods up north of here. . . . (*He nods toward the back wall windows.* I haven't enough men to stop you.

Thad: But you're taking my shotgun, my rifle and ammunition. And you already took my pistol.

Maxim: You're a smart kulak . . . You'll figure out ways to trap small game. You'll have the wife and kids out hunting berries, trapping rabbits, looking for mushrooms. I hear that bark from some kinds of trees can be eaten. Moss . . . some kinds of moss have nutritional value. . . . I predict you'll last a good six months.

Thad: You are Satan!

Maxim: That's right old man. Old fool. I'm Satan as far as you're concerned. (**Lev** *comes back in from the back porch.*)

Lev: The basement doors are open. (**Maxim** *goes out on the front porch.*)

Maxim: Leonid! Those doors are open. Clean out that basement. All the food . . . tools . . . knives . . . jars . . . weapons . . .

Lev: Things will get better. I promise you! (*He comes close to* **Tasha**, *but she turns away.* **Maxim** *comes back in followed by the two enforcers.*)

Maxim: Search all the rooms up here for food and weapons.

First enforcer: Yes, sir. (*Through the following, they search the left bedroom, then the room off left*).

Maxim: Remember, old man, this farm is now collectivized. All it produces belongs to the people. All the vegetables, fruit, corn, anything that grows on it belongs to the people. We'll be here, watching. If you steal some potatoes from the vegetable patch, you'll be shot. Understand? (*Pause. The Orlov family stare at him in silence, unable to entirely comprehend the cruelty of the orders he brings from the venerable Central Committee in Moscow.*) You can trap game in the woods. You can beg. (*He paces around the family with hate in his eyes and voice.*) You slaughtered the people's livestock. You cut yourself off from the Russian people. Now you're going to pay. You're going to pay the people for your crimes. (*He glares at* **Thad**.) You're going to watch as your wife and your children get weaker and weaker. You're going to watch as fear fills their eyes, day after day. You're going to watch them get thinner . . . and thinner . . . and then, even thinner than that . . . until you can hardly see them at all. And then . . . when you can't see them at all . . . old man, old fool . . . it'll all be over. (*Pause.*) You understand? (*There is a long silence. No one in the room speaks. Finally, the two enforcers return to the living room. They carry a shotgun, a rifle, some ammunition, the rabbit in his little cage, and the hog's heart in the jar.*)

First enforcer: This is all there is, sir.

Maxim: Take it all out to the trucks.

Lev: Wait a minute, Maxim. Wait a minute. (*The two enforcers pause by the doorway.*)

Maxim: For what?

Lev: Will you listen to me a minute?

Maxim (*after a moment*): Yeah, I'll listen.

Lev: That's Tasha's rabbit. And that heart in the jar, that belongs to Niki. His father gave it to him. Can't we leave them here? (**Maxim** *turns and looks out the window a moment, then turns back.*)

Maxim: All right. Put those things on that table. (*The second enforcer puts the rabbit and the heart on the dining room table.*) But take those guns and that ammunition out to the trucks. (*The two men leave by the front door.*) All right . . . all right. They've probably got some salt hidden somewhere. We'll never find it. They can salt down that meat and make it last a good long time. Can't you, old man? (**Thad** *does not reply.*) Let's go, Lev. And let's see how long four kulaks can last on a rabbit and a hog's heart! (*He goes out the front door followed by* **Lev**. **Thad**, **Anna**, *and* **Niki** *move over to the upstage window in the right wall and watch as the trucks drive away.* **Tasha** *stares out the downstage window.*)

Anna: My God! What's going to happen to us?

Thad: They may change their minds. Doing this will give them a bad reputation in Europe and America. The rest of the world hasn't gone over to the Communists.

Anna: But . . . will people in other countries find out what is happening?

Thad: It will get out, somehow. Witnesses will escape. . . .

Anna: But that will take years. And in the meantime . . .

Tasha: Well, at least we have my rabbit to eat.

Niki: And my heart.

Thad: Thank you, my children!

Tasha (*after a moment*): May I turn on the radio?

Thad: Yes. Switch it over to the battery. (**Tasha** *turns a switch in back.*) But don't play it very long. We'll need that battery.

Tasha: I won't.

Radio: —has reported to the commissariat for Agriculture that farmers in the Ukraine are joyfully handing over their livestock to the OGPU teams for transportation to the giant new Feliks Edirnindovich Dzerzhinsky Collective Stock Farm south of Kiev. It is expected that the program for agricultural collectivization in this state will be completed ahead of schedule. (*The stage lighting begins to fade down.*) In other news, a new regulation was announced today by OGPU headquarters in Kiev. In future, special permits will be needed to enter or leave the towns and cities of the Ukraine. This is an administrative procedure intended to help implement the new collectivization program. (*Pause. It is now quite dark.*) The weather for tomorrow—(**Tasha** *turns off the radio. The lighting has now gone down completely.*)

CURTAIN.
END ACT I.

183

ACT II

SCENE 1: *Six months later. Late afternoon in the spring of 1935.*
AT RISE: *Pale sunlight comes through the windows from off right. During the scene, the sun sets and it becomes dark outside.*

*The two rooms are almost bare. Nearly all the family possessions—furniture, dishes, most of their clothing—have been traded for food. In the living room, only the dining table and four chairs remain. The sink, stove, and icebox are gone and the water turned off. The butcher table on the back porch remains. On the table are four tin bowls, four tin spoons, and four tin cups. There is some water from the well in a tin pitcher. Also on the table is **Anna's** Bible. In the fireplace is a pot suspended from an iron tripod in which soup is boiled. Some wood is stacked by the fireplace. They have a few candles left and some matches. There is a candle on the table and another on the floor in the children's room.*

*The children have left only the clothing they wear, two mattresses on the floor, and a blanket each. **Tasha** still has some paper left and a pencil. She has also found a length of rope, which she keeps under her mattress with her paper and pencil. Her mattress is downstage, against the left wall, and **Niki's** is upstage of hers.*

***Thad, Anna, Tasha** and **Niki** are starving to death. They are thin, and their faces are pinched and haggard. Their stomachs are somewhat distended. Sometimes they stare vacantly about, seeing nothing. They move about the rooms like marionettes, in a halting, mechanical manner.*

The women wear ragged male clothing, as do the men.

*In the living room, **Anna** sits at the head of the table gazing numbly in front of her. She presses her hand against her stomach. Now and then she sips a little water from her tin cup. She tries to read her Bible but can hardly concentrate on anything except her ravenous hunger.*

*In the children's bedroom, **Tasha** sits on her mattress, cross-legged. **Niki** sits on the floor near her, holding his stomach. They try to play a game, "Famous People."*

***Thad** is out, begging for food.*

Tasha: Come on, Niki . . . you can think of someone. (*The children speak haltingly and often choke on their words. It is a continual struggle for them to keep from bursting into tears.*)

Niki: What was the letter?

Tasha: The letter is S . . .

184

Niki: S . . . (*He stops.*)

Tasha: Come on . . . we have to . . . do something.

Niki: S.

Tasha: That's right.

Niki: Is he a famous . . . composer?

Tasha: Uh . . . it's not Shostakovich. . . . Come on . . . give me another one. (*She coughs.*)

Niki: I can't.

Tasha: Niki . . .

Niki: I'm too hungry to think. . . . (*He clutches his stomach.* **Anna** *mumbles something, half-aloud, from Galatians 5.*

Anna: For all the law . . . is fulfilled . . . on one word . . . thou shalt love thy neighbor as thyself . . . but . . . if ye bite and devour one another, take heed that ye be not consumed . . . one of the other . . .

Tasha: Remember what Daddy said . . . think of something else and it isn't so bad.

Niki: Is he . . . he a famous general?

Tasha: He's not General Samsonov.

Niki (*with a weak smile*): I was thinking of the American general, Stonewall Jackson.

Tasha: It has to be his last name, silly.

Niki: I know. . . . (*He clutches his stomach again.*) Well . . . is it . . . uh . . . uh—(*Suddenly they all freeze as they hear noises outside the window in the living room down right.*)

Anna: Oh my God! Children! Come in here! (*She rises with difficulty, goes to the fireplace, and gets a poker. The children cling to her in fear. Outside the faces of starving people can be seen, pressed against the windows in the right wall. They are emaciated, elongated faces, like those of dead birds with sharp beaks.*)*

Niki: Mommy, look!

Anna: No food! No food! (*She waves the poker threateningly at them. There is a rattling at the locked and barred front door; then the faces disappear from the front windows. In a moment however, they reappear against the windows in the back wall as the procession of protracted death winds around the house.*)

Tasha: No food!

---

*These faces should be painted masks, as in a Greek-style chorus.

Niki: Go away!

Anna (*waving the poker at them*): We have nothing! We are starving too! (*The faces press against the windows, their eyes vacant, hopeless.*)

Tasha: Leave us alone!

Niki: Go away! (*Finally, the last face disappears from the windows and there is silence. Outside, it has been growing darker.*)

Anna: They're gone. Thank God! (*She puts the poker back by the fireplace.*) Back to your room. Both of you. (*She lights a small candle on the table and sits down again to continue reading her* Bible.)

Niki: Will Daddy come soon?

Anna: Yes.

Niki: Will he bring us some food?

Tasha: Niki, leave Mother alone.

Anna: Yes, dear. Daddy will bring us some food. (**Tasha** *and* **Niki** *go back into their room and sit on the floor by* **Tasha**'s *mattress.* **Anna** *turns the pages of her* Bible.)

Tasha: Come on . . . S. . . .

Niki: OK . . . S . . . is he a famous composer?

Tasha: I said he's not Shostakovich.

Niki: German composer.

Tasha: Uh . . . not Schubert.

Niki: How can I ever stump you?

Tasha: You'll think of something. (*Pause.* **Niki** *clutches his stomach.*)

Niki (*in despair*): Oh, Tasha! Aren't we going to get *anything* to eat today?

Tasha (*embracing him*): Daddy will be here soon with food. Believe me! (*Pause.*) You have to have faith.

Niki: In what?

Tasha: In God.

Niki: God hates us.

Tasha: No, he doesn't.

Niki: Yes, he does.

Anna (*reading from Lamentations 1*): "How does the city sit solitary that was full of people . . . a widow . . . becomes tributary . . . "

Niki: I'd rather be dead than live like this.

Tasha: Don't say that. We have to live . . .

Niki: Why?

Tasha: Something might happen . . . some good luck . . . (*Her voice trails off.*)

Anna: "She weepeth sore in the night . . . and her tears are on her cheeks . . . none to comfort her . . . all . . . have dealt treacherously with her . . . have become her enemies . . . "

Tasha: Come on . . . S . . . who is he?

Niki: If I were dead I wouldn't take up any more food. You all would have more to eat.

Tasha (*hugging him again*): I'd rather have you than all the rice in China.

Niki (*after a moment*): Was he a famous Chinese revolutionary hero?

Tasha: Uhhh . . . not Sun Yat-sen.

Niki: You're too good at this game.

Tasha: You're getting better all the time. That was a good question. I almost didn't know the answer. . . .

Anna: "Judah is gone into captivity . . . she dwelleth among the heathen. All her persecutors overtook her . . . "

Niki: I must have done something awful to deserve this.

Tasha: You haven't done anything awful.

Niki: I've had bad thoughts.

Tasha: Anyone can have bad thoughts.

Niki: But that's wrong.

Tasha: I . . . I guess so.

Niki: I've had bad thoughts about Communism.

Tasha: So have I.

Niki: And even . . . about Daddy . . . for killing our animals . . .

Tasha (*again holding him close*): Stop. Stop thinking these things. . . .

Anna: "Her adversaries are the chief . . . her enemies prosper . . . her children are gone into captivity before the enemy . . . "

Tasha (*after a moment*): Come on . . . who is he?

Niki: Is he a famous philosopher?

Tasha: Hmmmmm . . . oh! He's not Socrates.

Niki: Tasha . . . I know I did something bad. Or this wouldn't have happened. Can't hardly walk . . . can't go to school . . . can't see my friends . . . I want to die. . . . (*There is a long pause. Outside, it has become dark.* **Anna** *and the children are silent. They seem to fall into a kind of trancelike hunger-induced stupor. Finally, there is a knock at the front door. No one moves for a moment. The knocking increases to a pounding.* **Anna** *finally starts up from her chair and screams. The children come into the front room as quickly as they can.* **Anna** *again gets the poker from the fireplace.*)

187

Thad (*off right*): It's me! Unbar the door! Let me in for God's sake!

Anna: Oh my God—it's your father! (*She puts the poker down and goes out to the front door off right.*)

Tasha: It's Daddy!

Niki: Daddy! (*They wait by the door. Soon* **Thad** *comes in from the outside. He is thin and haggard, the picture of a desperate man. His eyes sometimes glance wildly about the room, and his hands often tremble.*)

Anna (*following him into the room*): Oh, Thad—Thad! I'm so glad you're back safe. (**Thad** *embraces* **Anna**, *then the children.*)

Thad: Yes . . . safe . . . for a little while . . .

Niki: Daddy! Did you bring some food?

Tasha: Niki! Give him a minute to rest.

Thad: It's all right, Tasha. . . . Yes! . . . Yes! . . . A little food! (*They all exclaim with joy.*) I was lucky. (*He takes four potatoes out of his pockets.*)

Anna: Oh, thank God!

Niki: Four potatoes! (*He can't help reaching for one.*)

Tasha: Niki, control yourself!

Anna: Yes, child. We'll all have supper soon.

Thad: Just two for today. Save the other two for tomorrow. (*Through the following,* **Anna** *puts two of the potatoes in a drawer with a padlock. She slices the other two, puts the slices in the pot hanging on the tripod, and pours in a little water. Then she lights a small fire under the pot and stirs the mixture with a wooden spoon.* **Niki** *sits on the floor watching the pot.*)

Tasha: How did you get them?

Thad: An amazing piece of luck, my dear. (*He sits at the head of the table.* **Tasha** *sits beside him and pours some water in his tin cup.*) I was at the railroad station. A train came in from Kiev and the OGPU thugs drove us away. There might be people on the train from foreign countries . . . they might see us . . . they might guess what our government is doing to thousands . . . and thousands . . . maybe millions of helpless people. . . . (*He pauses, exhausted from speaking, and sips a little water from his tin cup.*) Oh God . . . I'm so tired. . . . (*He gets control over himself and even manages a smile at his daughter.*) And what have you and your brother been doing today?

Tasha: We've been playing Famous People.

Thad: That's a good game. What's the letter?

Tasha: S.

Thad: S . . . hmmmm. Is he a famous Greek playwright?

Tasha: Uhhhhh . . . oh! It's not Sophocles.

Thad: Good. You are good at this game, Natasha. You are becoming an educated woman. I'm proud of you.

Tasha: I'm proud of you, Daddy. (*There is a quick embrace between father and daughter.*)

Niki: How did you get the potatoes?

Thad: Oh yes . . . oh yes. . . . (*His entire body trembles a moment; then he regains control of himself.*) Yes . . . I . . . I followed the train when it left the station. It wasn't going very fast . . . for some reason . . . just crawling along. . . . I followed it for quite a distance. It went around a bend . . . out of sight of the people at the station . . . and the police. (*Again, he sips a little water.*) And then . . . I thought I was seeing things. . . . A young woman leaned out of a window and waved at me. I waved back. . . . I ran along . . . don't know where I got the strength.

Anna: From God.

Thad: Yes. Yes, it must have come from God. Because . . . the woman threw me four potatoes out the window. I gathered them up. . . . By then the train was going faster . . . and when I looked up, I saw her in the distance. And she waved to me . . . again. . . .

Niki: Four potatoes! We'll all feel better soon.

Tasha: Yes! (*She goes over to the pot and sits on the floor beside* **Niki.**) I'll stir the pot, Mommy.

Anna: All right, dear. (*She hands* **Tasha** *the wooden spoon, goes slowly to the table, and sits beside her husband. During the following,* **Tasha** *stirs the pot now and then. Both children watch the pot fixedly.*)

Thad: Then some more luck . . . no one saw me pick up the potatoes. And no one robbed me on the way home.

Anna (*sipping some water*): Are things any better?

Thad: No . . . worse. Do you remember Zinaida Lvovna Kuskova?

Anna: From Bedichev?

Thad: She was seven months pregnant. They caught her plucking wheat. They beat her with a board. She died, soon after. . . . (*The children concentrate on the pot, trying not to listen.*)

Anna: Poor Anna Zinaida Lvovna . . .

Thad: And Yekaterina Dmitriyevna Dyakov . . . she had three little children. . . .

189

Anna: Wasn't her husband arrested last summer?

Thad: Yes . . . they sent him to Siberia. Well . . . (*he sips some water*) . . . she was digging up potatoes at night on the collective farm. A guard caught her and bayoneted her. Later on . . . her three children starved to death.

Anna: The Lord is punishing us for something. . . .

Thad: They say the Ukraine has been completely quarantined. All the food is shipped out and none comes back . . . except to the army and the police. And the people living in towns and cities. But us, in the farms and villages . . .

Anna: Are any churches still open?

Thad: I didn't see any. That big one in Kremenchug is being used as a transit prison. They lock up people inside until the train comes to take them to Kiev.

Anna: We can still pray . . . even if we can't go to church.

Thad: I've seen people praying. . . .

Anna: It's all we have left.

Thad: There are some priests living in caves in the woods up north of here. They hold secret services for kulaks.

Anna: We can talk to God without the priests.

Thad: They've all been arrested . . . sent away. . . .

Anna: I see God sometimes.

Thad: Anna, keep hold of yourself. The children . . .

Anna: I saw God this afternoon. (*She looks toward the front door as though in a trance.*) He came in the door. He smiled at me. He looked around the room. Then . . . he shook his head . . . and went away. . . . (**Tasha** *stirs the pot.*)

Tasha: How much longer do we have to cook the potato soup, Mommy?

Anna: Longer. . . .

Thad: I saw them plowing up a cemetery today . . . to plant wheat.(*Pause.*) The Communists destroy the bridge between the living and the dead. (*He sips a little water.*)

Anna: We will join the dead soon. . . .

Thad: I saw a band of people come to a tree. They . . . attacked it. They ate the leaves . . . the twigs . . . the roots. . . . Then they searched for kernels of grain in an anthill. . . .

Anna: God will send us grain. . . .

Thad: They say someone managed to cross the police lines into Kiev. He bought some food for his wife and children; then . . . when he tried to cross back, the guards shot him because he didn't have a border pass. (*He sips water again.*) I stopped by the Osorgin house down the road. Vladimir Nikolayevich and Anastasia Lyovna were lying on the floor . . . their faces and bellies bloated. Their eyes looked at me but didn't see me. . . . The children had little skeleton arms and legs . . . dangling from their bodies. . . . (*He passes his hand over his eyes, unable to get the images out of his mind.*) I had to turn and run away. . . . There are dead bodies everywhere . . . unburied . . . rotting . . . being eaten by vultures.

Anna: They are in heaven now. . . .

Thad: Alexandra Nikolayevna Platanov lost her son. She buried him with her last strength. But the OGPU enforcers came along and thought she had hidden food. They dug up the grave . . . found the body . . . then left her to bury it again. (*Pause. It has become very dark outside. Only the candle on the table illuminates the living room.*)

Tasha: Mommy, can't we eat supper?

Anna: Cook the soup a little longer. We must be careful how we eat . . . so as not to vomit. . . . (*There is a long silence. Then suddenly a loud knocking is heard at the front door.*) My God! They've come back!

Thad: Who?

Anna: Starving people, roaming about the neighborhood. (**Thad** *gets the poker from the fireplace. The others stand near him in the up right corner of the room.*)

Thad (*looking out the window*): Who is it?

Maxim (*off right*): It's us, sir. Maxim and Lev.

Thad: What do you want?

Maxim: We have to talk to you.

Thad: We have nothing to give you.

Lev: Please let us in, sir. It's important. (*Thad puts the poker back, then goes out right to open the front door.*)

Tasha (*clutching her stomach*): Mommy! I'm getting sick. Can I go lie down?

Anna: Yes, dear. (**Tasha** *goes into the dark bedroom left and lies down on her mattress down left. She pulls her blanket over her emaciated body.* **Anna** *and* **Niki** *sit down again at the table.*)

Thad (*off right*): Come in gentlemen. (*Through the following, he speaks to*

191

the OGPU men with utter contempt mixed with a natural courtesy that is part of his nature).

Maxim: Thank you, sir. (**Maxim** *and* **Lev** *enter right, followed by* **Thad** *after he has locked and barred the front door. The two OGPU enforcers have changed. They have witnessed unspeakable suffering, torment, despair, starvation, and death. Their faces are gaunt and expressionless. They wear dark blue uniforms, steel helmets, and heavy boots. Each carries an automatic rifle suspended from a shoulder strap and, at the belt, pistol, bayonet, ammunition clips, and hand grenades. They stand nervously near the door.*)

Lev: Thank you, sir.

Maxim (*to* **Anna**): Good evening, ma'am. *(Anna stares at him with undisguised hatred.)* You're Niki, aren't you? (**Niki** *nods but says nothing.*) I don't see your daughter, Tasha.

Anna: She is in her room. She does not feel well. . . . (**Thad** *has come back in and stands by the fireplace.*)

Thad: Well? What do you want?

Maxim (*looking about the room*): Been trading furniture for food, have you?

Thad: What if we have?

Maxim: There's a law against it, old man. But . . . we didn't come about that.

Thad: Didn't you? Well . . . you must have come about some other law.

Maxim: Maybe.

Thad: I just found out the other day there's a law against fishing. Did you know that?

Maxim: Yes.

Thad: A fellow got shot trying to catch fish in a stream up north of here.

Maxim: Did he?

Thad: What he didn't know was there's no fish in that stream. Never has been.

Maxim: A stupid man. You're not like that. (**Lev** *moves over toward the bedroom door.*) I can see that you're holding on. I thought you would. I told Lev you'd hold on. Didn't I Lev?

Lev: That's right, Maxim. That's what you said.

Maxim: You'll live to be a hundred, old man. . . .

Thad: Get on with your business. Then get out.

Maxim: All right! I've got another paper for you to sign.

192

Thad: Sign it yourself.

Maxim: Can we talk about it? Can we be reasonable . . . sir?

Thad: Yes, we can be reasonable. After all . . . I knew your father.

Maxim: That's right, sir. You knew my daddy. And I don't forget things like that.

Lev: Shall I take a look around? Hidden food? Weapons?

Maxim (*after a moment*): Sure, Lev. Take a look around. (**Lev** *goes into the bedroom left.*) And here's the paper I'd like you to read and then sign. (*He hands* **Thad** *a paper.* **Thad** *takes it and sits at the table with* **Anna** *and* **Niki**. **Maxim** *stands by the fireplace. In the left bedroom,* **Lev***, unable to see anything, turns on a small flashlight he carries. He shines it about the room and discovers* **Tasha** *under her blanket. He turns out the light and sits on the floor beside her. The following scene is played in darkness.*)

Lev (*softly*): Did Dmitri Yakovlevich come to see you?

Tasha: Yes.

Lev: Then you know I've been in Siberia all this time.

Tasha: Yes, Lev. I knew that.

Lev: And did he give you . . . my . . . my other message?

Tasha: Yes, Lev.

Lev: I couldn't write you.

Tasha: We kulaks don't get letters from anybody.

Lev: Tasha . . . like I told Dmitri to tell you . . . I love you. I've been thinking about you all this time. . . . (*He kisses her in the dark. She sighs with pleasure and despair.*)

Tasha: Lev . . . stop. Please stop.

Lev: I'm going to save you, Tasha.

Tasha: I'm dying, Lev.

Lev: No! I'll save you. I have a plan. (*He kisses her again. In the living room,* **Thad** *puts down the paper.* **Anna** *continues to stare at it in disbelief.*)

Thad: So we have to leave.

Maxim: That's right.

Thad: Leave our home.

Maxim: That's right, old man. (**Thad** *and* **Anna** *stare at the paper on the table.* **Niki** *tries to hear what is being said in the bedroom. left.*)

Lev: I have a passport for you. (*He shines his flashlight on a passport.*

193

Tasha *stares at it.*) I used that picture you gave me. Friend of mine in Siberia fixed it up.

Tasha: Do I still look like that?

Lev: Sure. Close enough. (*He turns off his flashlight.*) How do you feel?

Tasha: Oh, Lev . . . the hunger . . .

Lev: I know. . . . It must be bad. . . .

Tasha: I feel like I'm on fire . . . my stomach . . . and in my soul . . . (*He kisses her again. She sighs with pleasure.*)

Thad: Saturday morning . . .

Maxim: That's right. The bulldozer and the wrecking crew are due here early Saturday. Don't hang around and watch. Leave tomorrow afternoon.

Anna: This is monstrous!

Maxim: Decision of the Kiev Soviet.

Anna: What have we done to deserve this?

Maxim: You slaughtered your livestock. Stole from the people. You are kulaks. You will never accept Socialism. So . . . you must go. . . . (*His manner changes somewhat.*) Go into the woods north of here. Find those old caves. Maybe the people living in them will help you. (**Anna** *bursts into sobs.* **Thad** *tries to comfort her.* **Maxim** *turns away and looks out the window by the fireplace.* **Niki** *slips from the table and sits by the door to the bedroom, listening to* **Lev** *and* **Tasha**.)

Lev: Maxim has to go to Rostov tomorrow. I can use the truck. I'll be here about two o'clock. We'll go to Kiev—

Tasha: It's too late, Lev.

Lev: No, it isn't! Trust me. When we get there, my great-aunt will take you in and feed you. She's got medicine and vitamin pills. She works as a cleaning woman in a hospital.

Tasha: Too late. . . .

Lev: She'll get you well in no time. Then we'll get married . . . get you a job . . . and you'll be safe.

Tasha: Safe . . . ? Me . . . ?

Lev: Yes! You! (*Again he kisses her.*)

Thad: So the house will be torn down.

Maxim: And the lumber belongs to the people.

Thad: The people are welcome to it.

Maxim: That's a proper attitude, sir.

Thad: And the basement will be filled with soil.

194

Maxim: To grow wheat for the people.

Thad: But not for us.

Maxim: This place is now part of a large collective farm. By order of the Kiev Central Committee.

Thad: The Kiev Murder Committee.

Maxim: Don't slander the Party. You're still a free man. Slandering the Party can get you twenty years in Siberia.

Thad: How many years do I have left, anyway?

Maxim: Oh . . . I don't know. You're not dead yet, old man. And . . . since you knew my daddy . . . I've brought you something. (*From an inside pocket of his jacket he draws a bag of salt and a knife in a sheath. He drops them on the table.*) Two kilos of salt and a good knife. Bought 'em myself. That's all I can do. (*He turns back to the window right and looks out.*)

Lev: You got to be packed. Ready to go.

Tasha: That won't take long. All I've got left is what I'm wearing and my blanket.

Lev: We'll cross into Kiev at night. I know a place where there's only a couple of guards. They'll let us through.

Tasha: Will you take Niki? And Mom and Dad?

Lev: Tasha! How can I? The only passport I have is for you. If they catch me trying to save kulaks they'll kill me.

Tasha: So . . . it's just me?

Lev: Tasha, I love you! (*Again he kisses her in the darkened room. In the living room,* **Thad** *and* **Anna** *have recovered their composure.*)

Thad: Well . . . Mr. Malinovsky . . . thank you for the salt and the knife. I will accept them in the name of your father.

Maxim: Fine. That suits me just fine. Take 'em from my daddy. (*For a moment he seems to be gripped by some emotion remembered from the past. His shoulders shake a little as he looks out the window.*) If he'd had to face what you did, he'd probably have done the same thing.

Thad: Maybe. Maybe he would. And so . . . I still ask what I can't understand. Why create this hell on earth for thousands of innocent, helpless people?

Maxim: Oh, not everybody is starving. People have started to hear about what's happening to kulaks in the Ukraine. Collectivization is going very well in some places.

Thad: Is it?

Maxim: Yes, sir. So your sacrifice is not in vain. Look at it that way and you'll feel better. (**Thad** *and* **Anna** *stare at the salt and the knife on the table.*)

Tasha: Lev, why did you and Maxim come here tonight?

Lev: To tell you . . . you all have to leave tomorrow. They're coming Saturday to tear down your house. I brought you something . . . some powdered milk. (*He hands her a box of powdered milk.*)

Tasha: Oh Lev! Thank you. You've no idea how this will help us.

Lev: Drink it slowly.

Tasha: We will.

Lev: Will you be ready tomorrow? . . .

Tasha: Yes, Lev. I'll be ready tomorrow. (*He kisses her again. Then he gets up from the floor and goes into the living room.* **Niki** *returns to the table.*)

Lev: Couldn't find anything.

Maxim: All right. (*He turns to* **Thad.**) Will you sign the paper? So I can prove you know the wreckers are coming Saturday?

Thad (*shrugging his shoulders*): Might as well. It's all over now. (*He signs the paper.* **Maxim** *takes it, folds it, and puts it in an inside pocket.*)

Maxim: Thank you, sir. Let's go, Lev. (*He and* **Lev** *cross to the front door.*)

Lev: OK.

Maxim: Good-bye. I wish you luck.

Lev: Good luck. (*The Orlovs do not reply.* **Maxim** *and* **Lev** *go out the front door.* **Thad** *follows them out onto the front porch and bars the door.* **Tasha** *enters the living room.*)

Tasha: Look what I've got! (*She shows her family the box of powdered milk.*) Powdered milk!

Anna: Oh—thank God! We will eat well this evening.

Thad: Did Lev give it to you?

Tasha: Yes, Daddy.

Niki: Daddy, you won't take it away from us because of Lev, will you? (*Pause.* **Thad** *comes slowly to the table.*)

Thad: No. We'll drink the milk. (*He opens the box with the knife and pours a little of the powder in each cup. He then puts the box of milk, the knife, and the salt in the drawer with the padlock.* **Tasha** *pours water in the cups and stirs the milk.* **Anna** *has dipped the potato soup into the four bowls and puts them on the table.*) But we must drink it slowly, and in small amounts. We must make this milk last a long time.

Anna: Sit at your places, children. (*The children sit at the table, as does* **Thad**. **Anna** *sits down, then opens her Bible to read.*)

Thad: Something hopeful, Anna. (*She turns the pages slowly.*)

Anna (*reading from Psalm 18*): "I will love thee, O Lord, my strength. The Lord is my rock and my fortress and my deliverer; my God, my strength, in whom I will trust; my buckler, and the horn of my salvation, and my high tower. I will call upon the Lord, who is worthy to be praised; so shall I be saved from mine enemies." (*They all say, "Amen."*)

Thad: Now eat very slowly and carefully, children, so as to keep your food down. (*They all follow his directions.*) A bit of soup . . . a sip of milk . . . (*They eat in silence. Soon all the soup and milk are gone. A pause. The candle on the table throws a flickering light on their gaunt faces.*)

Niki: I'm still hungry.

Thad: We are all still hungry, Niki. But . . . at least . . . we ate slowly enough so we didn't vomit.

Tasha: It was good.

Anna: Yes. Our best meal in a long time. Think about that, Niki.

Niki: Couldn't I have just one more sip of milk?

Thad: No. We must save it for tomorrow. (*He rises from the table. The others get up, too.*) Time for bed. We have to pack tomorrow. We will have our last meal in our house in early afternoon. Then we will go. We will go into the forest north of here. And we will live!

Anna, **Tasha,** *and* **Niki** (*together*): We will live!

Thad: Again!

All: We will live!

Thad: To bed, children. (**Tasha** *embraces her father, then her mother.*)

Tasha: Good night, Daddy. Good night, Mommy. (*They respond with "good nights." She goes into the left bedroom and lights a small candle in a tray on the floor near her mattress.* **Niki** *embraces his father and mother.*)

Niki: Good night, Daddy. Good night, Mommy. (*They respond with "good nights."* **Niki** *goes into the bedroom.*)

Anna: Oh, Thad! What will happen to us?

Thad: Have courage, my dear. (*They hold one another close a long time.*)

Niki: Will read to me, Tasha?

Tasha: We haven't any books left.

Niki: Did you finish the story you were writing?

Tasha (*after a moment*): Yes. But you might not like it.

Niki: Read it to me! Please—I'm so hungry!

Tasha: All right. But let's wait until Mom and Dad are in bed. (*She blows out the candle by her mattress.*)

Anna: I love you, Thad. When I die in the forest, my last thoughts will be of you.

Thad: We will not die. (*He blows out the candle on the table. Then they cross in the dark through the children's room into their own room. The two rooms are now lighted only by a little pale moonlight shining through the back windows from off left. As the scene continues, this lighting brightens somewhat. After a few moments,* **Niki** *stirs on his mattress*).

Niki: Tasha . . .

Tasha: Yes. I'll read to you. (*She gets some sheets of paper from under her mattress, relights her candle, and crawls upstage by* **Niki**'*s mattress. There she sits, cross-legged on the floor, and reads him her story.*)

Niki: Is it a nice story?

Tasha: No. (*She begins to read.*) "The column of smoke from the bonfire was rising, thick. All the beauty of the day was gone. As he gathered up his rifle and ammunition belt, Sergei stared at the dying fire. The smell wasn't so bad now. The screams had died away into the cold, Siberian night. It was quiet now. Very quiet." (*She pauses a moment.*) "The Zeks hadn't put up much of a fight. They knew they hadn't made their quota. They were forty-four cubic yards of timber short. And yesterday—was it thirty-eight yards? And the day before, and the day before, and the day before. Short. Always short. Sergei was as sick of all this as the other guards. After all, who had to listen to the commandant screaming at them every night? The Zeks? They were eating their slop. Or already asleep in their filthy barracks. No, it was he, Sergei Sergeievitch Vorobyov, and his comrade guards who absorbed the tongue-lashings." (*She pauses and coughs a little.*) " 'Filth!' The commandant liked to compare his guards to things dirty. 'Filth! Foulness! Stench in the nostrils of the human race! You will be out there yourselves, soon, cutting down trees and sawing up the wood. You'll add fifty cubic yards to what they do. More, if necessary. Do you understand me, filth?' He paused. Stared at each guard in turn, his steel blue eyes glistening with the contempt of the righteous for the unwor-

thy. 'They make their quota tomorrow—or else!' He spat at their feet."
(*She pauses.*)

Niki: You're going away with Lev tomorrow, aren't you?

Tasha: No.

Niki: But I heard you. . . .

Tasha: I'm not going. (*She continues her reading.*) "The guards talked
quietly among themselves. Cpl. Vlas Petrov: 'The Zeks work very
hard. The quota is too high.' Sgt. Ivan Mersh: 'Don't make anti-Soviet
remarks, Comrade Vlas Nikolaevitch. Worse things could happen to
you than having to chop a little wood.' " (*She pauses, and again
coughs. The moonlight has begun to brighten.*) "Sergei Sergeivitch
tried to think. Was it right to work the Zeks to death? Should the quota
be reduced? Does one have a right to speak out? Sergei became tired
from his intellectual labors and went to sleep."

Niki: You're going to leave me.

Tasha: I'll never leave you.

Niki: But he can't take all of us. I heard him say it.

Tasha: Yes . . . he said that. (*She returns to her story.*) "Evening. Nearly
dark. The quota, short. Short by forty-four cubic yards. Sgt. Mersh
sipped from a metal flask of vodka. The other guards were sullen.
Day-long shouts and curses had had no effect on the prisoners. Now,
it was too dark to work any longer. The Zeks lay on the ground,
exhausted, hungry, trembling with fear and despair." (*She pauses a
moment to clear her throat.*) " 'Vlas, Sergei, build a fire.' When
Comrade Sgt. Ivan Ivanovich Mersh gave an order, it was obeyed.
Boris ventured a question, however. 'Aren't we going back to camp?
It's too dark to cut any more wood even with a fire.' 'I said build a
fire.' A note of menace. Ivan never raised his voice when he had
decided on something. He just gave an order. And it was obeyed."

Niki: Promise you won't leave with Lev tomorrow?

Tasha: I promise! (*She hugs* **Niki**, *then resumes her reading.*) "Soon, a
roaring fire. Built with three cubic yards of wood that had been
faithfully cut by the Zeks for the greater glory of the fourth Five-Year
Plan. A big, solid fire. The whole clearing was lit up. People warmed
themselves. A cheerful fire." (*She coughs a little.*) "Sgt. Mersh spoke.
'Throw them into it.' A moment of silence. Ivan held his submachine
gun carefully at the ready. 'I said throw them into it.' His voice had
risen only a semitone. But a finger flicked off the safety on his

weapon." (*She pauses again.*) "The guards lurched up from the ground and addressed their task. Orders were orders. They threw a Zek into the fire. He screamed. Tried to crawl out. The guards beat him with their rifle butts and pushed him back in."

Niki: If you leave me, I'll starve. Mom and Dad are dying.

Tasha: I won't leave you. I'll help you live. I know what I'm going to do.

Niki: What?

Tasha: Stay with you . . . and with Mommy and Daddy. (*She resumes her reading.*) "A moment's pause. Then they threw two more prisoners onto the funeral pyre. Black smoke mingled with the stench of burning human flesh. Shrieks of agony filled the air. Some Zeks tried to run away, but they were caught and dragged back. The guards now settled into an efficient routine. They stood like a bucket brigade leading from the Zeks to the fire, tossing the bodies on one at a time in regular measured intervals. Half an hour of hard work. Then silence. Comrade Sgt. Ivan Ivanovich gave the order to return to camp." (*She pauses and coughs again.*) "The fire was dying out. Sergei wondered what the commandant would say tonight. He stopped for a moment, turned around, and looked back. A blackened arm seemed to be waving at him. Then it dropped slowly down into the glowing embers. Sergei waved back. Then he turned and followed the others."

Niki (*after a moment*): Is that the end?

Tasha: Yes.

Niki: Some story.

Tasha: Did you like it?

Niki: Well . . . I don't know. But I think it was a good story. Where did you get the idea for it?

Tasha: Oh, something Mr. Guryev mentioned once . . . at school.

Niki (*nearly asleep*): Tasha . . .

Tasha: What?

Niki: Who was . . . "S"?

Tasha: Stalin. (**Niki** *is asleep.* **Tasha** *crawls back to her mattress. She puts her story under it and withdraws another sheet of paper, her pencil, and the rope. She blows out the candle and goes into the living room. There she puts the rope, the pencil, and the paper on the table and lights the candle. She sits at the table and writes a short note to her brother and her parents. She hesitates a time, then picks up the rope ties a slip knot in one end, and goes to the back door. She pauses a* *moment to take a last look at her home. Then she takes a chair out onto the back porch. Moonlight coming through the porch window throws shadows of her on the wall. She stands on the chair, puts the loop of the rope around her neck, ties the other end to the meat hook, then kicks over the chair. It makes a loud noise as it strikes the floor.* **Niki** *sits up in terror.*)

Niki: Tasha! Mommy! Daddy! Somebody's trying to get in the back door! (**Thad** *and* **Anna** *come through his room into the living room, pause, and then see* **Tasha**, *hanging from the hook on the back porch.*)

Anna: Ahhhh! Ahhhh! Ahhh!

Thad (*holding her close to him*): Anna! Control yourself! (**Niki** *has run into the living room.*)

Niki: Tasha! Tasha!

Anna: Niki! Stay here! (*She holds onto* **Niki** *as* **Thad** *gets the knife from the drawer, goes out on the back porch, and cuts the rope. He lays* **Tasha** *on the table and feels her pulse. After a moment, he lets her wrist drop. Then he slowly comes back into the living room.*)

Thad: She's dead.

Anna: Nooooo! (*She turns away and stands near the table.* **Thad** *holds onto* **Niki**.)

Thad: Quiet . . . quiet . . . we must control ourselves. For her sake . . . we must control . . . (*his voice trails off. There is a pause as the surviving members of the family struggle with their emotions.* **Anna** *finally notices the note* **Tasha** *has left on the table.*

Anna: She left a note.

Thad: Read it to us, my dear.

Anna: No! I can't! (*She moves convulsively to the fireplace as though trying to escape the reality of what has happened.* **Niki** *rushes to her and holds on to her tightly.* **Thad** *picks up the candle and then the letter. He holds the candle so that he can see to read the letter.*)

Thad: (*reading*): "Dear Mommy, Daddy, and Niki, I am writing you a letter tonight, but I won't be getting an answer from you . . . kind of a one-way correspondence." (*He stops a moment to control his emotions, then continues.*) "I am going to leave you all because I am a . . . a burden . . . another mouth to feed . . . and I want to end that problem forever. And also . . . I want to make myself . . . yes, myself . . . available to you for nourishment. . . . (*He stops a moment, then goes on.*) "Yes, Daddy . . . I ask you . . . as my last wish while I am still alive . . .

to butcher my flesh, salt it, and eat a little of it each day. Make it last as long as you can." (*Again he stops, then manages to go on.*) "Tomorrow, when you leave here forever, take me with you. In body and in spirit. Put superstition aside. These are hard times. Take strength from my flesh. We are all God's creatures. We are like cattle and sheep . . . and ducks and chickens . . . so eat me, too. Think of me as food for life." (*Pause.*) "Live as long as possible! I sure love you three!" (*Pause.*) Your Tasha. . . . " (*Lighting fades slowly down and out.*)

ACT II

SCENE 2: *Early afternoon, the next day.*

AT RISE: *Bright sunlight comes through the upstage windows.* **Thad** *is stirring the pot over the fire. He seems light-headed, almost giddy. His actions and remarks possess an air of the incoherent.*

    Anna *sits at the table in silence, staring straight in front of her, as though paralyzed. Sometimes she murmurs from the Lord's Prayer.*

    Niki *sits quietly at the table watching his father. His hunger is such that he is unable to think of anything but food.*

    In the left bedroom are three bundles of clothing wrapped in blankets and tied with thick string. The bundles contain the last possessions of the family, including strips of salted meat and some of the powdered milk for their journey to the forest up north.

Thad: Well—well! We eat soon! (*He stirs the pot carefully.*) Yes . . . soon . . . last meal in our old home. . . . *(He stirs the pot again.)* Potato soup with chunks of meat . . . and good milk to drink. We'll feel stronger soon. Protein and vitamins . . . (*He wanders down right waving the spoon.*) Yes . . . yes . . . our last meal in our old home . . . a feast! (*He smiles broadly at* **Anna** *and* **Niki**. *They stare at him, saying nothing.*) A feast I say! Fit for a king! (*He returns to the pot, which he stirs.*) Yes. A Christmas feast! All we can eat. . . .

Anna (*almost inaudible*): Our father . . . who art in heaven . . . (*Her voice trails off.*)

Thad: Ready soon . . . ready soon! Nourishment. Strength. Like Maxim said . . . we haven't given up. . . . We'll make it to those caves up north. . . . The people there will help us. . . . They've lost their land, too. . . . They'll help us find bark and roots we can eat. . . . (*He stirs* *the pot carefully.*) We'll find a small cave somewhere . . . facing south . . . we'll get through the winter . . . then spring and summer won't be bad. . . .

Anna: Hallowed be thy name . . .

Thad: We'll live. . . . That's what we're here for . . . to live . . . have to hold onto that. . . .

Anna: Thy kingdom come . . . thy will be done . . .

Thad: Purpose of life is to live. . . . When we die out . . . like the dinosaurs . . . life's purpose will be fulfilled.

Anna: On earth as it is in heaven. . . . (*There is a knock at the front door. They all freeze for a moment. The knocking is repeated; then* **Thad** *picks up the poker and looks out the window upstage of the front door.*)

Thad: Who's there?

Lev (*off right*): It's me—Lev. Let me in.

Thad: What do you want?

Lev: Let me in. . . . I need to see you. Please let me in.

Anna: Let him in, Thad.

Thad: All right. All right. Why not? Old friend . . . gave Tasha the milk. (*He puts the poker back.*) Let's have him in . . . have him to Christmas dinner with us . . . plenty for all. . . . (*He goes out on the front porch and unbars the front door.*)

Lev: Good afternoon, sir.

Thad: Good afternoon, Lev Petrovitch. Glad you came to see us. Come in.

Lev: Thank you. (*Lev enters right. He wears his uniform but does not carry his rifle, nor does he wear his steel helmet. He addresses* **Anna** *and* **Niki.**) Good afternoon, ma'am. Hello, Niki. (*They mumble greetings to him.* **Thad** *has barred the front door and now enters right.*)

Thad: We were just sitting down to Christmas dinner.

Lev: Is Tasha here?

Thad: No. She went out about an hour ago to gather berries for dinner.

Lev: Berries? . . . May I look around?

Thad: See for yourself. (*He motions politely toward the bedroom door.* **Lev** *goes into the left bedroom and looks about.*)

Lev: Tasha? Are you here? (*He looks in the room off left, then returns to the living room.*) I was supposed to meet her here about two o'clock.

Thad: Two o'clock?

Lev: Yes. (**Thad** *searches his pockets for his watch.*)

Thad: Sorry I can't confirm the time of day to you. . . . (*He stirs the pot.*)

Traded my gold watch some time ago for a dozen eggs and a kilo of bacon.

Lev: Are you getting ready to leave?

Thad: Yes. Leaving soon. Going north.

Lev: There's only three packs in there.

Thad: Oh, we don't expect Niki to carry anything. (*He stirs the pot again.*) Yes . . . traded my gold watch. Belonged to my daddy. Had a picture of his mother in the case. Remarkable picture . . . hadn't faded in over a hundred years.

Lev: Where is Tasha?

Thad: I told you. Picking berries.

Lev: What kind of berries?

Thad: Blackberries.

Lev: Where?

Thad: North of here a piece. She's found 'em before. Knows just where to look. (*He stirs the pot carefully.*) She'll be back soon. She wanted to have blackberries and thick milk for our last supper. With the milk you gave her. You remember giving her some milk?

Lev: Yes.

Thad: Good-quality milk. She shared it with us. Hope you don't mind.

Lev: No.

Thad: Join us for dinner while you wait?

Lev: No. Er . . . no thanks.

Thad: We have plenty. Been saving up for our last meal here. Milk, soup with meat and potatoes . . . berries comin'. Sit down.

Lev: Well, all right. Thank you. (**Lev** *reluctantly sits at the table in* **Tasha's** *chair.*)

Thad: Yes . . . plenty to eat . . . you've been nice to our Tasha. So we'll share our meal. Old Ukrainian custom.

Lev: I know the customs around here.

Thad: I know you do. You're not like the others.

Lev: Did she tell you I plan to take her to Kiev?

Thad: Yes, she did. Yes, she did.

Lev: I can't understand why she isn't here.

Thad: She'll be here in a jiffy. (*He ladles some soup into one of the bowls.*) Here . . . your portion, sir. (*He puts the bowl of potatoes-and-meat soup in front of* **Lev.**) Anna, give Lev Petrovitch some milk; then fill the other cups.

Anna: Give us this day . . . our daily bread. . . . (*As though in a trance,* **Anna** *pours milk into the four cups, then sits down again.* **Thad** *brings the next bowl to the table.*)

Thad: Niki . . . your bowl. . . . We'll keep Tasha's portion warm in the pot. . . . (*He puts* **Niki***'s bowl in front of him, then returns to the pot. Masking with his body what he is really doing, he pours all the rest of the soup into the two remaining bowls, then puts them on the table.*) And . . . soup for you, my dear, and my portion. (*He sits down at his usual place.*) Anna? Something from the Good Book?

Anna (*after a moment*): I no longer read the Word of God.

Thad: Well, Lev Petrovitch, take the first spoonful. Our guest . . . potato-and-meat soup. We kulaks know how to survive, as your friend Maxim Alexseyovich likes to say. (**Lev** *swallows a spoonful of the soup.*) How is it?

Lev: It's good. What kind of meat is it? Rabbit? Chicken?

Thad: Oh, various things. I put all the meat together when I salt it.

Lev: Yes. Very good. (*He eats his soup.* **Thad** *takes a spoonful; then* **Niki** *eats some, then* **Anna**. *They eat slowly, as before.*)

Thad: Well, Lev Petrovitch, how are things going for you?

Lev: Fine. Just fine. . . . (*He eats and drinks during the following.*) Resistance to collectivization is dying out. Capitalism and religion are dying out. (*Pause.*) People are beginning to accept Socialism. People are beginning to see the benefits . . . the beauty of Socialism. . . . (*They all eat slowly.*) The people own the land, today. Your little farm here is now part of the collective, "October Revolution," one of the largest collective farms in the world. . . . (*The lighting begins to fade down as* **Thad**, **Anna**, **Niki** *and* **Lev** *partake of the Feast of Thyestes.*) We will lead the world to socialism, peace and prosperity for all, universal comradeship. Soon there will be only one class . . . one folk . . . brothers and sisters all. . . . (*He takes a long drink of milk.*)

CURTAIN.
END ACT II.

205

Epilogue: On Violence

Joseph Stalin was not the only major perpetrator of genocide in modern times, his chief rivals being the World War I Turkish War Minister Enver Pasha, who ordered the slaughter of two million Armenians living in Turkey at the time, and Adolf Hitler, who saw to the extermination of six million European Jews between 1933 and 1945, an outrage that has come to be called the Holocaust.

A Holocaust Memorial Museum was opened in Washington, D.C., in 1993. Located on the Mall, the building houses many exhibits depicting the experiences of European Jews in the Polish death camps. The roof is designed to represent a series of camp watchtowers. In the Hall of Witness, the walls are pierced with the kind of ovens used to cremate the dead bodies. A railroad boxcar, of the type employed to transport Jews to Auschwitz, is on display. The whole story of the Holocaust is presented by means of films, photographs, human artifacts, and placard narratives. But a museum, no matter how imaginatively designed, can only hint at the reality of one of the monumental crimes of modern history.

Hitler's earliest specific plan for ridding Germany of the Jews was to deport them to Madagascar and place them under Vichy-French administration. A preliminary step was taken in October 1940 when 7,500 Jews from western Germany were shipped to France for transport to Madagascar. But this plan soon became untenable. Studies of the upcoming Operation Barbarossa, the invasion of Russia, revealed that the Germans would soon have to deal with another four million Jews, and Madagascar simply couldn't accommodate such numbers. Hence, in the spring of 1941, Hitler made the decision to exterminate the Jews of Europe and Russia. Secret orders were issued to the SS, which organized four *Einsatzgruppen* to do the dirty work in Russia. In the summer and fall of 1941, these special SS commando units murdered one million Jews in the areas or western Russia and the Ukraine that were occupied by the *Wehrmacht*. The killings were carried out in various ways—by mass shootings, by drownings, and by burning the Jews alive. In her book *A History of the Holocaust,* Yehuda Bauer quotes an eyewitness description:

> In August, 1941, German armies entered Uman, Ukraine . . . and on November 6–8, 1941, "actions" were committed. Groups of Jews were concentrated in synagogues, in the "Red Army House", and in many other houses in the old and new town. The houses were set afire and the people inside burned alive. Those who tried to jump through the windows were shot with automatic weapons . . . During these "actions", 18,000 people were exterminated. Jews who were caught after an action were mercilessly shot. Slowly, the Jewish artisans were also liquidated . . . Their property was stolen by the Germans and what was left was taken by the Ukrainians. (199–200)

But the more usual routine was to line up Jews in front of large open pits, shoot them, push the bodies into the pits, then cover them with dirt. The best known example of this barbarism was the murder of 100,000 Jews at Babi Yar, near Kiev, an "action" that has become infamous in poetry and prose and in the *Thirteenth* Symphony of Dmitri Shostakovich.

These "actions" in Russia came to be regarded in high places as unsatisfactory, however. Too crude. Too visible. Too noisy. Too messy. What was needed was a few remote places, designed specifically for the extermination of Jews by gas chamber and crematorium. They should be run quietly, efficiently, and out of the public eye. Located by a railroad, of course, but not on German soil. A final solution to the Jewish question—efficient, thorough, humane.

With these guidelines in mind, the SS, beginning in December 1941, established six extermination camps in the Polish cities of Chelmno, Treblinka, Sobibor, Maidenek, Belzec, and Auschwitz. Many eyewitness accounts of the proceedings in these camps have survived. At Belzec:

> As the train drew in, 200 Ukrainians detailed for the task tore open the doors (of the 45 cars holding more than 6,000 people) and, by laying about them with their leather whips, drove the Jews out of the cars. Instructions boomed from a loudspeaker, ordering them to remove all clothing, artificial limbs and spectacles . . . Then the march began. On either side of them, left and right, barbed wire; behind, two dozen Ukrainians, guns in hand. . . . Men, women, young girls, children, babies, cripples, all stark naked, filed by. . . . They walked up a small flight of steps and into the death chambers, most of them without a word, thrust forward by those behind them. One Jewess of about

forty, her eyes flaming like torches, cursed her murderers. Urged on by some whiplashes from Captain Wirth in person, she disappeared into the gas chamber. Many were praying, while others asked: "Who will give us water to wash the dead?" (Jewish ritual). (210–211)

At Maidenek:

You get up at 3 A.M. You have to dress quickly and make the "bed" so that it looks like a match box. For the slightest irregularity in bed-making the punishment was 25 lashes, after which it was impossible to lie or sit for a whole month . . .

We went in groups—some to build railway tracks, or a road, some to the quarries to carry stones or coal, some to take out manure, or for potato digging, latrine-cleaning, barracks- or sewer-repairs. All this took place inside the camp enclosure. During work, the SS men beat up the prisoners mercilessly, inhumanely and for no reason.

They were like wild beasts and, having found their victim, ordered him to present his backside, and beat him with a stick or a whip, usually until the stick broke.

The victim screamed only after the first blows, afterwards he fell unconscious and the SS man then kicked at the ribs, the face, at the most sensitive parts of a man's body and then, finally convinced that that the victim was at the end of his strength, he ordered another Jew to pour one pail of water after the other over the beaten person until he woke and got up . . . (212–13)

By far the largest and most efficient of the German death camps in Poland was Auschwitz. Begun in 1940 originally as a concentration camp for Polish and Russian POWs, it became a death camp for Jews in 1941–42. There were five gas chambers, each with a capacity of about one thousand victims, and many ovens in which to cremate the remains. Crystals of Zyklon B, or prussic acid, supplied by two German chemical firms, Degesch of Dessau and Testa of Hamburg, were dropped into the sealed chambers by SS guards wearing gas masks. When exposed to air, the crystals turned into a deadly gas that killed the victims after a few minutes of intense suffering.

The Commandant at Auschwitz, Rudolf F. Hoess, established a careful routine intended to keep the new arrivals just off the train from becoming unduly anxious about their fate. They were led unsuspectingly to "disinfection baths", something they would be glad to have after their long ride in the cattle cars. They undressed and were told to remember the number of the peg they had hung their clothes on so they could find them when they came out. Then they were invited by the SS guards to walk into the gas chambers, which had been constructed to look like large shower rooms. After they died, the *Sonderkommando,* special groups of Jewish prisoners, hauled the bodies out of the gas chambers, removed rings and any teeth with gold fillings, and stacked the corpses on elevators that lifted them to the floor above, where the ovens were. After the bodies had been cremated, the ashes were collected, loaded into trucks, and taken to storage pits. Later the Jews of the *Sonderkommando* met the same fate.

Hoess reported that peak efficiency at Auschwitz, reached only once, was the gassing and cremation of 9,000 Jews in one twenty-four-hour period. During the entire time of its operation, Auschwitz claimed about 2.5 million Jewish lives.

It has been said that any survivor of the German murder camps in Poland would be capable of witnessing the extinction of the human race with equanimity. During the years of the Holocaust, nearly six million Jews were murdered by the Germans—about a third of the total Jewish population of 1933. The only positive outcome of this colossal human sacrifice has been the reestablishment in Palestine of the ancient Jewish homeland after an exile of its populace lasting nineteen centuries. The historic vote in the United Nations that established the "new" state of Israel took place on November 29, 1947. This international act of redemption created a new feeling of confidence, and self-esteem among the Jewish people, and enabled them to defend themselves successfully during three short but vicious wars initiated by their Arab neighbors with the intention of "driving them into the sea." With the triumphant conclusion of these wars, centuries of Jewish self-hate came to an end.

The Memorial to the Jewish Holocaust in Washington inevitably suggests a need for other memorials to human violence and cruelty situated nearby. How about a Memorial to the Holy Inquisition? This sinister institution presided over five centuries of torture, and burnings at the stake of tens of thousands of heretics, witches, and Jews, all in the name of Jesus Christ the Righteous. What about a memorial to the first serious effort at genocide in the twentieth century—the Turkish campaign of extermination against their Armenian minority during the First World War? Memories of these atrocities slumber uneasily in our collective unconscious, and jogging unconscious memories into consciousness is the purpose of all memorials.

An excellent model for a Memorial to the Holy Inquisition already exists, in Carcassonne, a city in southern France. It could be duplicated or, better still—if the present owner were willing to sell it—dismantled stone by stone, shipped to Washington, and reassembled on the Mall. It is described by John A. O'Brien in his book *The Inquisition* as follows:

> Still surviving in remarkable completeness is the prison in Carcassonne with its towers, and narrow, dark cells wherein persons convicted of heresy by the Inquisition were confined. Thousands of people visit this museum each year to see the Torture Chamber with its instruments of torment. In the embrasure of a window in the upper story is the inscription made by a prisoner: "Give me food." The lower dungeon is reached by a trapdoor, and is lighted by three deep loopholes. The stone pillar, rubbed and worn by prisoners' backs, still has the chains riveted to it. (45)

The atmosphere of this edifying structure might be further enhanced by the inclusion inside of a copy of a steel torture chair from Cuenca, Spain, that resides presently in the Horniman Museum in London:

> It includes a movable seat with pinion and rack, manacles for feet and hands, and, most unusual of all, a skeleton helmet with screws to put pressure on the top of the head, to pierce the ears and to torture nose and chin.
>
> In addition, there is a gag for the mouth with rack-action for forcing the mouth open, and dragging forward the tongue, screw-forceps for extracting toenails, single and double thumbscrews, and various other padlocks, buckles, chains, keys, and turnscrews . . . Engraved on the mouth-gag are the words "Santo oficio caballero"—the noble Holy Office, namely the Inquisition, and the date of 1676 . . .
>
> Standing before that barbarous instrument, which sought to torture virtually every nerve in the victim's body, the spectator is afforded a glimpse into the incredible savagery with which the Spanish Inquisition sought to eradicate all so-called heretics, and impose Catholic faith upon Moors and Jews. (101–2)

Still another appropriate item for one of the larger rooms in the Inquisition Museum would be a copy of a picture by Picart, currently in the British Museum, titled *The Tortures of the Inquisition*. O'Brien observes that it daily attracts many visitors:

> In one corner of the dungeon there sits on the floor a handcuffed prisoner near a blazing fire. A torturer is holding a burning fagot close to his bare feet, causing him to shriek with pain. Another prisoner lies stretched out on a cot,

while his torturers are pouring a stream of water into his opened mouth. A third victim is suspended high in the air, and is about to be dropped within inches of the floor. The sudden jolt will almost pull his arms, tied together at his back, from their sockets. (112)

On special occasions, Good Friday, perhaps, or Easter Sunday, there might be staged in the vicinity of this Memorial—along the Mall—a reenactment of one of the religious parades so typical of thirteenth-century Europe: "A motley group of people, preceded by a trumpeter, each carrying a part of the partially decomposed body of one or more burned heretics."(73). Such parades doubtless warned the faithful of what could happen to them if they entertained thoughts that could be considered heretical.

In the year 1231, when the Inquisition was established, Europe was essentially a Catholic theocracy. Faith and nationality were so fused as to have become one. The rulers of the many entities of the Holy Roman Empire of the German States carried out church decrees, required all their subjects to pledge allegiance to the Pope, and used their police, and military forces to arrest, and torture suspected heretics. The idea of separation of church and state, so forcefully prescribed in our Constitution, is a very recent concept. In the Middle Ages, such a thing was unheard of.

Because of this, the Inquisition became the most feared judicial system the West has ever seen. Inquisitors strove to stamp out heresy by means of tortures that ranged from flogging to burning at the stake. Even convicted heretics who repented were usually condemned to life in solitary confinement on a diet of "the bread of sorrow, and the water of tribulation". Sometimes when a suspected heretic had died under torture, and been buried, if someone else who had known him revealed under torture evidence of the dead man's guilt, the Inquisition might order his remains exhumed, cursed, and burned to ashes.

In outward form, the Holy Inquisition consisted of a number of ecclesiastical courts, established in general principle by the Pope and in practice by the diocesan bishops, for the purpose of stamping out heresy. There were many objects of their zeal. Jews and Muslims who refused to convert to Christianity made up a large group. Another consisted of Cathari, religious fanatics who believed that all sexual relations between men, and women should be avoided, and suicide was not only lawful, but commendable. Obviously, if such a creed were allowed to spread, it could result in the extinction of the human race. The Inquisition devoted fanatical attention to witches, people thought to have been possessed by the devil and, hence, become enemies of Christ's church on earth. And finally, after Luther's confrontation with his accusers at the Diet of Worms, Europe's Protestants became the favored objects of the wrath of the Inquisition.

The courts operated by the rules of a standard procedure. A person accused of heresy was first interrogated about his beliefs. If he persisted in denying his heresy, he was tortured until he admitted it. His confession was then read to the Inquisitor, who considered a confession sufficient evidence of guilt to pronounce a sentence. No other evidence was needed. The heretic was then sentenced to life in prison if he repented, and to death at the stake if he didn't.

This vile conviction of the Holy Inquisition—that a confession extracted under torture was sufficient evidence of guilt—has persisted into our own times. The special political courts of Hitler and Stalin operated under the same infamous principle, as they tortured, then sentenced to death thousands of suspected enemies of the Third Reich, and the USSR, respectively.

The Holy Inquisition itself did not carry out the public punishments demanded by their courts—this service was performed by the secular authorities. After the Second Lateran Council in 1139, the secular princes were obliged to assist in the prosecution of heresy, on pain of excommunication. Since a person who had been excommunicated for a period of a year became himself a heretic, subject to arrest, torture, and death, all the princes of the Holy Roman Empire of the German Nations cooperated with the Inquisition, and provided whatever was required—police, dungeons, implements of torture, experienced torturers and executioners, sites for the public burnings, and space in the graveyards.

With the basic responsibilities established, Pope Gregory IX in February 1231 issued his *Excommunicamus,* which set up the first courts to hear cases of heresy, and mete out punishment. Inquisitors were usually chosen from the Dominican Order, well known for its zeal in denouncing heresy, and they soon became infamous for their indifference to the physical suffering of their victims. They were always present during the torture proceedings so they could take down a confession if one came out amid the shrieks of agony. For six hundred years, this repellent institution flourished in Europe, a symbol of pitiless cruelty, intellectual terrororism, and religious intolerance.

This unique body of law, established by the Papacy, was beyond secular jurisdiction of any kind. The courts of the Inquisition were a law unto themselves, and there was no appeal from their judgments. Perhaps the most remarkable aspect of their work, the element that set these courts off from all others known to history, was that the accused was on trial, not for something he had done, but for something that he may have thought; not for injuring someone or stealing something, but for harboring certain beliefs, doubts, and questions that were known only to himself, and to God. His Inquisitor might take note of his actions, but only as they confirmed or denied assertions made during his examination. He was on trial for his thinking, his beliefs, before a court interested only in thought control, and anything else he had done, whether good or bad, was outside the jurisdiction of these courts.

Perhaps most repulsive of all, was the belief of the Inquisitors that truth could be obtained from the accused only under the influence of unbearable pain. A person could not confess to heresy to avoid torture, because he might not be speaking the truth. He could be believed only when his confession was punctuated by shrieks of agony during the long hours he spent on the rack, while his arms and legs were being slowly drawn out of their sockets.

Torture, however, was only one of the many customs, rules, and procedures that set off the courts of the Inquisition from those of our own day. Many of the legal safeguards in our Constitution and the Bill of Rights were adopted by Congress in direct response to the barbarous practices of the Holy Inquisition.

For example, an Inquisitor could bring suit against any person accused of heresy, even if he were the object only of gossip, and rumor, and have him arrested and held in prison for interrogation as long as he thought necessary. The Inquisitor considered himself not only a judge, but also a church dignitary, a kind of father confessor deeply anxious to save contaminated souls from the eternal torments of hell, so vividly rendered in Dante's *Inferno*. Since his purpose was divine, he was able to ignore the earthly philosophical concept that the end does not justify the means. His sacred duty to save the soul of the suspected heretic permitted any means of obtaining information, and confession, including the most refined techniques of physical torture. One of the most infamous of the early Inquisitors, Jean Galand of Carcassonne, had suspected heretics tortured on the rack so savagely that later they could not use their arms or legs, and became totally helpless. Not surprisingly, many victims died in agony in the midst of their interrogation. Another famous torturer of the late fifteenth century, the Dominican Tomás de Torquemada, Grand Inquisitor of Castile, presided over the torture and death by public burning of over two thousand heretics, and, in so doing, earned immortality as a symbol of pitiless human cruelty.

Upon being arrested, and taken to the Inquisition interrogation chamber for examination, the accused was required to take an oath to answer truthfully all questions put to him, and reveal the names of all possible heretics known to him. If he refused to take the oath, the Inquisitor assumed that he was a heretic, and punishment followed on. He was never shown a copy of the charges against him, and was required to answer questions without knowing the drift of the hearing. Hence, nearly anything he said might be used against him. In short, he was required to testify against himself, a vicious judicial practice that is specifically prohibited by the Fifth Amendment to the U.S. Constitution. During the 1950s, this fundamental human right was ignored by the House Un-American Activities Committee, and the Senate Subcommittee on Government Operations chaired by Sen. Joe McCarthy of Wisconsin. Witnesses before these committees were called on to name other people they had seen at Communist party gatherings. If they cooperated, they were considered traitors by many. If they refused to cooperate, citing the Fifth Amendment, they were held to be in contempt of Congress, and sent to prison. And when they got out, they were often blacklisted. This period of "McCarthyism", with its concomitant display of Congressional contempt for human rights, remains one of the darker chapters in American history.

Before the Inquisition, a person accused of heresy was presumed guilty unless he could prove his innocence, not an easy thing to do in the world of thought control. All the rules of procedure favored the Inquisitor. Testimony against the accused was accepted from every kind of person in the community, including known thieves, murderers, blackmailers, whores, pimps, the excommunicated, heretics, mortal enemies or the accused, and people who were demonstrably insane.

Not only could the Inquisitor accept testimony from anyone to whom he chose to listen; he was further empowered to torture witnesses against the accused if he thought it necessary. Thus the Inquisitors were able to control the testimony submitted in their courts.

Both Stalin and Hitler grasped the efficacy of this concept, and made liberal use of it in the proceedings of their notorious political courts.

The accused was never told the names of his accusers, and could not question them face to face. Nor could his lawyer question them. He had no lawyer. More than most people, lawyers feared the consequences of thwarting the will of the Holy Inquisition. Nor could witnesses be found to testify in favor of the accused. Anyone who displayed sympathy for an accused heretic left himself open to suspicion of being a heretic himself, subject to arrest, torture, and burning at the stake.

Our modern rules regarding the admissibility of evidence into a judicial procedure probably were influenced by the outrages of the Inquisition. Sometimes depositions were planted in the minds of naive persons and their testimony then accepted by the court. Any kind of evidence was admissible—gossip, hearsay, inferences, remembered dreams, even statements made by demented persons.

Our modern conviction, that it is preferable for any number of criminals to escape punishment by one means or another rather than acquiesce in the punishment of one innocent person is exactly the opposite of the attitude of the Inquisitors. They held that the execution of a hundred innocent persons was preferable to the escape of one heretic.

Another modern response to the heinous practices of the Holy Inquisition was the concept of trial by jury, an effort to separate the process of determining guilt or innocence from that of passing sentence, since under Inquisition procedures the Inquisitor performed both functions.

He also performed the function of the prosecuting attorney. There was no wrangling among lawyers in the courts of the Inquisition, and all doubts were resolved "in favor of the faith".

Inquisitorial judgments frequently were influenced by the fact that the Inquisition could confiscate the property of a condemned heretic, a legal process that caused severe economic distress to innocent family members and heirs of the victim. The proceeds of the sale of such property were divided among the Inquisitors, church officials, and the public treasury. The argument was that the crime of heresy was a crime of treason against the church-state, punishable by imprisonment or death, and of forfeiture of property. A person was not even safe after he was dead. If the Inquisitors learned, by torturing his relatives and friends, that the dead man had been secretly a heretic, he could be declared contumacious, his bones dug up, and burned outside the graveyard, and the property he had left to his heirs, perhaps years earlier, confiscated. O'Brien notes that "of the 656 cases tried by Bernard Gui, no less than 88 were posthumous." (74)

The Inquisitors had other sources of income. They often extorted money from people threatened with a charge of heresy, who were glad to pay up to avoid interrogation. And after a heretic had been found guilty, a

sum of money placed by his relatives in the right hands might change the sentence from death by fire at the stake to life imprisonment. At a secular trial held in the Republic of Florence in 1346, a Franciscan friar, Alvarus Pelagius, testified that his fellow friars who were Inquisitors regularly pocketed money from their victims.

In fact, it seems clear that there was a direct relationship between the zeal for persecution of heretics, and the profits to be obtained thereby. The heretics themselves were forced to provide the financial means for their own destruction, just as the Jews in Hitler's time were first fined, then deprived of property and, later, sent to Auschwitz, where their gold teeth were removed after they died. The profits were deposited in the SS bank accounts in Berlin.

To assist the Inquisitors in their difficult duties, all judicial proceedings were held in secret. The initial examination, the taking of testimony from witnesses, and the acts of torture were hidden from public view. The sentence, however, was read in public and, if execution was pronounced, the victim was deprived of his life in a public ceremony known as the *auto-da-fé* (Act of Faith), in which scores of heretics might be simultaneously burned to death in the town square before a large and enthusiastic audience of true believers.

Inquisition proceedings were not noted for their speed. O'Brien mentions one victim, Guillem Carrec by name, who "was confined in prison for nearly thirty years before he was willing to confess before the Inquisition at Carcassonne in 1321." (43) In 1299, a certain Guillem Salavert made a confession that the Inquisitors for some reason found unsatisfactory. He was confined in prison for seven years, made another inadequate confession, then, after three more years, was let go with the mild penance of having to wear crosses (43). In Italy, the famous astronomer Giordano Bruno was interrogated, and tortured for six years before being publicly burned at the stake in January, 1600.*

Today our Constitution protects us from such savagery with its requirement that any person accused of a crime is entitled to a "speedy, public trial". Our laws also prohibit "cruel and unusual punishment", referring back, in

*His heresy consisted of persisting in the belief that all the stars in the sky are really suns, like our own. They are not as bright as our sun because they are very far away. The Inquisition felt that since the Bible speaks of only one sun, Bruno's theory was heretical. The scientist never renounced his findings, as did his colleague Galileo Gallilei.

all probability, to the barbaric means of public execution cherished by the Holy Inquisition. Among these were burning their victims alive at the stake, boiling them in oil, roasting them slowly over an open spit, and breaking their bones on the wheel.

But doubtless the most repugnant aspect of the Holy Inquisition was their employment of torture to extract confessions. The practice was sanctioned by the Papal bull *Ad extirpanda* of Pope Innocent IV (May 15, 1252), requiring all judicial officers to employ torture to force heretics to confess (14). Use of torture began in Italy, and soon spread to all other countries of Europe.

The most famous implement of torture favored by the Inquisition was the rack. On this triangular framework the prisoner was tied so that he could not move. His arms were stretched out horizontally and his feet vertically. To hands and feet were attached ropes that ran over pulleys to a sprocket windlass. As the windlass was turned, drawing the arms outward, and the feet downward, tremendous pressure was applied to the elbow and knee joints resulting in pain so severe that the victim usually fainted over and over during his ordeal.

The *strappado,* or vertical rack, was equally painful. The hands of the prisoner were tied behind his back, and he was required to stand on a table. A taut rope ran from his hands to the ceiling. Another rope around his chest was then used to raise him off the table toward the ceiling. The table was removed, and the chest rope released, allowing him to fall toward the floor. But before his feet hit the floor, his arms were jerked backward over his head, tearing the cartilage of his armpits. After he was allowed to swing awhile in this "butterfly" position, the process was repeated.*

Sometimes it was hinted by an Inquisitor to the torturers that it might be just as well if a certain prisoner died under interrogation. In this case, two methods were popular because they did not leave telltale scars on the victim's body. One was the technique of internal water pressure. The victim was tied firmly to his rack, a funnel was thrust into his mouth, and water was forced down his throat under pressure. His stomach gradually stretched

---

*This *strappado* technique was also favored by the North Vietnamese army torturers during the Vietnam War. An American prisoner would sit on the floor, and a chain would be fastened over his thighs. Again, his hands were tied behind his back and a rope from his hands over his head and forward of his body to a windlass. As the windlass was turned, his hands were pulled up in back until they reached over his head. Soon his arms would be twisted out of their sockets, and the prisoner would faint from the pain.

and stretched until it finally burst, whereupon the victim quickly expired in paroxysms of pain. The other method was quicker but more painful. The victim was tied naked on the rack face down. His legs were then spread apart, and a red-hot poker thrust up his rectum. After a few horrendous shrieks of pain, the victim was dead.*

The intense suffering of so many tens of thousands of people at the hands of the Holy Inquisition might be highlighted by means of somewhat detailed descriptions of what happened to a few prominent individuals of the period—for instance, Joan of Arc, Savonarola, Galileo, and Urban Grandier.

Probably the most famous victim of the Inquisition was Joan of Arc (1412–31), also well known as the Maid of Orléans. At the age of thirteen, she first became aware of voices giving her counsel, and advice, a clear suggestion of approaching schizophrenia. She came to believe that her voices emanated from certain saints and from God, and thus she was unable to resist their insistence that she go to Orléans, which had been surrounded by the English in October 1428, and lead French military units in the relief of the city. She had an audience with the future King Charles VII, who had not, at the time, been officially crowned. She told him she would raise the siege of Orléans, and enable him to receive his proper consecration in Reims Cathedral the following summer. The King believed her and sent her forth with an armed escort. Dressed in male clothing, and carrying a sword discovered in a church with help from her voices, the Maid led French forces against elements of the English army at Orléans, drove them away, and entered the city on April 30, 1429. In subsequent fighting she was wounded by an arrow in her breast, but she survived, and on July 17, 1429, she witnessed, as the voices had promised her, the solemn coronation of Charles VII as King of France in Rheims Cathedral.

After this high point of her young life (she was seventeen) her fortunes turned downward. In a military operation against the Burgundians, who were allied with the English, she was captured by forces of John of Luxemburg, who sold her to the English for a sum equivalent to about $110,000 in modern currency (149). The English were determined to put an end to her but couldn't kill her themselves simply because she was their prisoner. That wouldn't look good. So they decided to have her tried as a heretic by the French Inquisition.

*Edward II of England was executed in this manner.

219

This was arranged with the cooperation of the bishop of Beauvais, Pierre Cauchon, an unscrupulous prelate under the control of the Burgundians. During her trial at Rouen in 1431, some seventy charges were drawn up against her. These were based chiefly on the claim that her actions and beliefs were blasphemous: "She claimed the authority of divine revelation for her statements; she endorsed her letters with the names of Jesus and Mary; she prophesied the future; she immodestly wore men's clothing; and, she dared to claim that her saints spoke in French rather than in English." (150)

The charge that probably mattered most to the ecclesiastical authorities was that she spoke directly to God without the need of going through the factotums of the Catholic Church. As Bernard Shaw noted in his preface to *Saint Joan,* this talent made her, in principle, the first Protestant and if the possibility of personal spiritual intimacy with God came to be widely accepted by the masses, the basic need for the hierarchy of the Catholic Church would be revealed as nonexistent.

Under threat of torture she signed a confession of heresy, but later she repudiated it. On May 29, 1431, she was condemned as a lapsed heretic by the Inquisition, and sentenced to be burned at the stake. This sentence was carried out the next day in the square of the Old Market in Rouen, after which her ashes were thrown into the Seine.

Girolamo Savonarola (1452–98), a Dominican prophet and orator of exceptional gifts, Prior of San Marco in Florence from 1490 to his death, a post he obtained through the influence of the city's ruler, Lorenzo de' Medici, also attracted attention as a Protestant in principle. Savonarola preached fiery sermons to ever-larger audiences in the Duomo on the corruption of the Medici regime, and predicted that a divine chastisement would fall on the people of Florence for their gross and myriad sins. After the death of Lorenzo, Savonarola announced that Jesus Christ was King of Florence and holy protector of the city. As O'Brien observes, "the moral life of its citizens was regenerated. Many persons brought articles of luxury, ornaments, dice, playing cards, the writings of pagans, and lewd pictures of beautiful women to the monastery of San Marco where they were publicly burned." (161) Even Sandro Botticelli, convinced of the magnitude of his sins, burned those of his paintings still in his possession—not the only example in history of the defilement of art by theological fanaticism.

In Rome, Pope Alexander VI, learning of Savonarola's sermons attacking his family—the Borgias—became the mortal enemy of the prophet,

and set about to destroy him. Rodrigo Borgia, father of the infamous siblings Cesare and Lucrezia, had bought the votes of fourteen cardinals on August 10, 1492, and the next day was proclaimed Pope. Since Pope Alexander VI was the Pope denounced by Savonarola as the most immoral prelate ever to sit on the throne of Saint Peter, the struggle between Pope and prophet was probably inevitable. As O'Brien describes the situation:

"There is no doubt that the world has never seen a more total disregard of all law, human and divine, than that displayed by both the Church, and the laity during the pontificates of Sixtus IV, Innocent VIII, and Alexander VI." (165) But Savonarola's decision to challenge so formidable a man as Pope Alexander VI was ill-advised. In March of 1497, he addressed a letter to all the princes of the Holy Roman Empire calling on them to convene a council for the reform of the Catholic Church, which had become diseased under the reign of Alexander VI.

Copies of Savonarola's letter fell into the hands of the Pope's agents, and on May 12, 1497, Alexander VI excommunicated the prophet and threatened to place all of Florence under interdiction. Frightened by this threat, the Florentine City Council called on Savonarola to cease his preaching in the Duomo. He refused, and in April 1498, along with two of his closest disciples, Domenico Buonvicini, and Silvestro Maruffi, Savonarola was arrested by the Inquisition, confined to prison, and brutally tortured. He and his two brethren were subjected to the niceties of the *strappado* over and over, until they were incoherent with pain, and could not be questioned. Finally, Savonarola signed a confession of heresy but after a few days of rest he repudiated it, saying:

I signed because I was afraid of being tortured anew. I revoke my confession entirely. If I am to die, I will die for the truth. The truth is that God did speak through me to the people of Florence. I speak the truth now. I deny all your accusations. The Church of God will be purified. Florence too, after the scourging, will be purified and will prosper. (179)

In this moving statement of principle, Savonarola, like the Maid of Orléans before him, looked forward to the Protestant Reformation and to the subsequent Counter Reformation of the Catholic Church. His conviction that God could speak directly to any of his children and that anyone could speak directly to God if he possessed faith became the accepted doctrine of Christianity in modern times. The Pope ceased to be God's exclusive Vicar on Earth.

221

Pope Alexander VI had his moment of satisfying revenge, however. At dawn on May 23, 1498, Savonarola and his two disciples were stripped of their white Dominican robes, and other priestly vestments. They were then taken to the Piazza della Signoria, where a large crowd waited to witness the spectacle. The three Dominicans were hanged first, one at a time; then their dead bodies were thoroughly burned, and their ashes thrown into the Arno River to prevent the salvaging of relics.

In his Florentine studio, Botticelli permitted himself one more painting—*The Nativity,* of 1500. Above the scene of the adoration of the baby Jesus by Mary and Joseph are numerous angels in attitudes of joy while, below, angels welcome into heaven Savonarola and the two priests martyred with him. In the last ten years of his life, Botticelli painted nothing more.

A different kind of heretic was the Italian astronomer and mathematician Galileo Galilei (1564–1642). He was the son of the musician Vincenzo Gallilei, who had been a member of the Florentine Camerata and, with Monteverdi and others, one of the founders of the art genre of the opera in the early years of the seventeenth century. Galileo's heresy was scientific rather than theological, and he was in no sense a Protestant in principle. Nevertheless, his discoveries in astronomy, by means of the newly invented telescope, led him to a direct confrontation with the Italian Inquisition in Rome.

Up until a short time before Galileo's birth, the Earth had been considered the center of the universe, in the geocentric system devised by Aristotle, and Ptolemy. But in 1543 Nicolaus Copernicus advanced a heliocentric theory, in which the sun became the center of things and the Earth and other planets revolved around it in specific orbits. It was the search for evidence to prove the Copernican theory that dominated Galileo's thinking in all his scientific studies.

His publications defending heliocentricity by means of observations made through his telescope soon caught the attention of the Church. For a long time previously Church prelates had been challenging Copernicus by finding in the Bible apparent contradictions to his system. For instance, why did Joshua ask the sun to "stand still" if it never moved anyway? (Josh. 10:12–13). And the sun must be in motion because Ecclesiastes observes that "the sun rises and the sun goes down: then it presses on to the place where it rises" (Eccles. 1:5). Then, too, the idea that the Earth moves is plainly contradicted by the statement that God "fixed the Earth upon its foundations, not to be moved forever" (Ps. 103:5). Now, a modern scientist seemed to be challenging Holy Writ, and what might the consequences be? Could Galileo bring down the whole edifice of the Catholic Church, considered so carefully over a period of fifteen centuries? The question was taken very seriously in Rome. Some of the highest-ranking prelates in the Roman Catholic Church considered that Galileo was speaking blasphemy, and must be punished accordingly.

There had been a few arguments on the side of Copernicus over the years. Saint Augustine had declared that "the Bible was not intended to teach science, and consequently its authority should not be invoked in scientific disputes." (189) Also, many church fathers did not think the heliocentric system amounted to revealed truth. In his "Letter to the Grand Duchess Christina," Galileo answered his critics by maintaining that his faith in nature went side by side with his faith in God: "I think in the first place . . . that it is very pious to say, and prudent to affirm that the Holy Bible can never speak untruth—whenever its true meaning is understood. But I believe nobody will deny that it is often very abstruse, and may say things that are quite different from what its bare words signify." (190)

Nevertheless, he resumed his research, and continued publishing the results which, inexorably, tended to support heliocentricity. On September 23, 1632, Pope Urban VIII ordered Galileo to come from Florence to Rome to answer charges of heresy brought against him by the Holy Inquisition. After being shown some of the instruments of torture that might be used on him, he repudiated all his beliefs, and threw himself on the mercy of the court. He was sentenced to life imprisonment, but not in a dungeon. He was confined to his home in Florence, under the watchful eyes of the priestly police. He died on January 8, 1642, a broken man.

Another victim who was broken in body but not in spirit was the Jesuit priest Urban Grandier (1590–1634), Parson of Saint-Pierre du Marché in the town of Loudun, near Poitiers, in western France. Scion of a good family, Grandier was an outstanding student in the Jesuit college at Bordeaux, where he studied for ten years, and achieved the rank of canon. A handsome, learned, and elegant young man for whom the future looked bright, he accepted his appointment at Sainte Pierre in Loudun in 1617 and soon became a respected member of the community, at least for a time.

Shortly after his arrival in Loudun, a small Ursuline convent was established—in 1626—with some seventeen nuns under the direction of their Prioress, a young woman of twenty-five, of good family (as were all the nuns), named Sister Jeanne des Agnes. The nuns established in Loudun a private school for young ladies of quality, whom they taught catechism, good French, and courtly manners.

The Prioress, whose body was somewhat deformed, began to hear tales about Grandier that surprised her, and aroused her sexually. For it appears that young Father Grandier was something of a rake, who seduced several of his parishioners, including Philippe Tricant, daughter of the Public Prosecutor of Loudun. She became pregnant by Grandier, and had to be quickly (and inconveniently) married to someone who was willing to accept paternity of the child. For this Grandier earned the fierce enmity of the Public Prosecutor and managed to alienate as well a number of other prominent people through his arrogance and contempt for the people of his parish.

Somehow Sister Jeanne des Agnes became enamored of Grandier, from a distance. (They never met. He saw her for the first and last time as he was being carried to the town square to be burned at the stake.) When the spiritual head of the convent, Canon Moussaut, died, Sister Jeanne sent a letter to Grandier inviting him to become their director, and confessor. Grandier had no time for this sort of thing, however, and sent a polite letter of refusal.

The Prioress was deeply disappointed, as were the Sisters, and soon an extraordinary response to Grandier's indifference to their need for him began to manifest itself. They all became convinced that they were possessed by devils and that Grandier himself had sent them to ravish their bodies in obscene rituals to which they were forced to submit even in public. The psychology of this sexual hysteria is convincingly described in Aldous Huxley's book *The Devils of Loudun.*

About the same time, a political situation developed that also concerned Grandier. Cardinal Richelieu had persuade King Louis XIV to order the destruction of all fortress-castles in France so they could not be occupied by Huguenots in case of a general Protestant revolt. One result of this policy was an order for the destruction of the castle in Loudun, to which the Mayor, Jean d'Armagnac, with the moral and intellectual support of Father Grandier, vigorously objected.

Richelieu sent a personal emissary, Baron de Laubardemont, to the town with full powers to carry out the order. Upon sizing up the situation, the Baron concluded that if he could destroy the spiritual, and intellectual source of the town's defiance—Grandier—perhaps he could then bully the Mayor into accepting the King's edict.

224

In groping about for a way to deal with the Parson, Laubardemont heard about the strange antics of the Ursuline nuns and the efforts of some church prelates to exorcise the devils by giving the girls enemas. The fact that the nuns were convinced it was Grandier—through his devils—who was having sex with them every night struck Laubardemont as useful. Why not have Grandier arrested, and charged with sorcery? And tortured until he confessed? And then burned at the stake for his crimes against the Ursuline convent?

No sooner thought than done. Father Urban Grandier was arrested in 1634 on a charge of sorcery, and hustled off to a dark, airless prison cell where he was forced to sleep on a straw mat on the floor. The parsonage was searched, and among his books and papers evidence of sorcery was discovered by Laubardemont's police agents. And after further evidence was obtained from the nuns, who vomited up certain incriminating objects obviously fashioned by the devils inside them, Grandier was tried, found guilty, and sentenced to be burned to death in the public square on August 18, 1634. The death sentence included the proviso that Grandier must submit to the Question, both ordinary and extraordinary, during which time his confession would be recorded.

This "Question"—a euphemism for some of the cruelest tortures ever invented by the human imagination—was usually not to be avoided by prior confession to a crime, because the accused might be confessing to avoid torture. Only a confession shrieked in the grip of unspeakable torment was considered reliable. Still, after Grandier had been sentenced, Baron de Laubardemont offered to let him out of the torture if he would confess to sorcery. Why not? He was going to be burned anyway, but he could at least be spared the agony of the Question. Grandier replied that he was willing to confess to his sexual sins, but he was not a sorcerer, and couldn't, in all conscience, confess to such a thing. After he was taken back to his cell, Aldous Huxley imagines what happened next:

> The parson lay down again—but not to sleep. He had the will to heroism; but his body was in a panic. The heart throbbed uncontrollably. Shuddering with the mindless fears of the nervous system, his muscles were made yet tenser by his conscious effort to overcome that purely physical terror. He tried to pray; but "God" was a word without meaning, "Christ" and "Mary" were empty names. He could think only of the approaching ignominy, of death in unspeakable pain, of the monstrous injustice of which he was the victim . . . Gritting his teeth, he pitted his will against their spite. But the blood was still

banging in his ears, and as he turned uneasily on the straw, he realized that his body was bathed in a profuse sweat. (199–201)

The next day he was taken to the prison torture chamber and prepared for the administration of the Question. His hair, beard, and mustache were shaved. He was allowed a few minutes to pray and seemed to be equating his impending torment with his sexual crimes against the young women of Loudun. Then he was bound,

stretched out on the floor with his legs, from the knees to the feet, enclosed between four oaken boards, of which the outer pair were fixed, while the two inner ones were movable. By driving wedges into the space separating the two movable boards, it was possible to crush the victim's legs against the fixed framework of the machine. The difference between ordinary and extraordinary torture was measured by the number of progressively thicker wedges hammered home. Because it was invariably (though not immediately) fatal, the Question extraordinary was administered only to condemned criminals, who were to be executed without delay. . . . When the friars had finished their sprinkling (of holy water), and their muttering (of exorcisms over the wedges, and mallets), the executioner stepped forward, raised his ponderous mallet and, like a man splitting a knotty piece of timber, brought it down with all his force. There was an uncontrollable shriek of pain. Father Lactance bent over the victim, and asked in Latin if he would confess. But Grandier only shook his head.

The first wedge was driven home between the knees. Then another was inserted at the level of the feet, and when that had been hammered to the head, the thin end of a third and heavier wedge was tapped into position immediately below the first. There was the thud of the mallet, the shriek of pain—then silence . . . At the second stroke on the fourth wedge there was a loud cracking sound. Several bones of the feet and ankles had broken. For a moment, the parson fainted away. (211)

After a short respite during which the parson was revived, he was again offered the opportunity to confess. He said he was willing to confess to his sins of the flesh, but since he was not a sorcerer or a magician, nor had he ever had commerce with devils, he could not give them the confession they wished to hear.

A sixth wedge was hammered home, then a seventh, then an eighth. From ordinary, the Question had reached the traditional limits of the extraordinary. The bones of the knees, the shins, the ankles, the feet—all were shattered.

226

Their splinters projected through the mangled flesh, and, along with the blood, there was an ooze of marrow. But still, the friars could extort no admission of guilt—only the screaming and, in the intervals the whispered name of God. (212–13)

Baron de Laubardemont was disappointed that he was unable to obtain a confession from Grandier, but perhaps the wily culprit might confess at the last moment when, bound to a stake in the public square of Loudun, the flames from the burning kindling wood stacked around him began to sear his flesh. This was considered the ultimate pain of all and might achieve what the pain of the wedges had failed to do. Grandier was dressed in a shirt impregnated with sulphur and allowed to sit on a small iron seat attached to the large post, since he couldn't stand on his shattered feet. After he was securely bound to the post, the fire was started in the kindling wood around him. A large audience, sitting on a temporary grandstand, observed with pleasure the agony of Father Grandier as he was slowly burned to death.

But no confession. The executioner scattered four shovelfuls of ashes, one toward each of the four cardinal points of the compass, and that was that.

How many people died during the six centuries of the Holy Inquisition, as did Father Grandier on a summer's day in 1654? Records are scattered, but some figures are available. According to William H. Maehl in his book, *Germany in Western Civilization,* during the sixteenth and seventeenth centuries over one hundred thousand victims—some of them children—who had been accused of such crimes as inflicting a plague, famine, hailstorm, or flood on a community, hexing an army, striking livestock dead, causing cows to give no milk, and bear no calves, inducing sterility in women, administering adulterous love potions, or cursing with the "evil eye" were tortured into confessing their crimes, then burned to death at the stake.

In 1590 the Germans burned 1,500 witches. Between 1615 and 1635 some 5,000 were burned at Strassburg. In Würzburg 900 were sent to the stake between 1623 and 1631. In 1629 at Mittenberg 178 out of a population of 3,000 were burned. In Protestant Silesia at Zuckmantel, 152 were destroyed as late as 1651. In his time, the distinguished jurist, and professor of law at Leipzig, Benedikt Carpzov (1595–1666), in his capacity as supreme court judge at Leipzig, sentenced 20,000 witches and sorcerers to death. These figures diminished by 1700, but it was not until 1783 that the last bonfire was lit in Switzerland. (203)

Still, information on the total number of victims burned to death by the Holy Inquisition is hard to find. The few surviving records, written in Latin, and sequestered in monasteries, private libraries, and the Vatican, are not intended for prying eyes. It may be said, however, that between 1231 and 1834, at least a million victims were burned as heretics, and another million as witches, making the Holy Inquisition the perpetrator of a holocaust unrivalled in Western history for the cruelty with which it tortured, condemned, and burned to death its pitiful victims.

In addition to the Holocaust Monument in Washington and nearby (possibly) Monument to the Holy Inquisition, there might also be erected, in the general vicinity, a suitable monument to the memory of victims of the first official government effort at genocide in the twentieth century—the campaign by the Turkish Army in 1915 to exterminate the Armenian minority living in their country. In view of the way they did it—by marching tens of thousands of Armenian men, women, and children into the Syrian desert to die of thirst—the Monument might consist of a very simple large brick building with one surprising characteristic: no windows anywhere and only two doors, one in front, one in back. Upon entering the Memorial, the visitor would be confronted by a vast expanse of sand bathed in sunlight. Lines of stakes in the sand would lead to various "camps" at which large photographs on easels would depict the sufferings of the Armenian people at the hands of the Turks. The pictures would show Armenian girls being raped, hacked with knives, and tattooed before being sold as slaves. The men would appear naked in groups, burned, and shot to death. The children would be seen screaming in fear for their lost parents. Overhead would be a large banner on which would be printed in big black letters Hitler's famous words from a speech of August 22, 1939:

AFTER ALL, WHO SPEAKS TODAY OF THE ANNIHILATION OF THE ARMENIANS? THE WORLD BELIEVES IN SUCCESS ONLY.
                                                                    —Adolf Hitler

The visitor would be marched smartly along from "camp" to "camp" by Museum security guards wearing World War I Turkish Army uniforms and wielding rifles with fixed bayonets. The temperature inside the building would gradually rise during a leisurely tour to 125 degrees Fahrenheit.

A description of the ordeal of the Armenian people in 1915 would be spoken over the public address system in Turkish, punctuated now and then by short summaries in English. During his passage from "camp" to "camp", the visitor would, from time to time, come upon a small kiosk manned by smiling Turkish soldiers where he could purchase a cubic centimeter of water in a small plastic bag for ten dollars in cash, only one to a customer.

What would be the thoughts of a person confronted by such an engrossing exhibition? Would he wonder why the Turks hate the Armenians so? What had the Armenians done to the Turks? Nothing. But in their genes, many Turks carried hatred of Christians that resulted from the terror they experienced during a very violent series of events in their history: the Crusades. Launched in 1095 by Pope Urban II at the Council of Clermont, the Crusaders, in their zeal to free the Holy Land from the grip of the Infidel, for three hundred years committed countless atrocities against men, women, and children of the Muslim faith. The Turks retaliated with massive invasions of Europe that were finally stopped in the summer of 1683, with the raising of the siege of Vienna. Even today the Turks still fear the Christians, and with reason, as evidenced by the recent "ethnic cleansing" in Bosnia, site of the Turkish presence in Europe, as directed by the Orthodox Catholic Church of Serbia.

Does knowledge of the atrocities of history prevent future atrocities? Do we really believe that a Memorial to human savagery will help us make sure that "such a thing will never happen again"? The Germans knew all about the campaign of their Turkish allies of World War I to exterminate the Armenian minority in their country. There were many Germans in Turkey at the time, including the Commander-in-Chief of the Turkish Army, General Limon von Sanders, victor ever the British at the battle of Gallipoli. The German ambassador lodged protests with Enver Pasha, the Minister of War, but nothing came of it. Still, they knew about it, and their children in the Germany of the thirties knew about it, as Hitler's speech affirms. But this knowledge of the Armenian holocaust had no effect whatever on the course of the Final Solution. The idea that mere knowledge of the savage events of history such as the Crusades, the military campaigns of Genghis Khan, and Tamerlane, the hellish actions of the Holy Inquisition, or the vicious murders of thousands of their countrymen by Pol Pot, and Mao-tze Tung could prevent or even slow present-day violence against helpless minorities in any country in the world appears to be idealistic nonsense. Violence is an inherited characteristic of the human race, and it will survive until the demise of the human race.

In the preface to his book *Armenia: The Case for a Forgotten Genocide,* Dickran H. Boyajian notes that there have been many invasions in history that created havoc, horror, destruction, and desecration in the invaded lands, but "until the second decade of the twentieth century, one cannot find in any history the record of a plan comparable in savagery to the one set in motion by the Turks beginning on April 24, 1915. The word *genocide*—coined later—unquestionably applies to the Armenian massacres, for it was the murder of their race." (viii)

The "Young Turk" dictatorship that controlled the remnants of the Ottoman Empire in 1915 consisted of Enver Pasha, Minister of War; Talaat Bey, Minister of the Interior; and Djemal Pasha, for Marine. Their concern was that the Armenian Christian minority that had lived in Turkey for many centuries might prove troublesome if Turkey's allies Germany, Austria, and Bulgaria lost the war then being fought against England, France, and Russia. The historic homeland of the Armenian people lay across southern Russia, and northeast Turkey. Would the Armenians in Turkey, in case of a Russian victory, side with Christian Russians and attempt to annex their Turkish homeland to Russia? To prevent this eventuality, the three ministers agreed on a policy of extermination of two million Armenians living within Turkey's borders, and instructions were issued to the Army to carry out the policy.

Turkish persecution of the Armenians was nothing new, of course. In April 1909, thirty thousand Armenians in the city of Adana, and in villages of northern Syria were massacred in the cruelest possible ways, by shooting, by knife, and scimitar, by stones, by bastinade, by hanging, and by fire. Women were raped, children slaughtered, and entire villages wiped out all in response to the ambition of the Young Turks to "Turkify" the country, through attacks on minorities. One French witness to the savagery at Adana, George Brezol, recalled Victor Hugo's verse in *L'Enfant Grec*: " . . . all is in ruins, and mournful/ The Turks have passed by this place . . . ." (49)

The Turkish plan for the extermination of the Armenians was simplicity itself. They had no Zyklon-B, no gas chambers, and no cremation ovens. But they controlled the nearby Syrian desert, and they simply rounded up their victims, gathered them together in concentration camps along the Euphrates River from Meskene to Der el Zor, and then marched them into

the desert to die of hunger, and thirst. There was no special cost to the Turkish Army, and the lands and possessions of the evicted Armenians were seized by the government, and put up for sale at public auction.

In his book, Dickran Boyajian quotes an eyewitness account of conditions in the camps along the Euphrates:

The major portion of these miserable people brutally driven from home, and land, separated from their families, robbed of everything they owned, and stripped of all they carried underway, have been herded like cattle under the open skies without the least protection against heat, and cold, almost without clothing, and were fed very irregularly, and always insufficiently. Exposed to every change in weather, the glowing sun in the desert, the wind, and rain in spring, and fall, and the bitter cold in winter, weakened through extreme want, and their strength sapped by endless marches, deplorable treatment, cruel torture, and the constant fear for their lives, those that had some shreds of their strength left dug holes at the banks of the river, and crawled into them.

When the measures to transport the entire population into the desert were adopted, no appropriations were made for any kind of nourishment. On the contrary, it is obvious that the government pursued a plan to let the people die of starvation. Even an organized mass-killing such as during the times when liberty, equality, and fraternity had not yet been proclaimed in Constantinople would have been a much more humane measure, since it would have saved these miserable people from the horrors of hunger, and the slow death, and the excruciating pains of tortures so fiendish that the most cruel of the Mongols could not have imagined them. But a massacre is less constitutional than death by starvation. Civilization is saved.

What remains of the Armenian nation, scattered along the banks of the Euphrates, consists of old men, women, and children. Men of middle age, and younger people, as far as they have not been slain, are scattered over the roads of the country where they smash stones or do other labors for the Army in the name of the state.

The young girls, many still children, have become the booty of the Mohammedans. During the long marches to the destination of their deportation they were abducted, raped if the opportunity arose, of sold if they hadn't been killed by the gendarmes who accompanied these gloomy caravans. Many have been carried by their robbers into the slavery of a harem.

The entrance to these concentration camps could well bear the legend imprinted on the gates of Dante's hell, "Ye who enter here, abandon all hope."

. . . Everywhere I traveled I saw the same images; everywhere the terror-regime of barbarism, which has as its goal the systematic annihilation of the Armenian race, rampages. Everywhere one finds the inhuman bestiality

231

of these henchmen, and the self-same tortures with which these unhappy victims are tormented. From Meskene to Dir-ei-Zar—everywhere the banks of the Euphrates are witness to the same atrocities. (118–20)

Although the Armenian holocaust consumed nearly two million lives, a few lucky ones managed to escape. About four thousand men, women, and children took refuge on Musa-Dagh, an isolated hill in Lebanon on the northeastern coast of the Mediterranean Sea, near Antioch. Under the leadership of Armenians who had been trained in the Turkish Army, they managed to organize defenses efficient enough to hold off attacks by Turkish Army units for forty days, at the end of which time they were, fortunately, rescued by French gunboats that were patrolling nearby.

Some idea of the sufferings of the Armenian people was grasped by the survivors on Musa-Dagh, as they experienced—when the wind was blowing from east to west—the overwhelming stench of death coming to them from the Euphrates River, a hundred miles away. In his novel *The Forty Days of Musa-Dagh,* Franz Werfel writes:

But the death-rate of Mesopotamian spotted typhus often stood at eighty percent. It had descended from the cloud of disease that hovered above the steppes of the Euphrates. Ever since May, and June [1915] hundreds of thousands of dead Armenians had been rotting, on that very unconsecrated earth, in that godless common grave. Even wild beasts fled the stench. Only the poor troops had to force their way through that unspeakable mass of putrescent humanity. Columns of Macedonian, Anatolian, and Arab infantry, with endless baggage and lines of camels, were herded on in daily route-marches to Baghdad. The bedouin cavalry clattered among them. The worldly wisdom of Talaat Bey, in the Serail Palace of the ministry, might well have been confounded by the perception of what strange results may emerge from any attempt to exterminate a whole people. But neither he nor Enver let it perturb them. Power and the dullest insensitivity have gone together ever since there has been a world. (658)

In another novel, *Rise the Euphrates,* Carol Edgarion vividly describes what transpired in the town of Harput when the Extermination Plan was put into operation in May of 1915. The men of the Armenian quarter were rounded up first by soldiers who told them they were being inducted into the Army.

The Armenian men of Harput, who had reported to the government building that first morning, had been led into the building single file. Inside, they were

232

processed through a series of rooms, so none could see where the man before him had been taken. They signed papers, and checked their arms. Next, they were put in cells, hundreds of men to a room. The intellectuals, teachers, clergymen, and professionals were singled out.

The beatings began that first night. Some were bastinadoed, some whipped, others had their nails torn out, and the hair on their heads, and beards. That first night many died, so many, there was a question of what to do with the corpses.

The heroine of the novel, Garod, a child of nine at the time, watches as the men of her town are led away.

The men flowed from the city, as from a wound. Gared could not find her father, though she searched every face, every row. The men were bound together at their wrists, and waists; many were badly cut, and bruised. They seemed weak—she could not help thinking so—weak and already doomed; the sight of them filled her with profound shame. Though she was just a child, and could not assess such things, she believed each had failed her personally, and that they were the worst kind—victims. She watched their retreating backs, not a sword or weapon among them . . .

On June 26 a town crier ran through the streets accompanied by a small boy beating a drum. The crier announced that the government had ordered the deportation of every Armenian man, woman and child in Harput, and its neighboring villages. The Armenians of Harput City would go on Monday, July 5.

That night, and all that week, Turkish soldiers gathered in the central mosque, and prayed to Allah to bless them in their efforts to kill the Christians. (33)

Garod and her mother ("Mayrig" in Armenian) took care of the new baby, Sevan, as they waited in terror for the coming of the Turkish soldiers.

Garod was asleep when the soldiers entered the house. Rough hands grabbed at her; as she screamed and kicked she was tossed into the street. Mayrig was there, kicking, biting, crying out for the baby. The Turketa silenced her with the butt of a rifle; she fell like sticks. . . .

During the next hours several thousand Armenians were killed or maimed, their bodies left where they fell. It was nearly dawn when the gendarmes selected five girls, and tied their arms, and legs with rope. They strung them up by their thick black braids from the rafters of the government building. There was Ani, Shushan, Chortz, Nevart and Jilla, the eldest, just fourteen; Garod knew them all from school. . . .

233

Garod was stunned; her child's mind tried to grasp what terrible crime her people could have done to deserve this. And what was next?

The soldiers had an answer—it was a game they had perfected in other cities. Their leader, brought in for the massacre, mounted his horse, then trotted a hundred paces away. He turned, and, with a wave, motioned for the girls to be stilled. Then, holding his bloodsword high above his head, he spurred his horse, and galloped toward them. With one deft stroke, he severed four heads. The bodies dropped to the dirt like sacks of flour.

The troops cheered, and blew their whistles and, clapping their leader on the back, helped him from his horse. (34–37)

As the visitor in the Armenian Holocaust Memorial completes his tour of the camps in Syria where the Armenians suffered and died, he is shoved rudely out the back door onto the Mall, soaked in sweat and drained of any illusions he once may have had about the sanctity, the goodness, or the nobility of the human race.

An instructive Memorial. No admission charge. Salaries and upkeep on the building are provided from the sale of water inside.

Europe and the Near East are not the only sites of organized violence, and savagery among members of the human race. In Cambodia, in April of 1975, advance units of the Khmer Rouge entered the capital city, Phnom Penh and, after establishing security, began firing volleys into the air. This was the signal to begin the forced evacuation of the city, swollen by refugees to a population in excess of three million. All were forced to march out into the surrounding countryside. Sick people in the hospitals, women, children, old men, young men, businessmen, laborers, people of every class and category of humanity that make up the population of a modern city, were driven out with merciless cruelty of every kind—beatings, whippings, torture, and shootings.

Why depopulate a whole city? Because Pol Pot and his trusted comrades had studied at the Sorbonne in Paris, where such bloodbath socialists as Jean-Paul Sartre, and Bernard-Henri Lévy taught them that since Marx had declared money to be the heart of man's original sin and cities cannot function without money, then the logical first step of a "pure" revolution would be to destroy the need for money by destroying the cities. And Pol Pot set about this idealistic enterprise with an energy born of Marxist fanaticism. All the residents of Cambodia's urban centers were driven from their dwellings at a cost of over a million people dead of disease, starvation, overwork, torture, shootings, and decapitations. When asked by the United

234

Nations for an explanation of this carnage, Pol Pot replied to the effect that it was remarkable how concerned Western capitalists could be over the fate of a few war criminals.

Continental Africa, too, has seen a disproportionate share of violence, and bestiality over the years in such lands of suffering as Rwanda, Burundi, South Africa, Nigeria, Ethiopia, Liberia, Zaire, Somalia, and elsewhere. Tribal warfare (between, for instance, Hutus and Tutsies) accounts for most of the ethnic murders, and white-black confrontations account for the rest of the mayhem.

Violence is not limited to government-planned campaigns of extermination against racial, religious, and class minorities living within the borders of sovereign states. The U.S. federal government has never had a policy of violence toward a minority, slavery being a policy of several state governments. Even this policy died out with the freeing of the slaves after the Civil War.

In general, violence in the United States tends to be associated with crime. Americans rob, rape, beat, stab, and shoot people daily with an abandon that appalls the rest of the civilized world.

Properly directed, of course, violence in a human being can be a valuable commodity. In a football player, it is an essential ingredient of his talent. Not for nothing was Bill Bates of the Dallas Cowboys called the bully of the playground by his schoolteachers, and the same may be said of countless boxers, wrestlers, kung-fu types, bodyguards, hoods, and bouncers. The best soldiers in the army are violent men who can be trained to function as part of a military unit on a battlefield. And when a person's life is threatened, violence may be the most valuable of his innate characteristics as he struggles against his assailant to live a little longer.

Nevertheless, we all possess a consuming fear of criminal violence, as indicated by the number of pistols, rifles, and shotguns we own. We favor increasing city police forces. Our state legislatures build more prisons these days. Sentences are longer. In 1994, the total number of inmates in U.S. prisons reached an all-time high of 1.3 million—519 prisoners for every 100,000 people. In England, the rate was 93 per 100,000; in Germany, it was 80; and in Japan, 36.

Reports of criminal violence fill the columns of our daily newspapers. In Miami in April of 1993, Ms. Barbara Jensen Mailer, a physical therapist from Berlin, Germany, rented a car at the Miami airport and started off together with her mother, and two children, ages two and six, toward their vacation hotel. Ms. Meller got lost, however, and made the fatal mistake of turning off Interstate 95 onto a side road in an especially dangerous section of Miami. Suddenly she was hit by a car behind her, a popular technique employed by Miami highway thugs to induce their victims to stop. When she got out to check the damage, two men from the murder car beat her, threw her to the ground, took her purse and, as her children and mother watched in horror, crushed her head with their vehicle as they drove away.

Welcome to Miami!

Not long afterward, Uwe-Wilhelm Rakebrand, an agricultural engineer from Adendorf, Germany, drove his pregnant wife in their rented car, again from the Miami airport, toward a Miami Beach hotel. Herr Rakebrand was prepared for trouble, however. When he was bumped from behind, he refused to be intimidated, and resolutely kept on going. But this only infuriated his assailants, who gunned their vehicle and shot him dead as they went past. Rakebrand's wife grabbed the steering wheel and managed to bring their car to a safe stop. A few days later, the German government in Bonn formally warned German citizens against taking their vacations in the United States, a country where, they said, foreign tourists stood a good chance of getting murdered.

It should be mentioned that the Miami police displayed commendable competence in dealing with these outrages. They arrested two men in the Meller case, and charged them with first-degree murder. And in the Rakebrand case, a tip led the police to three youngsters who used a rental Ryder truck for their robberies. Against these worthies, the police obtained indictments for murder in the first degree.

About this same time, two Miami men who had abducted a black New York stockbroker from a shopping plaza, forced him to drive in his own car to a field, doused him with gasoline, and set him on fire were convicted of attempted murder, kidnapping, and robbery.

But Miami is not the only American killing field these days. White supremacists who attack Blacks, Jews, Asians, and homosexuals are making their presence felt everywhere. Recently the FBI announced the discovery of a plot by the Fourth Reich skinheads to slaughter the congregation of the First African Methodist Episcopal Church of Los Angeles, assassinate a number of prominent Blacks around the country, and send a letter bomb to a Jewish clergyman.

In New York City in 1990, the Doc Martens Stompers kicked a homosexual to death. Later that year, in Houston, two skinheads stomped to death a Vietnamese immigrant, Hung Truong, after he pleaded with them for mercy, and said he was sorry he had come to their country.

In Salem, Oregon, in 1992, three members of the American Front group fire-bombed the apartment of a black lesbian named Hattie Cohens, and her roommate, a gay white man named Brien Mock, killing them both. Well . . . "they asked for it." Earlier, in Birmingham, Alabama, three skinheads knifed a homeless black man named Benny Rembert, on the occasion of Hitler's birthday.

Hate groups are not without a philosophy of action. Tom Metzger, head of the White Aryan Resistance, calls for the expulsion from America of all Latinos and Asians, and the establishment of separatist black and white states. Minister Louis Farrakhan, leader of the Nation of Islam, demands a separate African-American state within the continental limits of the USA. And Christian Identity, whose members pay tribute to Odin, and other ancient Norse gods, regards Blacks as "mud people" that God created in error on the third day. Of the many leaders of hate groups in America, Louis Farrakhan appears to be attracting the most national attention after his "Million Man March" on Washington, October 16, 1995.

Car thieves have begun killing car owners as the most reliable way to gain possession of the desired property. In Maryland, Pamela Basa was dragged to her death trying to save her baby daughter when thieves drove off in her car. In Los Angeles, City of Angels, Sherri Foreman, a pregnant beautician, was stabbed by a carjacker who drove away in her car. Her baby died in an ambulance on the way to the hospital, and a day later she was dead, too. In Detroit, the amateur boxer Mark Rayner stopped his car at a phone booth, and was accosted by carjackers. As he attempted to escape by driving off, the thugs killed him with two bullets in his back. Then they drove away in his car. In Pine Hills, Florida, Philip Chandler was about to get into his parents' 1986 Ford Mustang when two teenagers forced him to get into the car's trunk, and took him for a long "joyride." He was later found in a parking lot thirty miles away, comatose from the 130-degree heat in the trunk, and permanently brain-damaged.

Once in a while, there does seem to be a certain rough justice out there. In Newark recently, three thieves stole a car, drove across a side street, sheared a power pole, and brought down some high-voltage transmission lines that promptly electrocuted them. But such episodes of cosmic retribution are not numerous.

Many young people carry guns these days. As in the Old West, "if you

237

ain't carryin' a gun, why ain't you?" Young people often buy guns from dealers parked behind fast-food emporiums, the trunks of their cars filled with weapons. A shotgun might cost only twenty-five dollars. A hacksaw can shorten barrel and stock, converting the weapon into a sawed-off shotgun with a pistol grip. Easily concealed. Easy to use.

According to the National Center for Health Statistics, gunshots accounted for one of every four deaths among teenagers—4,200—in 1990. Probably one hundred thousand children carry a gun to school every day for self-defense. Thousands shoot, and are shot at. In Omaha, recently, according to a *Time* article of August 2, 1993, Jennifer Rea, fifteen, shot her two younger sisters to death with a .22-calibre pistol. Carlos Fisher, sixteen, killed himself playing Russian roulette with a .38-calibre pistol. Travis Hogue, eighteen, shot and killed a rival for his girlfriend in the rest room of a McDonald's with four shots from his trusty .38.

But Omaha isn't so bad. Only sixteen residents were killed by gunshot from January to August 1993—hardly a weekend's worth in Los Angeles, murder capital of the world.

Besides self-defense, teenagers have another reason for packing a gun. "If you have a gun, you have power," as they say. Differences aren't settled by a fight after school anymore. Guns can do more damage than fists. And there's not much risk of going to jail. One can always claim to have been sexually abused as a child by one's parents, and the jury will understand. Take the case of Lyle and Erik Menendez, who, in February 1994, were charged with pumping sixteen rounds of rifle and pistol fire into Mommy and Daddy as they ate ice cream, and strawberries in front of the TV set. The brothers confessed to the murders but offered the defense that, over the years, they had been abused by their parents, and had killed them in self-defense. Their parents were guilty of encouraging them to be bad boys, so the murderers were really the victims, and deserved to go free. Their trial ended in a hung jury, though a second trial would convict them. But at first, victimology triumphed. The dead parents were found guilty of child abuse even though they hadn't had an opportunity to defend themselves in open court. But what did that matter?

Violence has overpowered idealism. Rock 'n' roll rules the roost. People today prefer "Weasels Gripped My Flesh" to "Singin' in the Rain." Millions have become enchanted with the hate lyrics of rap, rock, soul, and heavy metal. Heard on CDs, in movie houses, on cable TV, and in the plays of David Mamet, for instance, vile and vicious language profoundly poisons the daily conversation with which we engage in social intercourse. Vileness of speech discloses vileness of character.

The plays of Mamet, of course, are not the only examples of American theatrical sleaze. A 1993 piece, *The Kentucky Cycle,* by Robert Schenkkan, dramatizes the development of America from the Revolution to the present and, in doing so, depicts American character as essentially violent, deceitful, and cruel. Firearms and knives are employed generously among the many villainous characters of the work, creating a pervasive mood of treachery, betrayal, revenge, and greed. The play was well received on Broadway, and won its author the Pulitzer Prize for Drama.

Well, violence is not a recent thing in America. The first slave ship arrived in Virginia in 1619—beating the Mayflower by a year—and the three-century saga of American violence toward the races of Africa was under way. Stanley Feldstein in his book, *Once a Slave,* quotes many original sources written or dictated by slaves that describe the hellish nature of their servitude in America. William Wells Brown, a fugitive slave, wrote:

> Slavery . . . tore wife from husband, took child from mother, and sister from brother; it tore asunder the tenderest ties of nature. The system had its bloodhounds, its chains, its Negro-whips, its dungeons, and almost every other instrument of cruelty that the mind could invent. All this for the purpose of keeping the slave in subjection; all this for the purpose of obliterating the mind, of crushing the intellect, and of annihilating the soul. (28)

As early as 1774, slaves were recording the effect of slavery on themselves, and their families. In a protest to Thomas Gage, Governor of Massachusetts, they lamented the fact that they were "unjustly dragged by the cruel hand of power from our dearest friends, and sum of us stolen from the bosoms of our tender Parents, and from a Populous Pleasant, and plentiful country, and brought hither to be made slaves for Life in a Christian land." (31)

Frederick Douglass grew up in slavery. Later, when he had obtained freedom, and education, he became an articulate foe of America's "peculiar institution". One of the pro-slavery arguments was that the poor of Europe were as bad off as American slaves. Douglass replied that at least in Europe the poorest of the poor still had rights, but how was it with the American slave? Did the right to assemble exist for him? Were newspapers available to him? Where was his right to petition? Where was his right to speak out, his freedom of movement? "Had you asked the slave what he thought of his condition . . . you might as well address your inquiries to the *Silent Dead*. There comes no *Voice* from the enslaved." (33)

Once sold to their new masters, the slaves found themselves working on three kinds of plantations—cotton, rice, and tobacco. Working conditions varied from farm to farm, but violence toward the slave workers was a common denominator of their servitude. John Brown, a fugitive slave, wrote of his experiences on a cotton plantation in Georgia:

> If the women of the world could see the female slaves and the little children picking cotton in the fields till the blood runs from the tips of their fingers, where they have been pricked by the hard pod; of if they could see them dragging their baskets, all trembling, to the scale, for fear their weight should be short, and they should get the flogging which in such a case they know they must expect; or if they could see them bent double with constant stooping, and scourged on their bare back when they attempted to rise to straighten themselves for a moment . . . they would never in their lives wear another article made of slave-grown cotton. (47)

But if working the cotton fields was bad, the slaves who were occupied in the rice fields had it worse. As John Brown described it:

> Rice was grown in muddy soil into which the slave sank knee-deep, his own footsteps sending up the foul smelling vapors which inevitably caused fever, and disease. The heat alone, reflected back from the water, was intolerably painful and frequently brought on sunstroke. His feet would get water poisoning of a malady they called "the toe or ground itch", when the flesh cracks, and cankers. Rice plantation slaves would also attract the chigger, a small insect that punctured the skin under the toe, and deposited an egg. The egg would soon hatch, producing a very minute maggot which grew in the flesh, and caused swelling, and unendurable irritation. In addition, the field hand was constantly on his guard against being bitten by water moccasins. Fevers, agues, rheumatism, pleurisies, asthma, and consumption were among the illnesses contracted in the rice swamps. It was, to say the least, very much more trying than either cotton or tobacco cultivation. (49–50)

In the tobacco regions, again according to Brown:

> Planting time was extremely hard . . . especially for the children. They were considered better able than adults to creep among the plants, and pick out the weeds with their little fingers. It was, too, a difficult time for the aged slaves

who, from constant stooping, could not stand up straight to save their lives. The driver was very sharp, and active during this season; and if he sees a hand straighten up from his work . . . to rest his back, down comes the bull whip across the shoulders of the unfortunate man or woman, with a loud crack, like a pistol shot. (50)

The treatment of African slaves by the American people has been at least equaled in violence, and brutality by our treatment, over the years, of the descendants of those peoples who first came to North America from Asia about 12,000 years ago: the Indians. From colonial times to the end of the nineteenth century, America's relations with the Indians have been stigmatized by theft of their land, murder, rape, enticement to alcoholism, forced migrations, and broken promises. Perhaps the most famous example of American bestiality toward the Indians was the infamous massacre at the Sioux Indian reservation on Wounded Knee Creek in South Dakota December 29, 1890, during which the Seventh Cavalry took revenge for what had happened to Colonel Custer and his men on the banks of the Little Bighorn some years earlier.

Led by Colonel James W. Forsyth, elements of the Seventh Cavalry attacked the village after an accidental gunshot. As described by eyewitnesses in the book *Eyewitness at Wounded Knee,* by Richard E. Jensen, R. Eli Paul, and John E. Cantor:

Black Coyote, sometimes called Black Fox, had refused to surrender his rifle to the soldiers, and there ensued a struggle that resulted in an accidental gunshot. Almost immediately, fighting broke out on both sides. The few Indians who were still armed fought back, while others retrieved guns from the pile of confiscated weapons, and joined the fighting. The shock, the surprise and the pall of black powder smoke that obscured much of the horror of these first few minutes of fighting probably resulted in more than half of the fatalities. (19)

Peter McFarland, a government drayman present at the fight, reports that "the Hotchkiss guns on the hill fired into an Indian wagon. Several Indians were firing on the soldiers from behind the wagon. The shells sent into it knocked it to pieces, and killed a number of warriors." (106)

Charles w. Allen, a newspaper correspondent present at the massacre, reported:

The first gun had no sooner been fired than it was followed by hundreds of others, and the battle was on. The fighting continued for about half an hour, and then was continued in skirmish for another hour. When the smoke cleared away from in front of the tent where it began, there were forty-five dead Indians with their impregnable ghost shirts on, lying on a space of ground about two hundred yards in diameter. (108)

Dewey Beard, a Miniconjou Indian, took shelter in a ravine, and later described some of the action that took place there:

I was badly wounded, and pretty weak too. While I was lying on my back, I looked down the ravine, and saw a lot of women coming up, and crying. When I saw these women, girls, and little girls and boys coming up, I saw soldiers on both sides of the ravine shoot at them until they had killed every one of them. Later, I saw a young woman who was crying, and calling "Mother! Mother!" She was wounded under her chin, close to her throat, and the bullet had passed through a braid of her hair, and carried some of it into the wound . . . Her mother had been shot down behind her. (116)

On that bitter day in America's conscience, the Seventh Cavalry lost about 30 dead and 90 wounded. The mainly unarmed Indians lost 250 dead, and perhaps 750 wounded men, women, and children.

Why are we Americans—or many of us—such a violent bunch? Have we inherited our violence from our forefathers? The idea of inherited violence is gaining credence among evolutionary biologists, and the discovery of the genes that transmit violent impulses from one generation to the next may not be far in the future. Already the National Institutes of Health have linked low levels of a brain chemical, serotonin, to abnormally aggressive or violent behavior. And these low levels of serotonin may be caused by a genetic defect.

Who *were* our forebears? Who settled America? A mixed bag, to say the least.

According to the 1990 census, the largest minority group in America came from Germany (23 percent), followed by those from Ireland (15 percent), England (13 percent), and Africa (9.3 percent). American idealism, especially the belief that all men are created equal—the essence of the "American Dream"—seems to be the result of the eighteenth-century German *Aufklärung* (Enlightenment), the basic ethical principles of which were expressed by the slogan "*Freiheit, Gleichheit, Brüderlichkeit*" (Freedom, Equality, Brotherhood). This concept soon reached France (as *Liberté,*

Egalité, Fraternité), then England and, finally, the American colonies. As Benjamin Franklin once said, "Equality is the ethical essence of the Declaration of Independence", and most of the political and military activity in America from then on—including the Civil War—turned on the concept of equal rights for all.

The *Aufklärung* sparked many political revolutions—first in the British colonies in America, then in France, Germany itself, and many other countries. By the end of World War II, the great principle of liberal democracy had triumphed nearly everywhere, and the risk of large-scale military conflicts was greatly diminished.

After the conclusion of the American Revolution, migrants from England fell off, but they were replaced by migrants from other countries. The German minority started with a large group already here. Of the 30,000 Hessian soldiers rented by the Grand Duke of Hesse to his cousin King George III of England for use in the colonies, 6,000 of them decided to try their luck in Pennsylvania. Why go back to Fulda when you could live in Philadelphia? In subsequent decades, many more thousands of Germans, facing famine in their homeland, decided to opt for the new land of opportunity.

Tens of thousands of immigrants from other countries came, too, in order to accept the invitation inscribed on the Statue of Liberty in New York harbor, part of which read: "Give me your tired, your huddled masses, yearning to breathe free, the wretched refuse of your teeming shore. Send these, the homeless, tempest-tossed to me . . . ."

And, indeed, many of the new arrivals could well be described as tempest-tossed refuse from many a teeming shore: Irishmen and Scotsmen fleeing abysmal poverty back home, prostitutes shipped over by the boatload to New Orleans to mate with the colonists of Louisiana, desperate Italians fleeing the Austrian occupation and the Catholic Inquisition, hereditary bandit families from Sicily, penniless Jews from Poland and Russia, emaciated hunter-gatherers from the forests of Bohemia, shivering Scandinavians seeking surcease from the harsh living conditions near the Arctic Circle, and impoverished peons from Spain and from Spanish colonies such as Mexico, Puerto Rico, the Philippines, and Cuba. In short, much of our ancestry is derived not from the cream of European society, but from its dregs.

We also have forebears from other continents. Multitudes of starving Chinese peasants were brought to the United States under contract to work

243

as laborers on the construction of the great transcontinental railroads. And modern-day Afro-Americans are descended almost exclusively from slaves brought from Africa to America to work the Southern cotton, rice, and tobacco plantations.

So, it is indeed hard to refute the charge made by George Bernard Shaw that we Americans are "a mongrel race with no ancestral home of our own". We inhabit a country in which the only thoroughbreds are cats, dogs, and horses. No wonder our everyday speech is filled with obscenities that reflect a sick national character. No wonder we Americans are regarded in other countries as violent specimens of the human race, who carry guns everywhere we go and use them where and when we please.

What can we do to improve our reputation? Our image? Anything? The optimist will reply, "Yes". For a start, we could trouble ourselves to try to understand at least one of the sources of violence among us—racial prejudice.

In October 1995, the Million Man March took place on the Mall in Washington, D.C. Called to this historic gathering by the Nation of Islam leader, Minister Louis Farrakhan, hundreds of thousands of African-American males assembled in a spirit of atonement, solidarity, and self-esteem. President Clinton spoke later about the desire of the participants to renew their sense of responsibility for their families, to say "No" to drugs, crime, and violence in the streets, and to seek reconciliation with the white people among whom they live. Other speakers called for an end to race prejudice—prejudice of whites against blacks and prejudice of blacks against whites. The idea that whites intuitively hate blacks, and that blacks intuitively hate whites has been rejected by political and social idealism. Racial prejudice can be overcome by education, empathy, and goodwill.

But can it?

Does prejudice grow out of an inherited condition? Are people prejudiced against certain "others" *a priori*?

The answer seems to depend on the degree of our willingness to accept the following proposition: that race prejudice is the manifestation of a particular hate, that we hate what we fear, and that certain fears are inherited by all members of the human race.

Lately, more and more attention has been paid to the role of genes in determining human behavior. In the recent past, popular wisdom held that we are conditioned by the environment in which we grow up. Those who mature in big-city slums are likely to turn to violent crime. Abuse by a parent

244

might incline a young person toward homosexuality. If parents display hostility toward Jews or blacks, their children will learn to do the same.

As the result of many recent discoveries in medicine, and biology, however, we seem to be having second thoughts about all this. It has been ascertained that defective genes inherited from our forebears are responsible for many diseases, including hemophilia, muscular dystrophy, familial colon cancer, Huntington's disease, cystic fibrosis, malignant melanoma, sickle-cell anemia, Alzheimer's disease, amyotrophic lateral sclerosis, and Down's syndrome. Besides disease, we also inherit certain behavioral tendencies. Science is close to identifying genetic abnormalities that predispose their possessors to violence. People who like to fight in the school yard, in the streets, or in hockey rinks are often deficient in the brain hormone serotonin, a condition caused by a defective gene.

Other genes probably determine our talents, skills, and tastes, our attraction to certain members of the opposite sex or same sex but not to others, our inclination to take long solitary walks. One person plays baseball, another plays the violin, and a third plays roulette. Some people prefer writing novels to writing television commercials. Some people prefer Bach to rock. A gene has been identified that appears in homosexuals, but not in heterosexuals, a discovery that surprised no one. Nearly all homosexuals believe that their sexual orientation must have been inherited, not learned in childhood. How could someone be indoctrinated with homosexuality? How could someone imitate it from parental example?

If homosexuality, a physiological characteristic, is carried in our genes, perhaps prejudice against it is also inherited. Such a prejudice would likely be lodged in that complex of genes that directs our behavior toward the goal of survival of the human species. Over the centuries, we have developed prejudice against the homosexual because he is absorbed in carnal relations with members of his own sex only, and this preoccupation renders him unable to contribute to the survival of the species by propagating children. If all members of the human race were homosexual, the human race would become extinct.

We all intuitively fear extinction. Countless people today actively concern themselves with preventing the extinction of various animals, plants, and trees, an activity that clearly expresses the fear of extinction slumbering in us all. It is true that such a fear seems far-fetched, especially in view of the steady increase in world population day by day, but it is

245

perhaps the very irrationality of the fear that prompts the hatred felt by so many heterosexual people toward homosexuals.

It is beginning to be clear that many, if not most, of the impulses that determine our responses to the chance events of life are inherited. Our external appearance, our gender, the color of our akin, whether we are left-handed, right-handed or ambidextrous, our propensity to suffer certain diseases, all are aspects of the physical side of our inheritance. The mental side includes our talents, which are the source of our pleasures, and happiness in life, and our fears, which deprive us of our happiness.

What are some of the talents we inherit? Mozart inherited immense talent for music from his forebears. His talent was natural and was refined by his father, and other music teachers, but none of them could have "taught" him his talent. There seems to be no question that we inherit from our forebears our talent for such things as painting; acting; singing; dancing; for teaching (ability to teach well cannot be taught); for violence, which can lure us, into prize fighting, football, crime, wife beating, or the Marine Corps; for business, and finance; for law, and politics; for medicine, mathematics, physics, chemistry, and biology; for philosophy; for baseball, soccer, tennis, golf, billiards, bridge, and chess. Our talents, together with our intelligence, enable us to make our way through life while waiting for Godot (*der Tod*), a journey that is also plagued by our fears—of pain, of disease, of poverty, and debt, of hunger, of fire, of darkness, of snakes, of heights, of crowds, of loneliness, of death, of racial extinction. We can learn to erect defenses against our fears but, like the Turks in seventeenth-century Europe, they are never very far away.

Can fear of certain kinds of people be inherited? Animals inherit distinct fears of this kind. The image of a deadly enemy of a particular species can, over a period of time, enter its genetic structure and help the threatened ones to survive. An experiment demonstrating this phenomenon has been performed many times with newborn chicks, and the results are always the same. While the chicks are eating in a fenced-in open area, shadows of the wings of various birds are passed over the area. The chicks pay no attention to most of these shadows, but when the shadow of a hawk's wing is passed over the area, the chicks scramble wildly toward the edges of the enclosure in the desperate hope of escaping from a mortal enemy, exact knowledge of which they must have inherited.

In the human species, blacks appear to have inherited fear of whites.

And, for different reasons, whites seem to have inherited fear of blacks. And these inherited fears manifest themselves in the form of race prejudice.

The blacks of the world possess a very sound basis for the fear of whites that they carry in their genes. Over the centuries, white slave traders have preyed on the Black peoples of Africa to satisfy their customers in the Western Hemisphere, Europe, and Asia. The appearance of white men in black African villages signaled murder, rape, and the kidnapping of the best specimens of young people in the village, who were then sent to the slave ships. Fear of whites has entered the genetic makeup of blacks, and probably will never be dislodged.*

In Rhodesia, half a century ago, hatred of the white minority on the part of the Black majority was endemic. After elections that gave power to the blacks, a Constitution was agreed on that contained a clause guaranteeing the white population a basic minimum representation in the new Parliament. As black power became consolidated, however, this clause was stricken from the Constitution and the Parliament was soon all black. Today there are very few white people left in Zimbabwe, as the country is now called.

In South Africa, a country whose name surely will be changed soon, a single episode of 1993 may be taken as symptomatic of the hatreds that lurk beneath the apparently calm surface of social intercourse. In April, one of the most prominent leaders of the Communist-oriented African National Congress, Chris Hani, who had returned from exile in Zambia in 1990, was shot to death by two white men in his driveway as he got out of his car. The response was weeks of violence, strikes, black attacks on whites, burned cars, and looted shops. In the southern coastal town of East London, when blacks attacked the bar at the Highgate Hotel, firing guns, and throwing hand grenades, they killed five whites, and wounded many more. It took 23,000 police, and soldiers to restore a semblance of order, but the threat of violence remains a fact of life in South Africa today, and will continue to do so until all the whites are gone.

Blacks' fear of whites is not hard to understand, but why whites fear blacks is not so clear. Does it reside in our inherited fear of the dark? Perhaps

*In her book *Leni Riefenstahl, a Memoir,* the author describes an episode during which she tried to hire some Black Africans for a documentary film she was making on slavery, but as soon as they saw an Arab interpreter she had hired they became terrified, fearing that Riefenstahl and her assistants were slave traders (423).

the color of the Black man's skin evokes the darkness of the jungle, where he is at home and we are not. For white people, the jungle is an image of the primordial fear of the unknown, so memorably described by Joseph Conrad in his *Heart of Darkness.*

Death comes at night. Most people die between sunset and dawn. It is a universal belief if the sick person can "make it through the night", he has a chance to survive.

We sleep with the night-light on.

Probably we inherit fear of the night from our ancestors, who feared that predators would attack them while they slept, kill them, and take their food. Whatever prevents us from seeing—night, fog, darkness—arouses our fear, and fear is the source at prejudice. As long as the black man remains black, he will probably arouse prejudice in the white man.

Other examples of fear-engendered prejudice come to mind. Will the American Indians ever cease hating white people for what was done to them from 1492 to the present? Will Muslims ever cease hating Christians for the rape, murder, and pillage they suffered during the Crusades? Will the Armenians ever cease hating the Turks for driving tens of thousands of their forebears into the Syrian desert to die of thirst?

Prejudice against those who wreaked violent injury on one's forebears is comprehensible. A different problem in human prejudice arises however, when the victims of prejudice become objects of violent outrages without seeming to deserve such treatment, as in the case of the Jews. Why do Gentiles fear the Jews? Jews seem harmless enough. As one gets to know them, they appear to be agreeable, intelligent, humorous, admirers of art and literature, hardworking, and loyal to their friends.

And they like Gentiles. If a Jew lives in Poland, he likes Poles. If he lives in Germany, he likes Germans. And over here, Jews like Americans—well, most Americans. When the ancient, and venerable state of Israel was returned to the Jews by the United Nations in 1948, the Israeli government opened the gates to all the exiled Jews, everywhere. Yet today (1996), when one would expect almost all the world's Jews to be living safe, and snug in their own country, millions prefer to live elsewhere. Of the 13.9 million Jews worldwide, only 4.4 million live in Israel, while 5.8 million live in the United States. The rest live in many other countries, including some sixty thousand who live in Germany. These "exiles" continue to live where they were born because they have learned to like their neighbors.

248

And yet we all fear the Jews. Why? What do we fear that is universally associated with the Jews?

Debt?

It is only recently that owing money one couldn't pay has ceased (except in criminal circles) to be a fear-inspiring condition. In Europe, for centuries, people could be sent to debtors' prison if they couldn't pay their creditors. The sentence was indeterminate—they stayed in prison until they paid their debt. If they couldn't pay, they died in prison. Richard Wagner nearly "fell into the hands of the Jews" in the 1860s, until King Ludwig II of Bavaria paid his many creditors and provided him enough peace of mind to finish his *Ring* cycle. Wagner's anti-Semitism was doubtless exacerbated by decades of owing money he couldn't pay.

One of the more valuable recent improvements in life has been the institution of bankruptcy, in which a person who owes more than he can pay is given legal protection from his creditors while he seeks new ways to pay old debts. But from the Middle Ages to the recent past, fear of money lenders was universal and since the Catholic Church forbade the charging of interest on loans, the Jews drifted into the business of lending money, in part because their Bible said nothing against it. They turned out to have a racial talent for this occupation, and fear of the Jewish money lender soon entered the gene pool of European Gentiles—Shakespeare's *Merchant of Venice* provides a vivid image of the condition. As a result, European anti-Semitism became a matter of inherited behavior rather than something learned at home or in school.

Violence is the root of all evil. And if violence is an inherited behavioral characteristic in human beings, then hope that it may one day be controlled by means of gene therapy is not out of place. In 1994, an inherited disease called ADA Deficiency was treated at the University of Southern California by a team headed by Dr. W. French Anderson. The team extracted white blood cells from two young Ohio girls with the disease, inserted normal ADA genes into the cells, and reinjected them. The blood cells began churning out enough natural ADA to boost the immune system sufficiently to fight the disease. The technique was later improved by inserting healthy ADA genes into stem cells drawn from the girls' bone marrow. The altered cells were then inserted into the bloodstream, after which they found their way back to the bone marrow. The girls are now thriving.

This historic experiment in gene transplant therapy points the way toward a better future. From curing inherited disease to curbing inherited violence is doubtless a long step in the laboratory, but not too long for a caring mankind.